The Bronx Warriors

The Story of a Neighborhood Football Team

As Told to and Written by

Robert H. Nieder

Edited by

Ron Watson, Lt Col U.S. Marine Corps

Library of Congress Control Number 2021908646

No. 3 Publishing Co., L.L.C.
6861 Hills Drive
New Port Richey, FL, 34653
www.no3pubco.com

Digital Publishing of Florida
131 Burbank Rd., Oldsmar, FL, 34677
www.digitaldate-corp.com
813-788-3735

Manufactured in the United States of America for distribution in North and South America, or in the United Kingdom or Australia when distributed elsewhere.

Cover Design by Jeff Ortiz (photography) & Robert H. Nieder (layout)

Printed in the United States of America

ISBN: 978-1-7330733-0-1

Ordering Information:
Quantity sales. Special discounts are available on quantity purchases by corporations, associations, and others. For details, contact the publisher at No.3 Publishing Company address above. Also available on Amazon and other e-book retailers.

DEDICATION

***

Geraldine Loretta "Geri" (Wissler) Demers
May 1, 1945 – January 11, 2013

***

Francis "Frank" Demers
June 20, 1939- July 4 2018

***

Jeffrey Scott "Jeff" Ortiz
April 3, 1951 – September 1, 2018

Acknowledgments

To quote Stephen King, "To write is human, to edit is divine." Ron Watson is divinity. He was the editor on this project. Ronnie is one of us, a Warrior going back to P.S. 106. You will read a passage in this book about his background. If you should ever meet Ronnie, shake his hand and thank him for his service. If you should like this story, thank Ronnie. It could not have been written without his input, intelligence and his command. Thank you, Ronnie, for keeping it in the family. You made the Coach very happy and proud.

Every rock band has the sisters, the ladies standing in the background swaying and harmonizing. Cindy Yates and Jill Apel were my sisters. They transcribed everything I recorded. Jill is a family friend for many years and did a wonderful job when I realized my aging bones couldn't and wouldn't type as fast as I once did. Jill was a medical transcriber and had the time to help me out. Cindy is a whole 'nother story. I needed another transcriber as the recordings were piling up. My daughter, Lyndsy suggest that I go into her college and search the "job wanted" board. Well, in the twenty-first century, those boards don't exist. As I questioned someone in the registration area about needing a student that might want to transcribe and make a few bucks, from the corner of my eye I could see a petite woman race up upon me. I knew right then and there I had found my mark. Cindy was phenomenal, knocking out six conversations, each an hour or more long in a week. This book would have never been completed without the sisters.

Bronx County Historical Society – Special thanks to Professor Ultan and Ann Ryan of the Bronx County Historical Society. Two of the most accommodating people that I've met in a long time. Dr. Ultan is a font of Bronx history with a humorous and charming allure. He will educate you and put a smile in your heart. Thank both of you to giving access to Bronx Press Review articles that could not be found on microfiche at either Lehman College or the Schwartzman Library.

Many thanks to Ed Wallace, periodicals librarian at my quasi-alma mater, Herbert H. Lehman College. Ed Wallace is a gem. He was at my side each and every visit, not only assisting me in the pulling of microfiche reels but being younger and faster than me, he would actually sit at the machine and run the reels, find the article, and print. Every phone call made to Ed was always returned promptly. He was a godsend and a delight.

I would be remiss if I didn't express gratitude to the New York City Public Library's main branch, the Stephen A. Schwarzman Building. In particular, the staff in the Irma and Paul Milstein Division of United States History, Local History and Genealogy I don't know the name of a single person at this research center, but they were more than helpful and accommodating in my microfiche search when Lehman College's Library was under construction. Thank you all so much for your patience and to listening to my dribble.

I would like to also thank the Alvin Lee of the Samuel H. Coleman Memorial Library at The University of Florida A & M for access to New York Times microfiche. It was cheaper to make an eight- hour round trip car ride than a plane ride plus hotel plus car rental rates to Nu Yawk. Thank you, Al for teaching me how to operate the digital version microfiche machine. Much more advanced than what I used in 1970.

Special thanks to Digital Publishing of Florida located in Oldsmar. Jill and Ryan Illg are as accommodating as they are professional. Their personal touch and guidance have been of great help in the printing of this book, as they have done for me in the past.

I would like to acknowledge my good friend, Randy Nold. Randy, having no connection to New York City, let alone the Warriors was a great unbiased guide in writing this story. Your support and encouragement as well as your commentary helped me to forge on in the right direction.

Kudos to everyone who took the time to speak with me. A lot of you gave me hours of your time. Your recollections amazed me and gave me the confidence to continue this book. This story would have never been written without all of you. You will know who they are as you read on. As the cover states, "As told to". I could not write this history without all of their voices which is why this is not my story, but our story. But two of you stand out, head and shoulders. Jeff Ortiz, God, I miss you dearly, and Tommy McGurl. They became my historians, my libraries. Their recall was impeccable. A lot of this book was word of mouth. The stories become grander over time; the tales become legends…in our minds. But we are who when we were who we are. Jeff and Tom kept it on the straight, the narrow, and most importantly, the accurate.

Dr. Arthur Langer, we are honored to have you provide the forward. I want to express my gratefulness. Thank you so much for this, thank you so much for what you provide Veterans, and thank you so much for what you give to young people educationally. You will learn about Artie's exploits and endeavors in this book

My deepest appreciation to Joe Reich, a true Warrior captain and a leader. To borrow the phrase, you are a man amongst men. Joe is also another individual you will read about, so I need not say more about him. His story will touch you. We would not have completed this project without your generous financial backing. You made the Coach, Jeff, and me proud.

There is no one I could thank more than the Coach, Jerry "Jay" Demers. Jerry read everything, in draft, as I wrote. He was my director making sure my timeline was accurate and the passages were on track. He seemed to like it so as I said to my wife, "I guess I might be hitting the mark. I might be doing something right." Thank you, Jay for being my guide and being the father that I no longer have due to my father's passing. Dad loved you as well.

Of course, and without hesitation or question, a multitude of thanks to my wife, Carmen Iris, my best friend. As always, with every book that I write, she is the recipient of my torment and insanity in her efforts as proofreader, editor, and mental health counselor. She is a steady force and calming influence in the face of my mayhem. I love you forever.

Forward

Bob Nieder has done an outstanding job of capturing Jerry (Jay) Demers' lifelong accomplishments as founder of a football program known as the Bronx Warriors. However, this book is about much more than a football program, it's about the way Jay transformed the lives of the people he touched, how he helped boys to become men, and ultimately how he managed to create an organization than has spanned over forty years.

I am just one product of Jay's program. Growing up on a dead-end street in the Bronx, I as many kids of that time, was a child of a blue-collar family. Our parents were depression-era kids who worked hard and managed their children using strict rules. Both my parents worked to provide us with what they could, but believed that their children would have to find their own way and deal with the challenges of life. With this freedom, there were plenty of opportunities for us to get into trouble—any many of us did.

At the end of the dead-end street was a schoolyard, which we called "the park" and an adjacent public school called P.S. 106. The schoolyard had a park-house where Jay was assigned as the neighborhood's recreation director. It was here where Jay kept us out of trouble. I represented the second-generation of kids to come under Jay's tenure there. It was here where I first became a Warrior. Jay could be a friend but knew he needed our respect to ultimately coach us. Thus, he instituted rules of behavior in the park. For example, no one was allowed to ride a bicycle in the park, which I of course quickly violated. The punishment was swift—I was taken to the park house and spanked on the butt with a plastic whiffle ball bat—it hurt, and I never did it again!

Our football team, like many others, had a number of outstanding players. At 5' 7" and 135 pounds I was not one of them. I did not have the arm of Jackie Cawley, the speed of Joe Golio, the technique and size of Ronnie Watson, the strength of Mark Anderson, or the all-around abilities of Joey Reich and John Sullivan. I just wanted to play football and be part of a team. The book mentions how undersized our defense was—actually there were seven of us and we were known as the "seven dwarfs"! I played Defensive End.

During my seven seasons, I experienced many life lessons. I had bad games, good games, and made a play that might have made a real contribution towards winning the game. It taught me how to handle disappointments while being humble when being praised after making a great play. I remember those experiences and think about them often—more often than one might think after all these years. For example, I remember making an interception against the Road Runners and going head on head against an incoming tackler—I got my bell-rung and had to be helped off the field. Talk about taking a good play and looking dumb! But I also remember making a key tackle against the St. Albans Chargers. We were trailing 19-7in the fourth quarter at our home field called Rice Stadium and we needed to get the ball back for the Offense. It was pouring rain and their team ran a "screen" play, which might have gone for a long gain or even a touchdown—I dived, made the tackle and fell in a huge puddle of dirty water. When I came up for air with all kinds of mud and grass on my facemask, I was greeted by John Sullivan (Sully) our middle linebacker with a barrage of punches to my face and head—a strange way to congratulate me, but this is who we were. We came back and won the game when Tommy McGurl executed the perfect "hook in lateral" play, flipping the ball to Victor Fernandez who ran for the winning touchdown as the clock ran out. For me this happened yesterday and we talk about these games over and over again when we get together.

What made the Warrior culture so great was our bond beyond the practices and games. We had ski weekends, social events, and often would just hang out together and do crazy and funny things. Only a handful of the P.S. 106 Warriors ultimately played for the tackle football team. Those six or seven of us had a special relation with Jay because we were involved with him at a younger age. During this time Jay was more to us than just a coach. We went to his house, discussed growing up dilemmas like dating girls—you name it Jay was interested in our challenges and was approachable on things that we could never discuss with our parents. Even his wife Geri participated—we were a real family!

While writing this forward, I kept asking myself how I could convey to the reader why our story is so unique. Certainly, there must be kids that have had similar experiences with local sport programs? So, what sets ours apart from theirs? I believe I found the answer to this question after my recent participation in the inauguration of Dr. David Thomas as President of Morehouse College, the historical Black college that graduated such famous people as Martin Luther King Jr. Dr. Thomas was a professor at Harvard Business School and former Dean of Georgetown's Business School. He was instrumental in helping me launch my charity to help underserved young adults and veterans. We have been colleagues for years and I felt honored to be a delegate at the ceremony. During David's acceptance speech he talked about a touching conversation he had with his dad about good parenting. Surprisingly, David's dad explained that he could only ascertain his quality as a father by assessing the success that David had as a parent to his own children! The point is that one's success cannot be measured solely by what you accomplish alone during your life, rather it's the quality of influence you leave behind. At Columbia University, I always define leadership to my students as one's ability to influence the behavior of others without using authority. Jay had no real authority or force to make us productive adults; he simply influenced our behavior by setting an example.

I would confidently say that most Warriors are engaged in giving back to society in many ways, not because we are obligated to do so, but because that's what we were taught to do—it's the way we were coached! I spent years coaching in our local Pop Warner organization and also serving as their Vice President of Football. Many of our players returned to the Warrior organization to coach with Jay while others help in other service areas. So, like David Thomas' dad, Jay's accomplishments and his legacy will be judged based on the social accomplishments of his players! To me this is what makes our story so unique! A few years back I had an annual gala for my charity. Jay attended as part of our Warrior table. It was his 80th birthday year and I acknowledged Jay's contributions to an audience of over two hundred fifty people. There was no hesitation by the audience to give Jay the standing ovation he deserved. It did not take long for outsiders to recognize the extent of what Jay had accomplished.

I think it's important to mention a few Warriors that have left us too soon. Dougie Williams was one of our stellar offensive players. As Tom McGurl mentions in the book Dougie did not like too many people, especially defensive players. Dougie and I somehow formed a strong bond on and off the field, however unlikely that was. Dougie left us far too soon and I must say I really miss him and all those great times we spent together, especially at the ski weekends. I can still remember him running around in his white thermals and black socks (LOL). This year we also lost Jeff Ortiz. Jeff played for two generations of Warrior teams and was one of our original PS 106 players. He did a lot of work to keep us together and always sent me a text to see if I was coming to our Friday night dinner in the Bronx.

This forward would not be complete without mentioning my 40-year loving spat with John Macchiaroli (Match). We had a disagreement in the park house one day and we were immediately escorted to the sand box to iron out our differences. Boxing gloves were added and the fight began. Match, you know who really won that fight even though there was an early and unfair knockdown! See the pictures!

I played for the Warriors until I was twenty-two years old. During my last season I was married with a son who was in a baby carriage on the sidelines—it was difficult to finally leave the playing field.

I want to thank Bob Nieder for writing this book—it is a great accomplishment. And by the way, Bob was the best kicker in the league!

Dr. Arthur M. Langer

Warrior #51

Table of Contents

The Warrior Story

Chapter 1

The Reconnecting

Stock Photo of a Football Game-Central Park N.Y. circa 1958

This is the story of a sandlot football team in The Bronx, circa 1952 and which still exists to this day. From egg creams, sock hops, drive-in movies and life in schoolyards to sex, drugs and rock and roll to cell phones, iPads, and social media. This is also the story of one man who was the center of gravity for this enduring organization committed to sport and camaraderie.

***

We found our glory in the streets, some of us as young as eight years, in playgrounds maybe at age ten and on local gridiron fields, from blacktop to grass. A lot of us would continue playing until we were in our mid-twenties and beyond. We were all Warriors. When we put on our jersey, when we wore that uniform, we were bigger than life. We were kids and young teenagers growing up, in the Bronx, a great time to live in New York City. It has been quite some time now since we've all played and of course, our legends grow in our minds, our stories get better with age. But on that team, we were kings, we were champions.

Over time we grow up. We get married, have families, and real jobs beyond the supermarket, the drug store, and the candy store of adolescence. Some of us move out of the New York area. The neighborhood schoolyard or the local pub is no longer a meeting place. But our memories grow, and our smiles widen recalling our "golden" days. Some of us go on to do well in life and some of us get by. Some of us pass on, to be remembered affectionately forever and some seem to disappear off the face of the earth. Some of us fell into drug addiction and some of us couldn't handle the drink as well as others. But almost every one of us cleaned up and returned to living a steady if not fruitful life with our families and careers. But we are all Warriors and always will be, a bond we share, a common rite of passage proudly.

About ten years ago, maybe 2010, three of the guys from my playing days, Gary "Buck" Cosentino, John "Johnny Match" Macchiaroli, and Tom "Pich" Piccininni got together in a diner on East Tremont Avenue in the Bronx. They are life-long friends from their pre-teen youth, as far back as grammar school, St. Benedict's and Santa Maria in the Bronx. As one of them told me, "it was just three old friends who had gone through some rough times but were now back on track and wanted to reconnect". They enjoyed their encounter so much that they decided that they should do this more often., After a while, this small group thought to invite the coach, Jerry Demers. Jerry was the Athletic Director at the P.S. 106 school yard and head coach of the Warriors. Jerry always loved his guys and of course, he would attend. In a short time, the group grew. Comprised of Jerry, Match, Gary Buck, and Tommy, they were now joined by Jackie Cawley, Vic Anderson, Mark "The Bear" Anderson, and Joe Regina. It was Joe Regina who had the impetus to create a contact list. Over quite some time, he constructed a directory of all who had played on our team including coaches, almost fifty names. It contained player and spouse names, mailing addresses, a phone number, and an email address. Lord knows where he found the time to do this tedious task as this took quite some time, over a year's worth. All done during his tenure with the Wes tchester Square Merchants' Association working with merchants and community members throughout the Bronx to help develop the Business Improvement Districts (BID) and caring for his mom Eileen, age eighty-seven. Upon completion of this massive spreadsheet of information, he emailed it to each one of us. We now had the means to communicate and keep in touch with each other. What began as a casual get together in a diner grew into a monthly event for any and all. Every third Friday of the month, The Huddle, as it was named, was held in various diners, bar, and restaurants. Each month, Joe would send out a reminder to let everyone know where, when, at what time a Huddle was taking place. On one particular reminder, he indicated that a special guest would be attending the upcoming Huddle. That special guest was me. On May 17th, 2013, I flew up to the Bronx from Tampa, Florida to attend my first Huddle. As I walked through the doors of the Crosstown Diner, purposely late so that everyone would be there. I was greeted by an uproar from eighteen of my brothers. It had been about thirty-five years since I had seen these guys, but it felt as if I had never left. It was as if time had never elapsed from back then. We were always a close-knit group that cared about each other. There was always a charm and magic amongst us. Hugs came from everywhere, but none were as sweet as the embrace my coach and I shared. Tears filled my eyes holding onto Jerry as the memories flooded through me. My mind raced back to 1970, my second game with the Warriors. I had kicked a field goal under the worst of weather elements. We won that game 3-0. This clinch that Jerry and I shared reminded me of that day and coming back to the bar, Leonardi's, purposely late so I could receive the cheers and joy of my new teammates. Having my guys there made my day but having Jerry with me made my world. I soon sat down and over food and drink, the blarney flew about punctuated by laughter. In the Bronx, breaking horns is a sign of affection, A great night indeed.

It was maybe a year later that I was back up in New York and stayed at Tommy Piccininni's condominium in New Rochelle. As we sat in the living room, watching a Yankee game, Tom asked as to why I wouldn't write a book about "us". To explain, I had written two fictional novels that were self-published. Tom had read both of them but was particularly impressed with the second one, *Battersea Island*, a fictional tale with slight social, cultural aspects. When he asked me about writing about us, I questioned him as to who "us" was.

"What do you mean by us?

"Us, The Warriors. You know when we played."

"I don't know Tommy, I don't do fiction. And besides, a story about the Warrior goes far beyond the six, seven years that we were together. I mean the team started in 1952."

"Nah, just write about us, when we played. The championships, the ski weekends, the shenanigans, the guys. It would be great."

"I don't know Tom. Maybe, I guess. I'm just not a non-fictional writer."

On the plane ride home, I considered Tommy's proposition. Advocate on one shoulder and devil's advocate on the other.

Why not try writing it. You have nothing to lose. You're retired. What else do you have to do with your time? Do I write about "us" or the entire history from the very beginning? I should write the entire history. How do you capture events from before I played? Chrissakes, the team started the year I was born. I guess I could start by talking to Jerry. I know some of the older guys. And my worst-case scenario is if I write something that isn't good, I could hand it off to one of the other guys to continue on.

I got off the plane knowing I would not do this. Within a few months, I began to write my third book, *Lacey's Choyce*, another fictional story centered about a young main character with slight paranormal ability. I had found that as I was writing this, my mind would drift to the Warrior story. It was almost as if I was trying to write two different books at the same time. Ultimately, I did write the third book. Upon its completion, my mind and thoughts were now locking onto the Warrior story. About a year after staying with Tommy, 2015, I was back in New York and attended another Huddle. It was held at Jimmy Ryan's a bar and grill on Middleton Road in the Pelham Bay section of the Bronx. There were eleven of us that night, sitting at a long table in the dining area. As always, a great time. As it was getting late and a light rain began, the guys started making their way home. I was to stay at Tom's place once again. Tom was going to drive someone home. He gave me a choice to come for the ride with him or wait at Jimmy Ryan's and he would come back to get me. I wanted to wind down with one more beer, so I told Tom to come back and fetch me. I got my pint and wandered over to the front of the bar. I peered out the big window into the night, watching the rain dampen Middleton road. My eyes fixated on a building across the street, McNulty's Funeral Parlor. Again, the memories. McNulty's was, when we played, the Emerald Isle. A massive wide bar that maintained two back rooms, one behind the other. I was recalling that Wednesday night, December 1971. We were locked in a first-place tie with the Kiwanis Saints of Throggs Neck. We would be playing them that coming Saturday night, the final regular season game at German Stadium for the divisional championship. That particular night we were having what the coaches called a "skull session". This is where we would go over plays that we would run offensively and what we would be doing defensively. The session began in the Emerald Isle, farthest away from the bar. Most of the team was in attendance so there had to be about thirty of us. At some point, as the bar began to fill with patrons, Jerry, our head coach, decided we should continue in the back room, the second one. It was obvious, as this was the "big game" that Jerry did not want to chance someone overhearing us. We continued on in the back room. Someone from the bar, someone not on the team but who knew us, came into the back room.

"Two guys from the Saints just came into the bar," he clandestinely told someone. The message was delivered to Jerry. This was Halas and Lombardi all over again when Halas would spy on Lombardi's summer workouts. If you ain't cheatin', you ain't tryin'. Without hesitation, we moved into the third back room but within no time at all, Jerry instructed us to get into our cars and we would carry on at a small patch of grass off the Cross-Bronx Expressway, a little north of Castle Hill Ave behind P.S. 36. It was now dark, maybe about 6:30 but it was frigid out there, featuring a wind that was bone chilling. Not only were we going to go through our chalkboard session, but as we were on a field, we would walk through the plays, over and over again until we got it right. As a kicker, I had nothing to do but stand there and freeze. Someone did offer me a gulp of liquid codeine which I gladly accepted. It wasn't as good as blackberry brandy but it did the job. I stood there at the window recalling that moment with a slight smile on my face. A voice from behind startled me into the present.

"Hey Bobby, are you afraid of the rain?"

It was Jerry. I didn't respond immediately.

"Are you staying at Tommy's condo?

"Yeah. He went to take someone home and then he's coming back to get me."

"You miss the Bronx, don't you?"

"Yes, I do. I like the Florida weather and prices, but I miss the guys, my favorite foods and the New York City vibe. I'll always be a Bronx boy."

Jerry moved to my side. A moment of silence. I wondered if we were both being a touch nostalgic in that quiet instant.

Finally, I spoke. "Jerry, do you think it is apropos that a bar we drank ourselves under the table would become a funeral parlor? I mean as young guys we drank ourselves to death in that bar and now they're laying out the dead to rest."

Jerry laughed. "I never thought of it that way, but I suppose you're right. And the funny part is the funeral director, Pat McNulty played for us. He was a tight end after you guys left."

"Really?"

"Are you good for one more?" Jerry asked

"Sure, let's sit at the bar, I'm buying."

We ordered our draughts and shot the breeze. My mind was racing to the point that there was a jolt of an adrenaline boost. Out of the blue, I blurted it out, finally.

"Jerry, I want to write a book. I want to try to write about our history…from the beginning."

Jerry lit up. He spun on his bar stool to face me. "Yes, Bobby, yes. Someone should try to capture the Warriors' history."

"Jay, as he was always affectionately called, I'm not sure that I can do this, but I want to try. I have written three fictional stories…"

"Yes, I've been told."

"I'm not sure where to start but I want to give it a try. Tonight, is not the night to ask you questions, jeez, I've got a million questions, but I can call you. We can talk, and I can record you off my cell phone."

There, it came out, it was said. A five-hundred barbell was lifted off the back of my neck and shoulders. I had just made a commitment. Jerry was ecstatic, the gleam in his eyes told me so. I knew at that moment I could not disappoint my coach, as none of us would ever do. I have no idea how I would do this.

"Jerry, the Warriors started in 1952, correct?"

"No Bobby, 1948, it starts in 1948."

"1948? But you told me once that it started in 1952."

"Yes, it did but 1948, when I'm a ten-year-old boy, that's when I fell in love with football. That's where we start."

Chapter 2

The Beginning

Stock Photo Upper East Side, German Town, New York, N.Y – circa 1948

1948 was basically the mid-point of peacetime between World War II and the soon to be Korean "Conflict". These were the "good old times", an era when life was simpler were rolling. "Dewey defeats Truman[1]" yet somehow Time Magazine's Man of the Year, Harry Truman stayed in office as our President. On a wall in Jimmy Ryan's Bar and Grill is a framed public

---

[1] Chicago Tribune, Front Page, November 3, 1948

notice which reads as follows "Notice to Bronx passengers. Effective Sunday, July 11, 1948, the 167th Street Crosstown, 138th Street Crosstown, Westchester Avenue and St. Ann's Avenue trolley will be motorized. Effective same date, exchange of free transfers between the 167th Street Crosstown and the Broadway – Kingsbridge, Third and Amsterdam Avenue will be discontinued. A charge of two cents will continue to be made for transfers from the Williamsbridge Road, Eastchester Road and Throggs Neck buses to south bound Westchester Avenue Buses and vice-versa[2]." The sports world mourned the loss of Babe Ruth but a Baby Ruth candy bar, originally advertised as an "energy bar[3]" could be had for five cents[4]. A hot dog from the neighborhood deli was a better "meal" at ten cents but as every kid knew, a real treat was the ten cent hamburgers from White Castle[5]. The corner candy store was a better "restaurant" where for the price of fifteen cents an egg cream, could be enjoyed. I'm not sure what a pint of beer went for but a drinking man could go to the local tavern and bring home a galvanized metal pail of brew. We sat around T.V.s, if your parent had one, watching Howdy Doody while mom and dad would view Meet the Press and Philco TV Playhouse[6]. You could hop a ten-cent bus or subway ride to get to the Polo Grounds and watch the New York Giants, led by manager Leo Durocher, and purchase a seat in the outfield, lower deck, for one dollar and seventy-five cents[7]. With an average annual income of thirty-six-hundred dollars[8], (the minimum wage was forty cents[9]) dad could buy a suit for forty-one dollars and fifty cents[10] and mom could style in a fur coat affordable at three-hundred-forty-nine dollars[11], all at Sterns on Fifth Avenue. So, when one hears reference to "missing the good old days" what you are actually hearing are

---

[2] Poster at Jimmy Ryan's Bronx Grill and Bar, 3005 Middletown Road, Bronx, NY, 10461; Source Unknown; See Appendix Page 241

[3] Klein, Christopher (September 25, 2014). *"Babe Ruth v. Baby Ruth"*. *History* (network). *Retrieved October 29, 2017.*

[4] Candywrapperarchive.com/candy-collector/candy-prives-over-the-years/

[5] https://www.qsrmagazine.com/news/white-castle-offers-27-cent-burgers

[6] http://www.tvhistory.tv/1948%20QF.htm

[7] http://www.baseball-almanac.com/teamstats/roster.php?y=1948&t=NY1

[8] Revision of Estimate for Median Family Income in 1948; Federal Reserve Bulletin, Page 1324

[9] https://libraryguides.missouri.edu/pricesandwages/1940-1949

[10] New York Times, November 25, 1948, Page 34

[11] New York Times, November 25, 1948, Page 12

people saying that they miss the good old day prices. What they're not telling you is that they like today's conveniences.

Yorkville, in the forties, was a low to middle income, working-class neighborhood that became a destination for waves of European immigrants. The area was predominately a German community but also inhabited by many of Czechs, Slovaks, Polish, and Hungarian descent that came to America during the peak years of European immigration. The largest non-German group were the Irish[12]. The mix of people, the convenience of having "everything at your fingertips" and, especially, the pockets of Old-World culture that survived from a time, decades ago melted into this thriving blue-collar community which gave a lively Yorkville a distinct salt of the earth style and character.

I got together with Jerry and we commenced our deep dive into the genesis of the Warriors. Jerry's informative years were in the Yorkville section of Manhattan, the southern end of what they call the Upper Eastside. It was called Germantown back then.

"Bobby. even though I had an older brother, Frank, he was eight years older than me and I didn't get to see him much when I was growing up. He was either going to high school or college or in the army, so I was by myself a lot. I do remember as a young boy, I loved playing with my toy soldiers and my baseball cards. I used these baseball cards and played a game where I pulled back the lever and you hit a ball and it would be either a single, double, triple, home run. I had a whole league. I kept statistics and everything. I had a whole league and I would interchange players, make trades. I guess that's how I started. It was the early version of fantasy football. I was only maybe eleven twelve years old at that time I would love to play with the other kids from the neighborhood, in the streets of New York, 73rd Street between First and Second Avenues, which I believe is actually Lenox Hill. We all lived in pre-war apartment buildings. Five, six-story buildings built of sturdy brick and stone with high ceilings, probably about forty families to a building."

"The street right outside your apartment building was the playground, a meeting place for us young kids. On our block we played a lot of different activities on 73rd Street under the watch of the neighborhood moms who would sit on a fire escape, sipping a cool drink, knitting or

---

[12] Nicole Lyn Pesce, Yorkville vs. Park Slope: See how these New York City neighborhoods stack up". NY Daily News.12 December 2013.Retrieved 27 February 2015

reading a book. There was no air-conditioning back then so during the hot summer months, it was either sitting in the living room with a large window fan circulating hot air or it was the fire escape in the hope of catching a warm breeze. But of course, it was a safer time, so you could go out on your block and play until it was time to eat supper. Dinner time was announced by your mom, calling you from a window. Most of the games we played were stickball, stoop ball, slap ball, Johnny on the Pony, and a game called War. War was probably a leftover, I think from the Second World War. Who created it, I have no idea, but what would happen is that you would draw a circle and break up the circle into pie shaped slices and as many players as you had would stand around the circle and each would be representative of a different country, Italy, Ireland, Germany, England, America whatever they'd like to take at the time. The person who started off the game would go to the middle of the circle and bounce a ball as high as he could and call out a name, "I declare War on Italy". Whoever represented Italy would have to catch the ball on the fly while all the other players scattered in different directions from the circle trying to get as far away as possible. When you caught the ball, you would call out freeze, and everybody would have to stop. Some of them hid in doorways, some tried to go behind cars, and some were caught in mid-air on one foot. The person who caught the ball would then have the option of throwing the ball at the closest player to make that person "it". I'm forgetting the details of the game, my God it's almost seventy years ago from when I played but the object of the game was to acquire all of the other countries. Eventually, one player would end up with all the territories, thus dominating the world and winning the game. This type of activity was the same on almost every block in Manhattan at that time as there were very little structured programs in those years. Believe it or not, most of the games we played ended up with what you would call "asses up" where the losing person would go up against the wall, face the wall, bend over. Everybody would have a chance with a Spaulding ball from across the street to take a shot at his rear end. One of the more popular games that we played was stoop ball. Usually, it called for three players per team to play. You played from one side of the street to the other side. The batter would throw the ball off a pointed stoop. The objective was to hit the ball at such an angle off that point that it took off in the air as far and high as possible. Ground balls and line drives that were not caught were singles. Of course, if it hit a parked car and someone caught it off the car you were out. Any ball hitting the building on the other side of the street was a double and anything over the second story window was a home run. There weren't that many kids on the block but generally,

9

there were about six to eight kids, Luby, Henry, Bill, Ritchie, Steve Caputo, to name a few, with maybe one or two visiting kids from other blocks playing these games. Of course, the most popular street game was stickball. All that was needed was an old broomstick handle for a bat and a Spaldeen for a baseball."

A Spaldeen ball was sold in 1949. It is actually called Spaulding, the company name, but the New York City dialect affected its name. They were tennis balls that had been rejected for slight defects before the addition of the fuzzy coating. Rather than toss them in the trash, Spalding, based in Springfield, Mass., stamped the words "Spalding High-Bounce Ball" on the pink rubber rejects and sold them cheaply to wholesalers[13]. The old Spaldeens cost a quarter and sat on candy counters in most corner stores. The new ball would later be sold in sporting goods stores at a cost of two dollars and today they could be found on Amazon for almost six dollars.

"The Spaldeen was twenty-five cents at the corner candy store and of course, back then, we would have a few of us chip in to come up with a quarter because that was a lot of money for kids back then We played stickball by hitting the ball by yourself right down the center of the street, no pitching or running the bases, until we got older. Manholes covers were always home plate and second base and a fire hydrant or a parked car would be first and third base. Of course, in a narrow street we would unfortunately break a couple of windows or we would lose the ball up on a fire escape. Whoever hit it would have the embarrassing job of going into that tenement building, knock on someone's door and ask for the ball back, sometimes they would and sometimes they wouldn't. I guess after a while they got sick and tired of us or having us disrupt their daily activity, so they would just keep the ball, it depended on the person, much like today. Stickball was the most common game, the game we loved most. In the fall and winter, we did play a little football, but it wasn't easy to do that because the kids on the block at that time were very poor for the most part and I don't recall too many of them having a football. Once in a while we'd play touch football but of course, again, the street was a very narrow area, so you could either go long for a pass or fake going long and stop or do a square out in between two cars, that was the extent of football. In the very early days when we didn't have a football, we would roll

---

[13] https://www.nytimes.com/2005/03/13/business/yourmoney/the-spaldeen-is-back-even-if-the-dodgers-arent.html; Brendan I. Koerner

up newspapers, tie it up and use that as a football. But there wasn't that much football. I didn't have a true love for the game yet. That didn't happen until I started to see the Cardinal Hayes football games with my brother Frank. To play anything like touch-tackle football or baseball which we did, you'd have to walk from 73rd Street and First Ave to Central Park Sheep's Meadow which is a good mile and a half, I guess. But we did it without thinking too much about it, we just thought this is what you have to do if you want to play. So, we would walk over there and play baseball and football out on the big lawn. Today you can't do that since they put new grass down, you can only play Frisbee or lay around and watch the people walk their dogs so in those days there was a lot more activity in Central Park. It seems that they're always trying to close down activities for kids. But there were no Little Leagues that I know of in Manhattan at least on the East Side at that time. I guess in the outer boroughs or suburbs there were more Little Leagues and of course, today there are plenty of fields for kids and teenagers to play on. Back then, the Parks Departments started to build fields but, in those days, you had to be your own initiator of activities which we did. I am proud to tell you that at that young age, I was initiating and organizing these activities. We did a lot of running around back then and it got to the point, as new families moved in, where there were so many kids on the block that we actually separated the block into two halves. We had the Eastern half and there was another group from up the block, the Western half. We knew each other and sometimes we played games against each other, but basically, they had their own way of playing and we had our way of playing. Eventually, later on, as we became older, some of the guys up the block would become good football players with the Warrior Team."

"Of all the things that I loved throughout my life, including now, it was Frank who got me into football, history, model kits (soldiers, airplanes, and ships) and he encouraged me to have a sense of humor…he's responsible for everything. So, I owe him a lot. He was part big brother and part dad. My father, Joseph Albert Demers was an older man. When I was born in 1937, he was fifty-five already, so, he didn't have that energy anymore. He had fought in the First World War for four years, so he was kind of disgusted with politics and with people…he must have had a chip on his shoulder about which we never discussed but I'm sure that was a factor. Anybody that came back from the war looked at humanity in a different way. But yeah, so my brother took over a lot of the things like taking me to the park or doing this or starting a team or doing things a father might have done. My father was from Lachine, Canada, which was a city unto itself but today it is a borough within the city of Montreal. He was a lumberjack by trade. He moved to America after the war. He moved down to Detroit from Canada and was in the printing business. And then from there, he moved to New York which is where he met my mother. We grew up never knowing any of my father's relatives. They were all in Canada. We heard about a couple of them and once in a while, he would get a letter from them. I don't know if he wrote back, he may have. But my brother and I never actually saw them. Evidently, he didn't have a great desire to go back there. He had been married previously and also had a daughter from that marriage. They were separated or divorced in Canada so maybe he didn't want to go back for that reason. But he never kept in touch with his relatives up there. But when he got to New York, he married my mother, and he would be the superintendent, in whatever particular building we lived in. I say this that way because we moved around just about every year for a number of years. He worked as a "super" (building superintendent) fixing things and shoveling the coal in the basement for the building's furnace which was the heating system for the building, you might remember having a radiator in your apartment when you were young."

"Yes, I do. I remember that if the apartment was chilly during the winter, you could hear the tenants banging on their radiators with a hammer. The whole building could hear this including the "super". It was like code language telling the super to turn up the furnace and provide more heat. The cheap supers trying to pinch a penny, totally ignored this and never did turn up the heat."

"Well, my dad did this work because it would provide an apartment, rent-free. My father was a fiery man who had a bit of a temper. It was common for him to get into arguments with the landlord of the building thus getting fired. I can remember that we first lived on Summit Avenue in the Highbridge section of the Bronx and then we were on Pleasant Avenue and 122nd Street in East Harlem. We then moved to Yorkville. At 73rd Street, between First and Second Avenue, we lived in three different places. We stayed there up until we moved to the Bronx in 1957. My mother was a very quiet person, Geraldine, the same as my wife's name. Mom was born in Ireland and came to America in 1927 with her father, my grandfather, two sisters and her brother. My mom's mother, my grandmother, had died in Ireland from consumption which was rampant in Ireland. Her father, immediately went into the stock market. He was an engineer, but he lost everything in the stock market during the Depression. He came over at just the wrong time. My mom was a housekeeper, she worked at the Amsterdam Hotel on West 50th Street. I'll give you a little bit of my father's history in World War I. Unfortunately, the Germans had invaded, and they got most of Belgium under their control. But the King of Belgium insisted that the British hold onto this one section called Ypres and that's where my father was located. There was a lot of fighting going on there. The Germans wanted to take all of Belgium and the British wanted to hold it for the King of Belgium and they eventually did. That's the same area where Hitler was serving as a Gefreiter (lance corporal) in the Bavarian Army, on the opposite side. It's very strange that they were so close together, my father and Hitler. My father was a Sargent in the Canadian Army. He was wounded three times fighting and they sent him right back to the trenches each time because in that period the Americans were not in the war yet and they needed everybody they could get. Seeing the tactics that were going on where it was straightforward charges with machine guns mowing down everybody, that's got to affect a person in a big way. The French especially believed in what they called the 'offensive' which was simply a matter of the will and that all a soldier had to do was to go forward and charge. Unfortunately, I never asked my father too much about the war. As a kid, not being that interested at the time or that knowledgeable but I'm very sorry now that I didn't."

"As I was saying about my brother Frank, he got me into everything I love, especially football. I can remember vividly when I got that love of the game. My brother, God bless Frank, started to take me to his high school's football games, Cardinal Hayes, which is the high school I eventually attended. I believe all of their games, back then, were played at either Randall's Island or Baker's Field at Columbia University. It was Thanksgiving, 1948, again, I'm only ten years old. He took me to what is known as the Bronx Turkey Bowl. This has been a tradition for the last 76 years. Since 1942 Mount St. Michael and Cardinal Hayes have met on each Thanksgiving Day, a storied Catholic High School Football League rivalry showdown. The games were exciting for a young person like myself who had no knowledge of football since at that time I never had a television, so I didn't get a chance to be a fan too much. As a young boy, I didn't listen to the games on the radio but having Frank take me to a game and seeing it in person was special. Listening to the names of the various players as they were announced when they ran onto the field was exciting and a lot of fun. One player I especially remember was Jerry Perry of Cardinal Hayes High School and seeing eleven people on each team trying to do something on every single play affected the way I thought about a sports program. On that day in 1948, Thanksgiving, Frank took me to the Turkey Bowl at Randall's Island. It was a mild day, weather-wise. I remember that we took the bus to 125th Street and walked over the bridge to Randall's Island that morning to watch that game. That day, I fell in love with football."

"Do you remember who won that game?"

"No, I can't recall the score. Frank probably remembers."

I decided to give Frank a call. I do remember that I had first come upon Frank Demers at Westchester Manor, April 21, 2012. Until that night, I was not aware that Jerry had an older brother. That night at Westchester Manor was a retirement party for Jerry. This was a grand affair attended by somewhere between one-hundred-seventy-five to two hundred people. Our team was in full attendance as well as our predecessors, the touch-tackle team out of P.S. 106. We were joined by Jerry's family, his wife Geri, his daughters, Karen, Kerry, and Kim, and his son Ricky along with coaches and of course most of us with our wives. Councilman Jimmy Vacca was present. This was an incredible evening on many levels but in my mind, it was the first time that you had the two groups, the touch-tackle team and the tackle team in one room en masse. This is not to say that most of us did not know of each other. As a matter of fact, there were some of the P.S. 106 guys, Artie Langer Jeff Ortiz, George Nardone, and Joey Reich, that also played on the tackle team. But to have us all under one roof was quite the sight. It was as if an imaginary bridge had been built connecting the '60s to the '70s. It was that night that I had noticed an older gentleman, tall and thin, well dressed and distinguished. Perhaps I noticed him because he only mingled amongst Jerry and his family, some of the coaches and the Councilman. He had a sophisticated presence and for some unknown reason, for me, he stood out from the crowd. I would come to learn that this was Jerry's older brother.

A voice on the other end of the phone answered my call and I introduced myself to Frank Demers. We chatted a bit, mostly about the affair at Westchester Manor. At age eighty-six, I had found him to be very interesting, very sharp, lucid of mind, very vivid in his memory, extremely well-spoken, very impressive. I would come to learn that Frank went on in his life as an educator. He was a professor of sociology at Marymount College in Tarrytown (also known as Marymount College of Fordham University). He went on with pride about how proud he was of his little brother. From when Jerry was a young boy to the accolades and love that his brother is receiving at this time in his life.

"I can't believe that my little brother got more out of life than I ever did for what he did out of his heart."

"Frank, what was Jerry like as a young boy? Let's say in 1948."

"Bob, the one thing I can tell you about Jerry, even at the age of six, is that he was always organized. One of his favorite things to do was to play with his toy soldiers. He was very methodical in arranging the figures into battle formations. All his toys, books and stationary were kept in an orderly fashion. By the time he was playing in the street with the other boys, one could see that he had leadership qualities in him. He was always the one organizing the games and later on teams. He always had a plan as to what he wanted his team to do and they all would listen to him."

"Frank, the reason I referenced 1948 is that your brother told me about the day he fell in love with football. It was the Thanksgiving Day Turkey Bowl game. He doesn't remember the score of that game, but he thought that you might. So, won that game?"

There was a momentary hesitation.

"Bob, I believe it or not I don't remember either."

We ended our conversation with my promise to find out the score of that game. All I needed was the New York Public Library and a microfiche machine. My work was cut out for me.

I had put a call into the New York Public Library to see if someone at the library could pull an article from the New York Times, November 25th, 1948 from their microfilm files. I was told that they could do this but quite a cost. They also told me that if I could get to Florida A&M University, that their library had New York Time's newspapers on microfilm going back to the 1920s. Driving to Tallahassee was a lot cheaper than getting on a plane to Manhattan. I called the university to make sure that they did have these files. They assured me that they had them and that even though they were in the middle of their spring break, the library would be open. I chose to make the drive, a tedious four-hour ride, most of which was on a one-lane blacktop that traveled due north through desolation and seemingly nowhere. But I was on my mission to find out if Cardinal Hayes won that day. I got to the university's library only to find that the entire staff had just left for lunch. I waited in the lobby for almost a full hour. While they were out, and

15

not being a patient person, I wandered about, found their microfilm files and pulled the New York Times reel that had the 1948 newspapers. Using the microfiche machines back at Lehman College during my days as a student, I was able to thread the reel onto the machine. My problem became technological advancement. Whereas the machines were fully manual back in 1970, today they maintained a digital program that I was unfamiliar with. Eventually, the staff returned, and a young man showed me how to work the program. Soon enough I had that machine humming as the reel whirred in high-speed motion. The actual reel contained the years 1945 through 1949 so it took a while to get to 1948 but there I was. The edition printed on Friday, November 26th, the day after Thanksgiving where the results of the previous day's game would be chronicled. The front page proclaimed that the "Pacific Coast Dock Strike Settled; Atlantic Men Expected to Ratify Terms of Agreement Here Tomorrow". This was the ILWU, the longshoremen union ending a ninety-five-day strike that tied up West Coast ports from San Diego to Alaska. This was news indeed as this strike was waged shortly after the passage of the Taft-Hartley Act[14]. I slowed the machine down so that I could go page by page to get to the sports section. As I advanced the reel, I came across many post-Thanksgiving sales from Macy's, Gimbel's and Saks Fifth Avenue. I guess the fore-runner of black Friday. I finally came upon page seventeen, the local sports section. I let out a whoop and a clap of my hands upon finding the article. The vacant facility echoed with my excitement. The headline read "Hayes High Rally" but I was aghast when I saw the score. The article read as follows;

"Striking back after being two touchdowns behind at half-time, Cardinal Hayes tied undefeated Mount Saint Michal, 13-13 in their annual Thanksgiving Day football game at Triborough Stadium yesterday. A crowd of 15,000, the largest ever to watch a scholastic contest at the stadium, witnessed the battle between the two Bronx schools. Howie Smith's well-schooled Mounties scored twice in the second quarter. Joe Ahearn scored the first touchdown when he smashed off right tackle for twenty yards shortly after Don Ciliotta ran back a Hayes kick from his own 38 to the opposition's 25. Four plays later Ding-Dong Bell plunged over from the four for a tally. The Cardinal got their first trying markers in the third quarter. The first came when a Fred Roselli swept his right end for 19 yards with Bill Bradshaw adding the extra point. A twenty-yard pass from Bob Tighe to Bob Davolin in the end zone deadlocked matters."

---

[14] Harry Bridges Center for Labor Studies, University of Washington, Ashley Lindsey, 2013

I drove home in a typical, torrential Florida downpour, barely able to see out my front windshield. And all I could think was that I spent an entire day making this miserable ride only to find out that nobody won this game. The actual headline to the article read, "*Hayes High Rally, Gains 13-13 Draw*".

I called Frank the next day.

"Hello Frank, how are you doing?"

"I'm fine Bob, how are you?"

"I'm not sure Frank and I'll tell you why. I spent a ten-hour day, eight-hours driving and two-hours in a library at Florida A&M in Tallahassee pulling the New York Times from November 26, 1948. I now know the score of that fateful game"

"Really? Did we win?"

"Nooo! Nobody won, it was a 13-13 tie. I spent a whole day out of my life to find out that nobody won. I feel cheated. I wanted a winner, preferably Cardinal Hayes. I was rooting for you guys almost sixty-years later. Geez, makes me remember the old New York Rangers coach declaring that a tie was "like kissing your sister through a screen door".

Frank laughed heartedly as did Jerry when I called him after Frank.

***

A few days later I sat with Jay at the Crosstown Dinner. We sipped some coffee followed by a full breakfast.

"Any program that lasts as long as sixty-four years must have had a strong motivation to start it out. The Warriors started in 1952," Jerry grinned with a big smile. "When I was fourteen, my father got a television and I was able to watch Notre Dame football which is when I became a big fan. This was even more impressive because I got a lot of the things that we do now from watching Ralph Guglielmi (Quarterback 1951 – 1954[15]), and watching their offensive sets as well as how the Notre Dame defense defended. In 1954, when I went to high school, my horizons and availability of meeting people opened up a little bit more, so it was more than a

---

[15] und.com/news/2017/1/26/Notre_Dame_Hall_of_Fame_Quarterback_Ralph_Guglielmi_ Dies.aspx?path=football

block team. The block team had started in 1952 and we would play other block teams in Central Park. We'd lay down our bags and jackets for the sidelines and just measure out a field that way," Jerry recalled in a laughing manner. "Sometimes my older brother would referee the games and we would play against another team. Frank was the first Warrior coach. Gradually, we kept playing and the teams that we played against, when they broke up their players would come and play with us because we still had a team. Consistency was very important in the early stages of the Warriors. We were still in Manhattan and I think by 1957 we were really forming what was an organized team that was pretty good because it had absorbed all these players from the Yorkville area. We had a darn good team. Myself and a gentleman named Ray Cullen who was older, but had played against us (laughing) he was a man and we were kids, teenagers, but we were strong, and we thought we could do anything. Ray came over and became the first defensive coach of the Warriors and in 1957 we started to really organize. That same year I moved to The Bronx and we played a couple of teams in The Bronx with all our players coming from Manhattan, traveling up to The Bronx to play. That same year Joey Salomini came around and was handing out flyers about a meeting to form a league. So, I went to the meeting and met Dan Salomini, his father. That's when we first started to play league football. Joe had two brothers, one was Danny Salomini (Jr.) and the other was Tom Salomini. They were all referees, but Joe was the top referee. The league was called The Bronx Umpires Alliance, in The Bronx, and we decided to go to the meeting they were having. They did form the league and we did enter in 1958 which was the first year that the Warriors played actual league football with a schedule and regular referees and regular different teams to play each week. We were very good in 1958 (definitive statement stated boldly, with pride) thanks to most of these Manhattan players and a few Bronx players who started to come onto the Warriors from teams that we would play. These were guys that had played in the past for teams such as the City Island Giants. We were 10 & 0 that year and won the championship. That was our first taste of glory."

"The quarterback was a gentleman younger than me who was one of the best we ever had. I was now the coach and this quarterback was my friend. His name was Bernie Lyons, since deceased, but he is remembered for his great ability and leadership. He was better than me, so I relinquished my position to him. Talk about leadership, he really was an outstanding leader and player and very calm on the field, a great passer, a great, great passer. In 1959 we were disappointed to be beaten by a team that was composed primarily of Monroe high school players,

18

they were very good, and they beat us in back then. We finished second but the following year we were able to pick up some of their players as their team disintegrated. We picked up their star running back Richie Paililo who was really small but had outstanding speed, cutting ability, and a great football sense. In 1960 we won another championship in the BUA and then the following year we went into another league called the Bronx Manhattan League, because of our ages. The Bronx Manhattan league was run by a gentleman name Eric Lociali. Whichever was the best league for us to get into, because of the age of our players, that's the one that we would go into, for that particular year. I believe we finished second. A lot of the teams were from the West side of The Bronx. It was the heyday of sandlot football in The Bronx. There being a lot of teams all over the place and no distractions such as video games, etc. which had not been invented yet and no soccer because there hadn't been a big influx of other nationalities. Baseball and football were the big games during those years, the late '50s and early sixties. Here's a footnote about the start of the Warriors. Initially our name was the Eagles in 1952 when we started. My brother who previously played for a team from Eagle Avenue in The Bronx thought that would be a good idea to name the team the Eagles since his team was the Eagles and I, of course, agreed so we were the Eagles from 1952 and 1953. In 1954 the players wanted to take a vote on what name the team should be. At that time someone suggested the Warriors and after the votes were counted it turned out the Warriors was the winning vote and we became the Warriors. I believe that's the last time I let any of the players or coaches or parents vote for anything in the history of the Warriors. I found that if you're doing all the work you've got to make all the decisions. But that was a good decision, I like the name Warriors even though I believe the Eagles was a better name. So that's how we started, 1954 with the name change from the Eagles to the Warriors. And a word about the jerseys, which essentially started in 1952. I'm not sure where I came up with the white and red. Hayes was maroon and gold, I guess it's as close as you can get (chuckle). It was probably some sort of a bargain deal, shirts on sale kind of thing, so I decided to get white jerseys with two red stripes on the sleeve and numbers on the front and back. I guess a little bit later when I started watching Notre Dame we might have gone to blue and gold but then again Mount St. Michael's colors were blue and gold. Mount St. Michael and Cardinal Hayes were definite archrivals, so I don't think I would have made the Warriors colors blue and gold. So, we went with white and red and stayed that way to this day as our team colors. Some years later on we would have red jerseys with white numbers but basically, our colors are white and red. There are a few guys that I played with back in my Yorkville day that you may want to speak to. Luby (pronounced Luby) Mlynar, Steve Caputo, Bill Henry, and Henry Helenek."

Well, I found that the phone number Jerry gave me for Luby was a bad number, it led to a business/sales division of a U.S. company in Canada. Steve Caputo had passed away. For Bill Henry, I was only given an address in Sequim Washington but no phone number. Despite all my efforts, I could not locate him. Henry Helenek was someone I did get a hold of.

"Hello. Yes, may I speak with Henry Helenek?"

"Yeah, this is he."

"Uh Henry, my name is Bob Nieder. I played football for the Bronx Warriors during the early seventies under Jay, Jerry Demers. I am attempting to write a book about the history of the Bronx Warriors and Jay, Jerry, he gave me your phone number. He said you played on the original team in 1952. Am I correct?"

Henry lit up, his voice was suddenly enthusiastic. "Yes, 1957. from fifty-two to fifty-seven we were working on the organization. I was about seventeen years old in 1957. Jerry is about two years older than me. As you probably know we grew up on the upper east side. Yorkville, Lenox Hill, mostly the Yorkville area. We called it Yorkville back in the day. That's where all the guys were from that were on the team. Back then Jay had set up the core of a team. He had, I remember, about seven guys who used to go out, this is in the early fifties, and would throw the ball around you know. Jerry was a friend of mine who I went to grammar school with at St. Catherine of Siena. He said he saw a site to play football and asked if I was interested in playing on a team? and I said, yeah, I'm interested. Then a third person joined us, I think it was Bill Henry or maybe Luby Mlynar. What happened is we eventually got up to a playable number and by about 1956 we had about, I'm gonna count, two, three, four, five, six, seven., maybe sixteen, seventeen players. We considered Sheep's Meadow in Central Park as our home. What we did is we just set up oh, what the hell did we call those things? Scrimmage games, yeah. We didn't play any real games you know. But what we were doing was testing where these guys should go for their position. Then when we had those scrimmages, a couple of the players from the opponent's team would come over to our side. Then before you know it, we had a pretty good team. We were able to field a team by the end of 1957. That's when we picked up a lot of good guys. It was all from Yorkville. So, the next season and I think sometime during that time,

Jay had moved from living on 73rd St. to the Bronx. But Jerry stayed focused on us and the team down here. So, in 1958 we thought we were ready for what was called the Bronx Manhattan League."

"You see they had the scandal in college sports in New York City, most famous, the point-shaving scandal in basketball, at this time which ended the college programs. Most of the college football players began to play football in leagues around the city. They formally call it sandlot football. We knew it was more than that. The fact is that it was a higher level of ball because these were the guys that stayed in New York, not wanting to transfer out to another college. Back then we had about ten different college teams in New York City. These guys would have been the core of those teams. So, we went into that league. I was a little apprehensive myself because it was unlimited in weight. I didn't know how we were gonna do but we went in there in our first season and went undefeated. Bernie Lyons was our quarterback. He was an unspoken leader out there. He was this kind of guy, he had this charisma. He didn't have to speak or do anything. You just knew what he was doing, and he had control of the situation. Very soft spoken in the huddle. And it was kind of a little bit of a democracy in the huddle. I can remember a couple of times that I would come back into the huddle and noticed the possibility of a big play that we could run. You know like a hole I could open up on my side of the line. So, he would call the play and tell everyone where the opportunity was to make a big play against the opposite team. Every now and then Jay would send in a play. I remember we had a run off of a reverse handoff on a kickoff. That was a play that Jay called, I'll never forget that one. It just sucked the kicking team to the center of the field. It was perfect, it worked out perfectly. Jay was the coach and then Ray Cullen came on as an assistant coach. At that time, I think Frank, Jerry's older brother, was in Florida working on his masters. He was our first coach from the neighborhood. A very smart man even back then. he stopped being involved with us the year before we entered the league. I don't know what role he and Jay had. Maybe they got together on things. I don't know, but in 1956 I know Frank was working on his thesis, so he didn't have the time to devote to us. I was the right guard which is all about being tough and having no brains (he laughs). But the football you see on tv today is not the football we played back in the day. Yeah, it's a different game. I was two-hundred-twelve pounds, I think. That's a big guy back then. I just found out about a celebration they had for Jerry's retirement. I saw that and said, 'Holy maceral, the Warriors are still going'. And you know I recently saw Jay and we kinda touched base again. You know, talking about all of this, just like the good old days. I got to tell you. The one thing I can say about Jerry is that he always had a calming demeanor but with a sense of humor. He definitely had leadership written all over him. Looking back, I would say that is quite an unusual quality for a ten-year-old. Anyway, back in those days as I was saying the usual weight was like one-hundred-eighty pounds for a tackle. It was all leverage, you know? It was like wrestling. You go for the joints like you were gonna tackle someone. You go for the knees and lift them, and you throw them off balance. A cross body block where you hit the guy in the waist. That's one of the defending points you know. And there weren't that many injuries. The only injuries I can remember is when a guy would block a punt. That's when the face masks started to come in, they put a bar across the face of the helmet. The worst injuries we were seeing were guys' teeth getting knocked out by blocking kicks. But anyway, we didn't need size we had uh, sort of dexterity. Well…back in those days, that's all I had, and we were taught not to use our head for blocking or tackling. When I was a little boy, like in junior high school. I was a heavy kid, so I would play middle linebacker and fullback. They always said, to use your shoulders to block. Put your shoulder in the guy's chest and wrap your arms around him to get the leverage for a tackle."

"You said you went undefeated that year correct?"

"The first year, right. I played for five more years. I remember the second year we came in second to the Luigi Rams. The Luigi Rams had a lot of ex-high school players. and these guys were good, but at the end of the season they broke up and half that team joined us. They were from the Bronx. Those guys played together on a high school team…James Monroe. Also, there was another team out of the South Bronx, the Apache's. They played in a little park, St. Mary's park. They were the top guns, but we knocked them off. A pretty close game, six to nothing. But we picked up some of their players after that. We picked up six of their best players. So, what happened as we went along, the teams that broke up after we defeated them, we would take their best players. By the time we got to 1960, it was a wonderful team. One game that I remember is when we played the Navajos. We played them for a championship that year and with our defense, they couldn't move the ball. So, what they would always do is kick on third down, quick kick, and get field position if they could. We won that year and, in sixty-one we lost a few players and the team was pretty slim that year. Jay joined us with the Archer Street team. We just didn't have enough players. We really had a bad year that year. It was 1962. Yeah, that was a bad year. That's when I quit the team. That was a disappointing season for us. First Bernie Lyons left the team and I don't know if you know much about Bernie Lyons. You know they used to have this PAL softball league during the summer for indigent kids. And they were putting something like twenty-three hundred teams that were entered into the competition from the city. St. Catherine of Siena, a Catholic church on East 68th Street between York and First Avenue, was in it and Bernie Lyons was the pitcher. He was a hell of an athlete. He pitched a perfect game. And in front of the whole city, a perfect game. And that's in the newspaper. He was a natural born athlete. He had everything that it took. I mean he could read the field as a quarterback and he was open to suggestions when we were stuck. But most of the time, ninety-five percent of the time he called the plays. Again, every now and then Jay would call in a play. But going back to 1962 when we had to join up with the Archer St. Rams, I was not too happy with that at all. Again, I only had one more year to play."

"Where'd you go to school Henry?"

"Cardinal Hayes and then from there I went to City College. Then to get my doctorate, I went to Brown University. I got a degree in geology and worked as a geologist for the government putting together geological surveys. I remember receiving a grant to do work around the West Point area. Most of my life I spent teaching at Bradley University here in Peoria, Illinois. But I think that the highest achiever that was ever on the team was Dennis Kent. He played right after me on the Warriors. I think he started in sixty-two. He is now Dean of Rutgers. He did ground-breaking work in geology. We only got to know each other very briefly. Now I'm retired in Peoria, Illinois. But I've gotta go at this point but thanks for the call. I enjoyed my trip down memory lane."

"Thank you and good-bye."

I had enjoyed this conversation with Henry and was now intent to trying to track down more of the "old gang". That evening, while I was out at an affair with my wife, Carmen, my cell phone rang and displayed a phone number I didn't identify, but it did show that it was a New York call. I answered as I began to move away from the dining area so that I could hear better.

"Hello, may I speak with Bob Nieder?"

"Speaking"

"Bob, my name is Luby Mlynar. I got your phone number from Jerry Demers. He told me to give you a call."

A wave of excitement ran through me as I had another one of the legends from the past. "Yes, yes, thank you for calling me."

"Jerry tells me that you're writing a book about the Warriors."

"Well Luby, I'm trying to write a book", I answered with a laugh.

"Is now a good time to talk, I hear music in the background."

"Now is a good time I'm at a small affair with my wife and her friends from work. A whole bunch of women talking shop. So, it gives me an opportunity to step out for some fresh air and have a cigarette. Now is perfect." I was about to be transported back into 1948, the upper east side of Manhattan. Just two guys "tawkin'" on a cobblestone street on First Avenue, surrounded by Packards, DeSotos, Fords, and Chevys.

Luby began his journey. "Well, my experience was a bit different from Jerry and Frank. I was born overseas. In Poland, southern Poland, I can't remember the name of the town. We moved to the US when I was nine. It's a long story. My father was an American soldier in the Army, stationed in Poland which is where he met and married my mother. After the war, we were able to leave there. Anyway, he wound up back in the United States and lived on Sixth Street in lower Manhattan. I was about eight, nine years old at that time. Then we moved to the Yorkville. Let me see. That was the seventh grade, so I was twelve or thirteen. Something like that. That's where I met Jerry, I was twelve years old. Yeah, that's right. I met Jerry probably somewhere around twelve, we were in seventh grade. I got to know him in that time span and we got to play out in the streets you know. He just lived a few blocks up from me. He lived on 73rd and I lived in 70th. So anyway, we got together playing stickball and a few other games like stoopball, war. Later on, as we started to get a little bit older, we started to play football. A lot of two-hand touch in schoolyard parks in New York City, that's where you played, the parks. Jerry really was the guy who organized all that activity, the football team. You know we were all football fans, so we organized a team and eventually, the team started to scrum with other teams. Then it developed where we played other teams. Teams from the west side. Teams from the other neighborhoods. It was not a league but with Jerry there, as he got to know other guys, we get them on our team and we played at Sheep's Meadow in Central Park. That was sort of our home field. There were goal posts, but they were meant for soccer. But nobody played soccer, so we used them for football. As we started to play more games, things got more organized as a league and Jerry would have the stats about that. Yeah, I would think that Jerry would have all the stats. As a matter of fact, Jerry would have it written down. You know we took film of a lot of the games. They weren't Hollywood quality, but they were continual motion. He had one of those old-time cameras. I don't know what happened to them, the films. I assume Jerry has them somewhere. When we moved the team up to the Bronx, we used to go to Rice Stadium in Pelham Bay Park, near where the police have their shooting range and play on both of the playgrounds there. If there was an open field, we were there playing as a team. Jerry was the organizer. He was also the quarterback, kind of like Eddie LeBaron, being of shorter stature. It wasn't that easy for him to do. He used to pass on occasion, and he could run pretty well. Eventually, Bernie Lyons joined the team. The two were friends. You know we were all friends out there. Bernie, he was quick, and he had a good arm. He was a natural athlete, so he was the quarterback for a number of years. Bernie later became a policeman and I assume he went on to bigger and better things. I don't know what happened to him. As time passes, you kind of lose part of the neighborhood. But as I was saying, there were no leagues back then. There were no coaches. Jerry had his uncle or someone he was close to."

I thought I would help Luby along, "It was probably Frank, his brother because I spoke…"

"No, no, no. No, it wasn't Frank. Frank was always around but back then he wasn't really involved with our team. It was all Jerry. I'm trying to remember some of the names of the guys on that team other than Henry, Bill, and Steve. There was a guy we called Sparrow, I forgot his real name. He was a Czech kid that was very quick. Then there was another guy that was bigger, Frank. He became a policeman too, but I don't remember his last name. We had Nick on the line. We had the Gasparig brothers. Louie and his younger brother. Louie Gasparig was about three years older than the rest of us, but he played tackle. He had great moves too. He was a tall guy, not heavy but tall. He'd pull out from his position and was able to cross body block two people at one time. We were great at running the corner to the right. As long as Louie was there that day, he could knock out the linebacker. I played center linebacker and guard or tackle. You know, at the beginning I was the defensive captain. Then we had Ray, did he tell you about Ray the painter?"

"Yes, he did."

"He had this station wagon that we would pile people in to. As many people as we could to go to the game. We could put three in the front and four or five in the back." Luby began to laugh so hard that he had to stop talking. "Sorry about that. But those were good days with Jerry and his big brother Frank. Frank was always the rational one. You know the super calm guy. Not that Jerry wasn't but Frank being older, he was like a father. You know, the big brother, father figure back then. You know Frank was in the Army. The two of them lived on 73rd street, the fourth or fifth floor when I met him. Then later they moved but that was it. Other than that, Jerry, as a person, was a nice guy. He was a very personable guy always with a joke. He was the coach. He put plays in and make people practice a bit. It couldn't be easy coaching back then because you know you're dealing with fourteen and fifteen-year-old kids. We had some guys there that could play football but not all of them. You know everybody can't be good, I guess. But the team firmed up and we had a good team. In terms of playing teams from all over. There were the ones from the Westside. I forget the name of that team. They had black and yellow stripes on their uniforms. We even played one time a team from Harlem. That team came out and you know we didn't have any black players. There were hardly any blacks in the neighborhood. But anyway, they came out and they had on uniforms. We had uniforms, sort of. Everybody on our team had a different helmet. Kind of a little bit like Charley Brown style. We all looked at each other and we kind of knew it was going to be a battle. (laughing) They were nice, but they were not that good as ballplayers. In football, you have to have the initiative. You have to get the football and have the personal drive to do better. If you do it mechanically then it's not going to work. We were spirited, and we thought that we were indestructible. Back in those days, that was the idea. And so, we were aggressive in the football sense. We didn't have a problem beating that team, but it was an interesting experience. I do remember that, (again laughing) after all those years. Otherwise, other than that, I don't know what more I could tell you. Sorry I couldn't give you more."

"Luby, that was great, just perfect. Thank you so much and have a good evening."

Lubomir Mlynar, is of Austria-Hungarian descent which could hear clearly in his accent. He went on to attend City College of New York graduating in the field of chemistry. He was drafted by the Army serving two years from 1961 to 1963 but never left the United States as he worked in the Army Chemical Corps in Baltimore as a chemist. After his discharge, he went to work for Rohm and Haas, an industrial chemical firm outside of Philadelphia. He would be transferred to Zurich where he met his wife who was from France, Michelle, another chemist. She still carries the most delightful Paree inflection. Then, he was relocated by his employ to France, where they had two daughters. Luby came back to America in 1983, finding residence in Blue Bell, Pennsylvania and continued to work for Rohm and Hass. He retired after thirty-six years with them. Luby did tell me that his name, Lubomir is a classic Slavic name. Lubo means love and Mir is the world of peace. He teasingly explained that he is a lover of either the world or peace. He had made up the nickname Luby as he found that Americans had difficulty with Lubomir. He would come to learn that everybody loved Luby as "I love Luby" was the slogan for Luby Chevrolet, one of the oldest car dealerships in the United States.

At this point, I was hell-bent on speaking with Bill Henry. I was in the middle of drafting him a letter when I decided to go on a search for his phone number through the computer. It took quite a while, but I did find a Seattle area phone number. I gave Bill a call and left him a voice message. A good two weeks had passed, and I did not receive a return call. Maybe he wasn't interested in talking to me, this had been the case with a few others. Perhaps he was ill of health or worse, this happens with eighty-year-old individuals. I put Bill in the rear-view mirror of my mind. Early, one Friday, my cell phone announced a Seattle call. Heart be still, I thought to myself. Could it possibly be?

I answered with anticipation. "Hello?"

A strong voice replied. "Bob, how are you this morning, or afternoon as the case may be where you are. This is Bill Henry. You left me a message about writing a book regarding the Warriors."

"Bill, thank you so much for calling and I am just peachy on a beautiful Friday here in sunny Florida. Actually, I'm writing so I have no clue what time it is. Alright Bill, what I'd like you to talk about, what I'm looking for is you growing up in that neighborhood as a young boy.

1948 is the year that Jerry points to when he was ten years old. What was it like? I imagine you grew up in that Yorkville area, the Upper East Side."

"We lived just down the street from Jerry. His address was 345 East 73rd Street as I recall, and I lived at 308 East 73rd Street."

"Oh, ok. So, you've known him since…"

"I've known him since he moved to that area. We went to grammar school together, St. Ann's of Siena. It was 1948 and we got out in 1952, so it was fourth or fifth grade I guess."

I was trying to do my best Dan Rather. "You were on that first team in 1952. Can you tell me what that was like?"

"It was fun. My high school didn't have a football team. Jerry's did but he didn't play for the football team. He got the Warriors going. We had all the neighborhood guys. There were several of us who grew up and went to grammar school together that played on that team. I'm going to keep looking to see if I can find an old team photo. If I do, I'll get it copied and I'll send it to you. I just have to dig it up. But the Warriors back then was a neighborhood group and we would practice in Central Park where there were no lines or anything. Then we would play games. I think some of them were in Central Park. I think we set up bags, coats, and stuff to make boundaries, sidelines. Then up in the Bronx, we played some games too at McCombs Dam Park. It was a baseball field right next to Yankee Stadium."

"Who were some of the guys on that team? I mean I've spoken to Luby and Henry Helenek. I've had great conversations with them. They pretty much paint quite a picture. Jerry, of course, paints the whole mural. We've sat for hours on the phone, at diners, at his house talking about the games that were played on the streets and what it was like in those days. There probably isn't much that you could say that someone else hasn't said. Even from guys in your era to our era, to the guys beyond me. It's all the same but what was Jerry like as a ten-year-old?"

"He was a rabid baseball Giants fan. He loved to play ball, but he wasn't the best athlete in the world. Just like I'm not. But he loved it and he loved the strategy of it too. So, he played quarterback. One of the things I remember most about Jerry is that he almost killed me.1951, late September, Bobby Thompson's shot heard round the world. I was at Jerry's house and we were

28

listening to the ball game and when Thompson hit that home run, he just came crossed the room and hit me with a tackle. I was standing by the window on the fourth floor and he tackled me so hard that I almost fell out of the window. And I had the last laugh because the Yankees won that World Series and I'm a Yankees fan. And you asked about people on the team. I believe George Milicheck but I don't know where he is. Luby may know. The next name I'm going to give you is Richie McQuade. And I keep in touch with Richie during Christmas time. He and his wife visited us in California. His late wife now. His brother Tommy McQuade was also on the team. Tom passed away several years ago. Jimmy Long. We all went to grammar school together except for George. Bobby, Richie, Jimmy Long uh, all of us went to grammar school together. Vinny Bistazio, he may be a little later, but I think I played with him. He went to Notre Dame. There was another kid who played guard and I'm trying to dredge up his name, but I can't do it."

"It'll come to you tonight."

"I know what you're going through with writing because I just finished a chapter for a book that the University of California is publishing. It has been non-stop and now we're starting to get some of the publisher's clearance information."

"What was your career Bill? I assume you went to college if you are writing books for the University."

"I have a Bachler's Degree in Civil Engineering from Cornell University. A Master's Degree in Civil Engineering from Stanford and an MBA from George Mason University in Virginia. I always worked for either an engineering consulting company or an engineering construction company. I started out as a very technical engineer. Then I moved into management and marketing. Some of the real highlights, I was the President of the American Society of Engineers. The ASED is about a 140,000-person organization. Then I was a chair of the American Association of Engineering Society, AAES. They had about 100,00 engineers."

Bill paused as if to gather his thoughts. He changed the course of our exchange. "The last time I saw Jerry was in 2006, I think. I was back in New York City for a convention and, I called him. We spent the afternoon together at a restaurant in a midtown hotel and he was still going strong. He had a heart attack, but he had recovered. Let me ask you a question…"

Bill asked a slew of questions in an attempt to catch up on Jerry's life. It started with me giving him Jerry's phone number. Of course, he asked and of course, I told him of Geri, his wife, passing away and that Frank also had recently passed. He was grateful as he informed me that he didn't want to approach Jerry with a conversation that would make him uncomfortable. We decided to call it a night for now.

"Okay Bob, so I'll give him a call later on today and I will look for that picture."

Absolutely, give him a shout. And I would love that picture because we have team photos of the other groups. There is no photo of that original team. If you find it, it may go into the Smithsonian, Bill."

In talking with Bill, another name had surfaced, Rich McQuade, living somewhere in Florida. About six months later, we had tracked Rich down and I spoke with him over the phone. The conversation was short and sweet as Rich, now eighty-two professed that he couldn't remember much for those early years. He did, however, tell me that he was the one who would set up events, like dances, to raise money for the "young Warriors" to buy their own jackets. The next day, I got in contact with Jerry to tell him that I had spoken with Rich and relayed our conversation. Jerry was elated.

"How did Ritchie sound Bob?"

"He sounded good, very clear, strong voice, full of information but unfortunately not so much with old Warrior days in the Upper East Side." I did mention to Jerry that Rich talked about holding dances to raise money for the team to which Jerry let out a laugh.

"Ritchie was always doing something or other to raise money for us. I'm not going to say he was very successful but that was his thing. Did he tell you what he's up to now?"

"Well, he just got back from a trip to Israel."

"Really? With his wife Gladys?"

"Unfortunately, Ritch told me that his wife passed away several years ago. Hey, did you know that your buddy became a Vice-President at Citibank?"

"No. I do remember when he started, I believe it was then the First National City Bank and he was just a clerk. I know he went to night school and graduated from the Institute of Banking but no, I didn't realize he rose that high in banking."

"Yeah, that he told me quite a bit of. He told me as he was ascending from clerk to branch manager and higher management, he was very involved in the credit, lending side of the business dealing with risk management and securities. It was very interesting as all your friends are."

"Interesting indeed. You know he had a brother who played with us, Tom McQuade, but he's long since passed away."

I informed Jerry that I had passed on his phone number to Rich and to expect a phone call from him soon. I had done this very same thing with each of the guys I had talked with and reconnected the dots for this group.

***

Talking with Jerry and his old neighborhood buddies about the early days was incredible for me. It was like a journey back in time, both historical and educational all at once. I felt as if I was there on those cobblestone streets of Yorkville. And in these conversations, I had found it an honor to get to know Frank Demers, a true gentleman of wit, charm, and intelligence. And it was a pure delight to speak with Henry Helenek, Luby Mlynar, Bill Henry, and Rich McQuade. These are impressive men in their personalities and in their careers. At ages seventy-eight to eighty-two, through the course of our phone calls, they all became young boys at heart.

At that point in time, 1948, in the streets of Upper Manhattan and 1952, the official beginnings of the Warrior football team, these young boys had no idea what they would build. This is our legacy. The Bronx Warriors that started in Manhattan, in Yorkville during the fifties. This is our history.

The section hasn't changed much, judging from today's foto. The large hall on the right in both fotos is the Bohemian National Hall, which was built in 1896. It is a meeting place for about 51 societies of Czechs and Slovaks. They keep alive their national customs with song fests, dances and plays. Every year, on Decoration Day, they parade through the district in their Old World costumes.

SUNDAY NEWS, MARCH 1, 1959

If you look close enough, the Chief circled his apartment

Jerome & Francis Demers

The Coach 1952

Original Warrior Team 1952

Original Warrior Team 1956 – Jerry Demers #14, Rich McQuade #33, Bill Henry #72, Tom QcQuade #70

Tom McQuade, Bill Henry, Jerry Demers et al.

Bill Henry 1952

Berlin Bar on the southeast corner of 3rd Avenue and 86th Street in 1955,

Chapter 3

P.S. 106 - The First Half

P.S. 106 Parkhouse, Parkchester, Bronx N.Y.

We, as young boys, the baby boomers, played, in the fifties exactly the same street games as did Jerry in the forties and curiously, as my father did in the thirties. There was one that was popular that Jerry did not mention which was the glorified game of tag known as ringolevio. There were two sides, the more the merrier, that demanded teamwork and strategy. The game would commence with one team running off to hide while the other team counted up to a particular number, much like hide and seek, Once the magic number was called out, that team would look for the team in hiding in an attempt to "capture the enemy" and take them, prisoner, putting them in jail. Jail could be a fire hydrant or a certain stoop. Any and all captive(s) could be freed if one of their guys swooped in on the jail, untouched and tagged them. The game ended if one side was completely caught but that rarely ever happened. The game was endless.

Another game was skelzie, also known as scully. All that was needed was a big, fat chalk and a bottle cap filled with melted crayon. You could pick out the future Hippies. They were the ones mixing wild colors like purple and yellow. With the chalk, a big square containing smaller boxes was drawn on the asphalt street as pictured below.

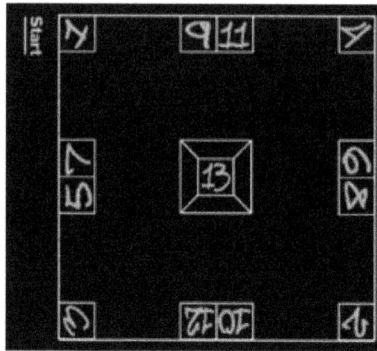

On hands and knees, we would go in order positioning the weighted cap between the thumb and middle finger and flick it into the box, working in numerical order. Shooting the cap within the box would allow that player to proceed to the next box. Hitting an opponent's cap advanced the opponent into the next box, without shooting, and giving him an additional turn. The first player into the thirteenth box was the winner[16].

Another street game was slug or "Chinese handball", an "upside down" version of handball which was played, of course, with a Spaldeen against the wall of an apartment building. Facing the wall, three or more guys would line up side by side but separated by the square in the sidewalk pavement. The winner of the last game would be the "Ace" which was the first box, followed by the "King", the "Queen" and the rest. The ace served the ball which had to hit the ground before it hit the wall. A player not returning the serve out of his box went to the end of the line. The object of the game was to get into the "Ace's" box and hold onto it as the others would send "killers", "slices" and "babies" your way. If the ball should hit a crack of the sidewalk or some other object which caused the ball to take an unnatural bounce, "Hindu" was shouted out. For some undefined reason, "Hindu" meant a do-over. "Hindu" would lead to many

---

[16] Popik, Barry (2005-04-05), *Skelly (or skelsy, skellzies, scully, tops, caps)*, retrieved 2008-01-05 – SELZIE

long and heated arguments[17]. Of course, the losing player, the guy in the last box, was subject to "asses up", as well explained by Jerry.

We honed our athletic skills on those Bronx streets playing stickball and touch football We could be Mickey Mantle, Willie Mays or Duke Snyder, by going into the streets and pretend to be and go to bed fantasizing of making that game-saving catch or hitting the winning home run in the bottom of the ninth, with two outs of course. Stickball was still king in New York City. The cobblestone streets gave way to smoothly paved blacktop which improved the quality of the street games. Ankles were now safe from torn ligaments caused by stepping wrong on an uneven stone. There was a drop in reported twisted ankle injuries. Consequently, statistics compiled from our street games, i.e. home runs and doubles in stickball and passes caught and touchdowns scored in touch football, could not be compared to, let's say, Jerry's era, much like the dead ball era vs. the modern era of baseball. There was nothing better than to get up early on an already warm summer morning and race out of your apartment to be one of the first out onto the street. This guaranteed one to participate in the first game as the others began to congregate. This was important because as the morning became afternoon, the older and bigger guys would take over and you were done for the day, at least in stickball and touch football.

Certain situations could halt a stickball game altogether. That Maris shot sometimes would hit a window and break it. We would all freeze and watch to see if the wooden frame of the window, of that very same six-story pre-war building that Jerry recalled, was raised and some old battle-ax was going to admonish us to hell., threatening to tell our parents and having them pay for the damage. If there was a sighting of someone approaching the window, we would all scatter like a scene from the Little Rascals. On occasion, a Mantle shot would "roof" the ball. Not a one of us would go up to the roof as that was taboo, forbidden by our parents. No one dared to be sighted by one of the neighbors doing these things, broken windows, going on a roof, or cursing. God those moms, who sat all day on the fire escapes, were the street police. Of course, sometimes, in the course of the game, a ball not caught would roll down the street, to the corner, and into the sewer opening. Normally, we would take a collection of twenty-five cents,

---

[17] Robert Wood, "Chinese Handball the Sport." Topend Sports Website, Dec 2014, https://www.topendsports.com/sport/list/handball-chinese.htm, Accessed 2/11/2019 -SLUG

all pennies and nickels, go down to the corner candy store and buy another ball. But other times, rather than spend the twenty-five cents, because that was a lot of money back then, the older guys would pry open a manhole cover, the one closest to the sewer opening where the ball disappeared. The youngest of the group, would make his way down a metal ladder and lo and behold in the muck of the crap and piss and rotten food and whatever the else was thrown down a sewer, there would be our ball. Sometimes there might be three more. It was like found gold. Play continued. Of course, we would only stop playing these highly contested games when it started to get dark and we couldn't see the ball, or someone's mom hung out of the window, yelled your name in a manner unheard anywhere else, and told you that your father was home and it was time for dinner. You didn't want your name called but it didn't matter because someone's mom was going to call. Once a player or two was removed, the game was done. And that youngster who went down the sewer hole, well, upon entering the apartment he would hear his mother shriek, "You smell like crap. Go take a shower." And off to the side, behind mom was dad who had a little grin on his face. Dad knew exactly how you got that stench. The young man had to take his shower, but also knowing that one day, he would not be the youngest. This was a rite of passage and payment of street dues.

As fall approached, there came a slight brisk in the air. This signaled the beginning of the football season. Football, on those same streets, was played by a quarterback and a giver and anywhere from a receiver going against a defender or three receivers, three defenders. The giver would flip the ball underhanded to the quarterback and count Mississippi's as the receiver(s) would run a route/routes up the street. At six Mississippi, the giver could "rush" the quarterback and if he tagged the quarterback with both hands that would end the play. I guess this was our version of the sack. Three receivers were the best. Bunched up alongside the quarterback, who was the guy with the best arm in the neighborhood, who could throw the ball a city mile. One receiver would run a square out to the '58 Crown Victoria, one would run a square in and the fastest guy would go deep on a fly pattern. Lord knows how many parked cars took out a receiver. We might get a few plays off but the inevitable cry of "car" would be announced and in the middle of a play, we would all retreat to the safety of the sidewalk to avoid a car coming up the block. God forbid that you might jump up and sit upon one of the parked cars because you would hear admonishment from one of those windows, "get off the car". In the fifties, you were not allowed to sit on someone's car. And of course, if a brand-new Caddy rolled up the street, we would all gawk in admiration and respect, much like looking at royalty.

The sweet taste of victory was always celebrated at Jacks candy store on Starling Avenue. Chocolate egg creams at the cost of fifteen cents and flavored fountain sodas for a dime were had by all. Maybe a Baby Ruth or Snickers or a bag of Wise potato chips, all for a nickel, on the way out. For a lot of us, it was a pack of Topps baseball cards, five cents a pack. Five cards and a powdered stick of stale gum that cracked when you stuck it in your mouth and chewed. Back then we didn't know that a 1952 Topps Mickey Mantle card would someday be valued at $2.88 million dollars in Heritage's auctions[18]. These were the very same cards that we would flip in the street. Flipping cards was a skilled game that consisted of two guys which was played as follows; "from a standing position, the first player would take a card, hold it along his side and then, with a flip of the wrist, let it drop to the floor. It would land either with the picture facing up (heads) or the stats facing up (tails). The second player would then flip his card and try to match the card. If they matched (both heads or both tails), the second player won the cards, if they did not match, the cards went to the first player."[19] Of course if you were fortunate to own a bicycle, you would clothes-pin baseball cards to the spokes of the wheel to give your ride a cool, motorized sound. God knows we had no clue as to what the cash value of these cards would be someday. Our cards were frayed and creased.

As we got a little older, say about twelve years old, we graduated from the neighborhood street and gravitated to the schoolyard. A marvelous, wonderland of a sports sanctuary that housed a softball field, basketball courts, and a handball court. The softball field served as a football field, played from the first base foul line to left field, and a roller hockey rink. Hockey was street hockey played on foot as the rough concrete could not handle roller skates. It also had more kids there, so we were assured of playing an actual softball or a touch-tackle game or spending the day shooting hoops. You name it we were playing it. Our parents didn't mind us going there as they knew that it was a safe haven. During the late fifties and most of the sixties, most playgrounds had a park attendant or "Parkie" who managed the park. The Parkie was there to lend you equipment, if needed, out of the park house. He was also the law of the land, making

---

[18] Forbes Magazine; David Seideman; April 29, 2018; forbes.com/sites/davidseideman/2018/04/29/forget-the-2-9-million-mickey-mantle-card-there-are-three-worth-10-million/#220032103a99
[19] streetplay.com/thegames/baseballcards.shtml

sure that order was in place and everything and everyone was under control. But life in the schoolyard was a whole 'nother social environment. It was littered with neighborhood athletes from superstar to wannabe, to bruisers, to hippie-types, and adoring girlfriends. You had to have a thick skin to make that first entry into the schoolyard. As a rookie, especially if you want to ball, you were going to be subject to getting razzed from the older veterans. It could get vicious. As dad once told me, "kid, if you can't handle the schoolyard, don't go there". The process of proving your worth, perhaps with that first at-bat or first big catch, was nerve-wracking. But, somehow, someway, we came through it all. A lot of who we are is the culmination of our genetic make-up, our parents, and the environment we grew up in. The schoolyard was that environment. It was an alternate form of an education. But the only bad day back then was waking up on a summer day or a winter weekend only to find that it was raining. A rainy day meant no game today.

***

The Big Apple has always been one of the world's most hopping cities -- and the 1960s were no exception. See the hustle and bustle of a city in transition during the rocking decade ... New York City's skyline was in for a massive change in 1961 when the Port Authority proposed building the World Trade Center in the Battery section of Manhattan. While the idea of establishing a World Trade Center was first proposed in 1943, it was put on hold in 1949[20]. America would "Sing Along with Mitch" as they were already "twisting" to Chubby Checker[21]. That new Ford or Chevrolet family car might stretch the budget at $2,850 but gas would be no problem at twenty-seven cents a gallon[22]. Bob Dylan would move into town and Alan Shepard would be the first American to leave town by going up into space. New York's winter of 1960 - 1961 was the coldest in twenty-eight years. It was brutal with a record cold wave lasting seventeen consecutive days of below-freezing temperatures from January to February and a record snowfall of over seventeen feet of snow[23].

---

[20] www.nydailynews.com/new-york/new-york-city-1960s-gallery-1.1038782; George Mattson

[21] Whitburn, *Joel (2000). Top Pop Singles 1955-1999. Menomonee Falls, WI: Record Research Inc. p. 32*

[22] www.thepeoplehistory.com/70yearsofpricechange.html

[23] National Weather Service Archives

The Bronx in 1961 would be the magical year of Mantle and Maris, the M & M boys. A home run derby between teammates as unseen in the history of the game as they assaulted Babe Ruth's single season record of sixty home runs. Mantle would be injured, falling victim to an abscessed hip on September 25th. He ended the season with fifty-four homers while Maris went on to break the record with sixty-one on the final day of the season. It was that team, that year that set the record for most home runs in a season, 240. Powered by the bats of Yogi Berra, Elston Howard, Bill "Moose" Skowron and Johnny Blanchard each hitting more the twenty round trippers and steadied by the arm of Whitey Ford who was backed up by Luis Arroyo out of the bullpen, the Yankees would go on to have a 109-53 record. They won the World Series beating the Cincinnati Reds to earn their nineteenth championship in thirty-nine seasons. I would later learn that Tony Arroyo, a Warrior on my team, was a relative of Luis Arroyo. The Yankees would defeat the Cincinnati Reds in the World Series in five games. Perhaps it was appropriate that the "Yanks" would go against the "Reds" as the Cold War was in full bloom. On the gridiron, the New York Giants would go to the championship game led by Y.A, Tittle throwing bombs to Del Shofner and a stout defense spearheaded by Sam Huff. Unfortunately, they would lose to Lombardi's legendary Packers in Green Bay 37 - 0. The Knicks and the Rangers both had nondescript seasons, once again.

***

The dawn of P.S. 106 begins in 1959, growing into a phenomenon throughout the sixties. P.S. 106 is a New York City grammar school which back then went from kindergarten to the sixth grade. It is tucked away off the east side of Parkchester, on St. Raymond's Avenue, bordered by Purdy Avenue and Odell Street with Starling Avenue behind it. St. Raymond High School sits across the street and J.H.S. 127, the junior high school is one block over.

I sat with Jerry in the living room of his new apartment on Lawton Avenue in Throggs Neck. We sipped freshly brewed coffee as he chatted about his start back then.

"Bobby, I graduated from Fordham University in 1960. I received my degree in history. While at the university, I enrolled in the ROTC program and enlisted in the Army. I was with the Army Reserve for thirteen years. We did our training on 238th Street, the Spuyten Duyvil neighborhood of the upper west Bronx. It's south of Riverdale, west of Kingsbridge and east of the Harlem River. I was there until 1973 when the armory moved to New Jersey and I didn't want to travel that far. But when I graduated in 1960, I didn't have to serve my military duty until February of '61. There was a big gap there and I decided to take a N.Y.C. Parks Department job as a Recreation Leader for six months. So, I did that and in the interim, I was sent to two or three places. I started at Loreto Playground in Morris Park and then I went to the playground at the Eastchester houses. I was there about a month and then I moved over to P.S. 106. Eventually, I became a Recreation Leader at P.S. 106 and was there for nine years. In those nine years, they never gave a test for the next higher promotion, which was called Supervisor. Finally, they gave one in 1969 and I was very high on the list. I was promoted to Supervisor, so I had to leave P.S. 106, but from Supervisor I was eventually promoted to the Borough Commissioner. While I was Supervisor, I was the head sports director for the Parks Department for all the city-wide programs. We had CBS sponsor our hockey program, our softball, and other programs. I worked with three other guys who were great guys. We were down in Flushing, Queens in an office there. Well to tell you the truth, I felt like the Parks Department was asking too much of us. I got so p.o.'ed, I wrote a letter to the Commissioner saying that there was too much work for the money I was making, something like that. They called me, and they said: "well okay if you feel that way, we're going to send you to St. Mary's Park in the South Bronx" which they did for a while. Of course, I went there, I had to go to keep my job, but fortunately, I was on the early tour only because the late tour supervisor was a teacher, so he had to have the late tour due to school hours. I was lucky I got the early tour because by night that park got rough. But shortly thereafter, I must have called the Department's bluff because it must have been a couple of months later that they called me back into the office and promoted me to the manager of Queens. Two years later the administration changed over again, and the new Recreation Commissioner brought me into the office and he made me the head of the whole five boroughs of Recreation. So, I went from the lowest position to the highest position. I was the youngest Chief of Recreation in the history of the Department which wasn't that long."

There was a New York City Parks Commission, but it only oversaw Central Park in Manhattan. My God, this was created in the mid-eighteen-hundreds under Mayor Boss Tweed. It wasn't until 1934 that a unified city-wide Parks Department was established. The first park was Seward Park, in the Lower East Side of Manhattan which opened in October 1903. The first Bronx park, believe it or not, was St. Mary's June 1914. About a week later, Pelham Bay Park was launched in 1914 as a public access park.

Jerry continued, "But yeah, I first showed up in P.S. 106 back in 1960. We were very successful in the late '50's'58,'59, but 1960 was the beginning of the end of the original Warrior team. The guys coming up from Yorkville were older now. Some of them were going away to college, some of them stopped playing but it ended around 1962. At that time, I got friendly with another recreational director, Ed Stack. Ed worked at P.S, 102 another elementary school, which was located off the west side of Parkchester on Archer Street. That school closed down in 2014 and was replaced with two smaller schools a couple of years ago. Anyway, when I joined the Parks Department, Eddie was already a recreational director. Back then, we would have District meetings and that's how we first met. I started to go over to 102 at lunchtime and developed a friendship with Ed. He was only a year older than me and I found that he had the same standards as I did. He always did the right thing and that's what I did. When it came to his team, the Archer Street Rams, he believed in fair play. He never used illegal (overage) players and always encouraged kids to do the right thing. We became close associates but competitive in nature. He was more of an athlete. He could bat right handed and left handed in softball. I might have been a better quarterback than him, but he was the better athlete. In a fight, he would have thrown me off the building. He was one tough Irishman. We became good friends. I would regularly go over to his neighborhood, Archer Street, which was walking distance from 102 and I became like a family member over there. As I told you previously, as a kid we used to move every year and from one ethnic neighborhood to another, but Ed Stack's neighborhood was Irish, and it was the first time I was able to experience the Irish experience so to speak. In 1961, we combined teams and became the Warrior Rams in 1961 and 1962. In 1963, when I was working in the playground, a young gentleman, a close friend of mine now, Anthony Vastola brought me a little list on a piece of paper and on it he had listed about twelve names and he said "Jay why don't you coach us in football. We would like to have a football team. We'd like to have it named the Vikings". So, we looked at the paper and we decided to go ahead with that since the older team was beginning to fade out. We took some players from the older team, we took some new players. Players came out of the woodwork it seemed for the 1963 team, which was called the Viking Warriors because their softball team, Tony Vastola's softball team, and the kids he brought were called the Vikings. So, for a year again we changed the name to the Viking Warriors, but it was still the Warriors. That team included Danny Miller and Jimmy Oliveto, Tony Vastola, and Biff Bafundo, future great coaches with the program. That team played three years from 1963 through 1965. At the end of that time, they all stopped playing. Since there was a draft in those days, they all decided to join the Marines. I mean seven of our players must have joined the Marines from that team, so the team ended at the end of the 1965 season.

We had a lot of great games playing down in Mullaly Park over on Jerome Avenue. We even played in Eric LoSalle's Bronx Manhattan football league one year, so we played over at Inwood Park, we played at Van Cortlandt Park and our home games were at Rice Stadium in Pelham Bay Park. We've had home games at Rice Stadium since 1958 so that's really a long, long time to have the permits at one field (laughing). Now we get them five or six days a week whenever we want them because we've been there so long, we have tenure as first come first serve. We get a lot of arguments these days from the soccer players who want to play on the field. They want to know 'why are you always on the field, why can't we have the field' and we tell them why because we have a permit for the field. So, they're not too happy about that and they go on the side of the field and play on the grass, but we do share the field during practice sessions as much as possible. Saturdays, the field is all ours and Sunday mornings, also."

Jerry and I decided to call it quits for the night. We agreed to carry on with this conversation.

The next day I was taken by storm by a phone call from Jimmy Oliveto, "Ollie" as he would always be called, went on later to be one of our assistant coaches, as did Tony Vastola, Danny Miller, and Bill Bafundo when I joined the team in 1970. All great coaches, dedicated to teaching us more than just a game, all great guys, under the tutelage of Jerry. Obviously, Jerry had called Ollie and told him to speak with me about his beginning days with the Warriors. I didn't expect to be schooled, much like a grammar school student being lectured by a stern teacher. If I told you that Ollie was emphatic in his conversation, I would be putting it mildly.

"I'm going to allow Golio and Botti, Cawley and Match and McGurl, and the rest of the younger guys to tell you the story of the 1969 to 1974 Warrior team that you guys were members of in that era but I'm going to verify and expand on some thoughts from before that. Now I knew Jay starting around 1961, 1962. I was young in high school at that time. He was working as a recreational director at P.S. 106 and he met Tony Vastola who was the organizer of our little neighborhood football team called the Vikings. It was a team of about 20 or 25 young guys from the Castle Hill area. Jerry took us under his wing as a football team and then he did what I

46

learned that he would do for the rest of his life. He became not only our coach and our mentor but a father figure to us and I learned that he was an organizer. I will expand on this. Here's what he did. Our football team was just a little bunch of guys. In our first year, we did virtually nothing. We just played whatever little teams we could find. But he organized and adapted. He got together somehow with maybe three or four other small teams from around The Bronx. There was a team from the Pelham Bay area called the Blue Devils. Dan Miller was a member on that team and on that team were probably eight excellent football players including a guy who turned out to be one of the best football players the Warriors ever had back in those days, Marty Kelly. Jerry incorporated the Vikings from my neighborhood with the Blue Devils from Pelham Bay. My neighborhood again is Castle Hill. Then he formed an association with a team from City Island called the City Island Giants. That team was probably thirty to thirty-five guys as we ended up getting another ten or fifteen excellent football players from the City Island Giants. So now you had a combination through Jerry's personal skills and his coaching of three small neighborhood teams and turned them into the Bronx Viking Warriors at first. A little later on the Viking name was dropped, it just became the Warriors. And we played as a team I would say probably 1962 or 63 up to 65 or 66, around that era. It was a combination of the Vikings, the Blue Devils, and the City Island Giants. Jerry also incorporated another group of guys from down in the Yorkville section where he had come from. I don't remember if they had a name, but I do know that they were all Central European immigrant kids. Their parents had come in from Czechoslovakia and Hungary. They were the toughest, most physical bunch of guys that I ever met. They played alongside with us but when we first met them, we would practice against them in tackle games, I was about thirteen or fourteen, and they physically beat the snot out of us. They turned out to be great teammates and very, very physical guys. We had toughness, and they taught us to be tough football players when they joined the Bronx Warriors. Right up until the middle of the Sixties when the team broke up due to the draft, mainly with guys going into the Army and the Marines and so on, those guys were part of the team. So, we were basically four teams combined, The Vikings, the Blue Devils, the City Island Giants and the group from down in Manhattan. They used to take the subway up to practice and play. Those four guys became Warriors and we did very well for the three or four years we played together. The only reason the team broke up was again, 1965, 1966 there was a draft that was instituted and a lot of guys were going to be eighteen and if they didn't go to college, they were getting drafted to serve in

Vietnam. There were a lot of guys who were leaving and six of us also from the team all joined the Marine Corps Reserve. We had to go away and spend months and months on active duty. The team broke up, unfortunately, a little earlier than we would have liked, but the point is Jay was the organizer. He was only maybe five years to six years older than us. I can't remember exactly but he was like a father to us and he was an organizer. In his own right way, he was the strictest, the most organized guy I had ever met. He demanded excellence and if you were not excellent, he told you. No loud mouth, no screaming and yelling but you knew that you had been chastised. I missed a practice because I was playing baseball for another team. He actually wrote me a letter and told me that I was suspended for one week because I had missed the practice and that I had made the choice to not come to the Warrior practice but instead played baseball."

"Hey Jimmy, is it possible he suspended you because you didn't let him know in advance?"

"Exactly, that was exactly what it was. Now he also did it in a comical way. He wrote the letter, and I answered him in a letter. I told him about unforeseen circumstances, that I could not make both practice and baseball. He wrote a second letter back and he said exactly what you just said, Bobby. He said if you chose, without telling me, to go to the other sporting event, as a Warrior you should have shown up and explained it to me so for that reason you are suspended for one week. We laughed later on about it but he was serious about it. He was making his point to me. He was making the point that as an adult, here I am I was about fourteen or fifteen years old, and as an adult he expected me to be upstanding and do the right thing and he taught me a lesson that day.

He was teaching us, always teaching us. His brother Frank, who was a professor later on at Fordham University, was also a wonderful guy who got to know us really well. It was a great, great experience. Later on, a couple of years go by and he wants to form the team that you guys eventually played for and he took on Dan Miller, Tony Vastola, myself, Biff Bafundo and I think there was one other guy as assistant coaches…Jimmy Sherry. The first meeting he had was held at his house on Hobart Avenue. He had moved from his first little apartment. He has this meeting and it's a Sunday and it was after the first practice he had ever held with the Warriors. We go into his house he takes us out to the back porch, he hands us each a folder and some cards, and he asks us to write down what we had just accomplished at that practice and what we planned on doing on the next practice. We had no idea what he was talking about. We were flying by the seat of our pants as ex-football players. We were just repeating what guys had done to us prior. That afternoon he insisted that we make a schedule, minute by minute, of what was going to happen at the next practice and we had to do that every single practice. We had to let him know that for the first five minutes there would be stretching and for the next fifteen minutes there would be calisthenics…" what kind of calisthenics?", "how much running?", "what drills?", "how are you running the drills?", "what part of the team is going into those drills?". He taught us how to coach in that one afternoon sitting on his back porch. It was a memorable moment for me and Danny and Vas. We live with that forever. I remember Dan who was almost four years older than me, he said to me "I can't believe we've got to do this". It was school work, but he taught us how to coach and that stayed with me through all the years as a coach later on with the Warriors and the Archer Street Rams. And I used that later when I coached in high school and even on the college level. The same method, organized minute to minute of what's going on and don't waste a minute of your practice time and your procedures on game day…what are you going to do first, second, third prior to the game, and at halftime. Nothing was done flippantly, it all had to be organized and that was the beauty of Jay Demers. He got it across to you very, very politely, very, very succinctly, there was no bullshit. You had to be on call and he would call you sometimes right in the middle of a practice and say, "come on over here, show me your cards, what are you going to do this practice". He was amazing and for that I thank him, all the time besides the friendship and the great times we had with him back in the neighborhood when he was a recreational director. The number of people that he affected, I was a teacher for thirty-four years and I know that by myself I ended up teaching over hundreds and hundreds and maybe even thousands of people over the years but the level of the effect that he had on the thousands and thousands of guys that played football for him or knew about him, even from other teams, was beyond belief. Everybody got to know him and his teams, we were always respected for our fair play and our organization. Real quick and I'm going to cut this short…when Joe Reich had his accident (1972) our biggest rivals in the neighborhood, guys that we had physical altercations with as young boys playing against them in baseball, basketball, football was the Archer Street Rams, they came from the west side of Parkchester. I had actually played three years for the Archer Rams later on after I came out of the service but in any case, they were our arch enemies. When we had a charity dinner to raise funds for Joe Reich, it was a nighttime party on Morris

Park Avenue, the Knights of Columbus, and we raised a lot of money for Joe so that he could get one of those cars that can be driven by hand. That night, late in the night, unbeknownst to us, the Rams had had a similar charitable party to raise funds for Joe Reich and later on that evening they came over and gave us a check. I can't remember the exact amount, but I know it was in the thousands, it might have been two thousand, three thousand dollars but they came over and gave us that check. I can remember sitting there with their coach, Eddie Stack. Well, he and a couple of other guys came over with the money and it was just an astounding night. They had done this because of Jerry. Jerry and Eddie had worked together, and because of the relationship of those two guys, at that time, this was amazing stuff. Some of the guys on that team the Diehl brothers are guys I still see occasionally, the whole bunch of them, they were really great guys. So, Jerry was a very important guy growing up as a football player, to be his coach and for all you guys in the next generation, a wonderful man. Those lessons that he taught you and me and everyone else as young guys. If you were that kind of person that was open to those lessons and accepted them, you carried it on in life and it made you successful. It did for me in business, I did it in education for thirty-four years, I was a teacher, a dean, an assistant principal, and acting principal. Every meeting I ever had was planned minute to minute. That all comes from that meeting that was held back on that afternoon on Hobart Avenue, on that back porch where he was demanding that you organize all the time, organize, organize. I taught my own children about it. My wife in her teaching career, she's still that organized and it all stems from and going back from what Jerry instilled in us and the demands of being an intelligent and thoughtful person. Great guy.

Here's a quick one, one of the guys that came from Yorkville that came up to play with us, I'm talking about my team back in the sixties…one of these guys, a Hungarian guy, had just come out of prison. He was that tough a guy. He had just come out of Sing-Sing. He was on the football field with us. I had battles with that guy. As great a football player that he was, Jay would not let him play. He had brought up a fellow, Mike Yurcik, who was much bigger than the rest of us, he was the first quarterback we ever had. I played defense at the time. Well this guy Mike, on a quarterback sweep, put his helmet into my stomach in a practice in Pelham Bay and taught me that this is what football is all about. He knocked the wind out of me, He knocked me silly. I got back up and realized I could survive that and I said to myself, "never again, I will never let somebody get that close to me on a football field or I'll kick their ass, I'm dishing it out". But those are the type of team guys he brought up. So many guys that he brought up from downtown, but he also had these tough guys from Pelham Bay and from City Island and kind of, without cutting anybody, he weeded out, by his demands, guys who were the lesser players or who didn't have the gumption to keep playing football. He ended up with the cream of the crop from each of these small teams. And he did that all along the line. I remember guys showing up at our practices when you guys were playing, and they either told us later on "this is not for me or wow I love this team". They weeded themselves out and we ended up with the best of the best. And just to go back to the guy who went to Sing-Sing. He got arrested for some crap he pulled down in Manhattan and that must have happened in the late fifties. Jerry would not let him play because of his arrest. He subsequently got locked up. Football on the Warrior Team in P.S.106 was more than a casual choose up game. It was a commitment to Jerry's rules and requirements of conduct. But anyway, he's out of jail, it's around 1962 or so, and he's out playing football with us one or two days in J.H.S. 127, on the playground. We're playing touch tackle with blocking and I realized how tough these guys were. Physically so tough, I mean they took no crap. It was supposed to be two-hand touch, but you got your ass kicked. They were just tough dudes and it was really a great experience as far it was to learn to grow up. You have to defend yourself, you have to play at that level and it made us better ballplayers. The rest of those guys from down there were wonderful guys. When we grew up in the streets, you had to be a tough dude to get on the playground. Either it scared you and you went back home and never came back out or it made you a tougher guy for the rest of your life. It was your physical toughness, it was your mental toughness. It was also a step up in confidence, I can survive this. I told you this guy used to block me, and he knocked me silly one day. There was another guy who was a little older than me, from the Italian neighborhood on Zerega Avenue, who hit me in J.H.S.127, when we were playing touch tackle. He hit me so hard one day that he broke my belt. I was wearing a belt on my pants, my belt broke, the leather broke, that's how hard he hit me. Knocked me silly. I cut my hand, I cut my wrist and he broke my hand in one shot. And it turned out he was a really, really nice guy. That's how hard he hit me. And I realized that I could survive this. And mentally it made you a little more understanding of what life was about. It built your confidence in that you could survive that and come back. The whole experience starting with Jerry back for me in 1961, '62 every which way was a positive, positive experience and I'm so glad that I was able to coach with Jerry to get to know all of you guys on your team which was fantastic."

51

Later on, I connected with "Bif," Bill Bafundo who spoke at length about his days with the Warriors as a young player, alongside Ollie, Tony Vastola, and Danny Miller.

"Bobby, I think I started knowing Jay around fourteen, fifteen years old so that would make it 1962. He was a Parkie at P.S. 106. He was sort of quiet back then. He had the Warrior team with a bunch of other guys and for some reason, either they stopped for a year or they were losing players, but they wanted to keep the team going. He asked me and Ollie and Vas and the guys in the neighborhood, Bobby Ferness if they would be interested in playing. We used to play two-hand touch but that was as kids. We were never very good, we didn't play a lot of football, but we did play a lot of sports. Okay so in the early 1960s we met Jay at the playground, and he was a Parkie. He asked us to come join the Warrior football team. So, we did, and we practiced. I remember we used to get the gym at 127 Junior High School. Dennis Kent, did you get the name Dennis Kent yet?"

I replied, "Well I put an email out to him. He's the dean at Rutgers University today and he hasn't answered as of yet. I might try to call him, but I'm sure he's a very busy man."

"That sounds like Dennis. You know when he got older, he used to talk in the huddle, he was an offensive lineman. I had no idea what he was talking about. Just way too smart for me, way over my head. But anyway, Dennis at that point was going to Stuyvesant High School and he played football on the Stuyvesant team, but he also played with us. Which he wasn't supposed to because if you play high school ball you cannot play in any other outside league. Back then, it was a bunch of guys from Jay's old team in Manhattan and he was mixing us together to make the team. And we had a pretty good team. We would practice, I think it was a Wednesday night at the J.H.S. 127 gym, the junior high school on Castle Hill Avenue, and Saturday afternoon, outdoors on the softball field, and then Sunday we played. Kind of like you guys did. Jay was a tremendous, tremendous coach."

"How so? How so Bill?

"He just had a handle on the game. He would, if I can remember right when I used to coach you guys, he actually came to me a couple times. He would say, "I need you to work on a couple of plays. I want to do some stuff with the tackle. I want to do this right because I know this team will be looking for something different." I remember Danny Miller and me or Danny Miller and Ollie used to go on Sundays after your game or before, scouting other teams. We used to scout them. Just like high schools used to scout them. Jay would ask us, "number twenty-four the running back, how many plays did he go off tackle? How many plays did he go around the end? How many passes did they throw? Did they throw them all on third down? Did they do a quick kick on third? All of this stuff. I got to say, we were much more prepared than a lot of those other teams. And probably won some games we weren't supposed to because of the organization and preparation. It was all Jay's doing. "I need you to do this. We gotta do this." And in the same token, he just instilled this, this… what is the word I'm looking for? He instilled this kind of confidence. You know what I'm saying? He would tell us, the coaches, I need this, but I want you to come up with it. And if he didn't like it, he would tell us and kind of massage it a little bit but that was his way and that always made me feel better. He was always so much a part of the game. This was the kind of coach we had. I have memories of when we were playing. I'll never forget one day. We had a guy on the team named Morty. He was one of the older guys on the team. I think it was when we played in the BUA [Bronx Umpires Association] league. It was up to seventeen or up to eighteen years old and you were allowed to have three nineteen-year-old players on the team. Why they did that, I don't know. Like Miller and his friend uh, what's his name? He's a cop. What the hell is his name now? Ronnie…Ronnie something. Anyway, Danny and he were really good friends. They came on the team together. They were the two of the nineteen-year old's you were allowed. Now this guy named Ronnie, I'll never forget this, we're getting dressed one morning at Van Cortlandt Park and Jay says, "Ronnie's not going to be here today." Ronnie was our defensive end, I think. I asked, "Well, where is he?" And Jay answers in disgust. "He's in jail." But that was Ronnie. You never knew. You never knew if he was going to make it through the weekend or not to play on Sunday. But as far as Jay goes, he is an amazing individual. I always said to Ollie, "Who the hell could have imagined in their wildest dreams that our team from 1963, would have turned into the organization that it is today and that was all because of Jay. He had support putting that whole thing together. He had tremendous, tremendous support but all from his efforts."

"Let me ask you this Bill. What does Jay mean to you? How did he affect your life? The relationship you had with that man."

"Well in a way I never really thought about it, but I would have to honestly say that it's gonna sound a little corny but the things that I do today reflect back to then, because of what Jerry taught me. Like I said earlier, he gave me my confidence. And he taught me about responsibility. He showed me what responsibility was and he led me through the paces. You know he was always there for the guys. Luckily, we were never the type of guys that needed help with the police or anything like that you know. I mean he always was there on the playground and was there to tell you what was needed to win, to succeed. When we were you, in our teens, we needed that type of thing. You could just tell he was a solid guy. I gotta believe part of what I am today, as you grow up and you evolve, I think Jay started all of that. You know there was no fooling around, no drinking, no drugs. We had a couple of beers here and there but no bad stuff. Like I said don't I think anybody did except for that guy Ronnie. For me, he molded me, he started me on my way. He was like a big brother. But I can remember when we finished coaching you guys and Jay said something about starting a younger team. It was almost as if he got it in his mind to start a new era. You know he went to OLA to ask for the use of the gym. You remember Our Lady of Assumption, the Catholic grammar school off of Bruckner Boulevard on Parkview Avenue. He said he was going to start a football team of grammar school kids and he was starting to sign them up using OLA as a base. We got the okay from the nuns to use the gym. We were going to start coaching and I remember I hung in there for about three or four months, going down to the practices at the gym. This might have been in the mid-seventies. Tony Vastola took over your team and Jay went off to OLA. I had to drop out because I was living in Connecticut at the time and it just got to be too much driving to the Bronx all the time. The first couple of practices that I did go to, Jay did ask me to hang in there. Just to get the kids set up and running. I can remember one practice in the gym, we got tackling dummies. There was this one kid and I'm showing him a three-point stance. I'm telling him, "Okay, when I say hut, I want you to come up out of your stance and I want you to bang this dummy. Alright?" He says, "Okay" and then the kid gets up and puts his hands out in front of him like he was gonna dance with it, he just kind of bumps it. "No, no, no, I call out. "You gotta hit it. Give me another kid." Next kid gets up as do several others after him and they all do the same thing as the first kid. I'm getting a little frustrated, not use to working with grammar school-age kids. I plead with them, "This thing is not gonna hurt you. Knock it down." They wouldn't and then after three or four more of them go, I decided that I would show them how to do this. I get in the three-point stance and I hit this dummy so hard that I fell off balance and almost broke my hand. I didn't want to show the kids that I was hurt. "See." I turn around to the kids with their mouths are open. They have got these looks on their faces like they're scared. I tell them, "Look don't be afraid. This is not going to hurt. This is just a padded thing." So, you know the next kid stepped up and a couple more and they started to get the hang of it. I said to myself, "This could be fun with these kids." But I had to drop out. And looking back, after all these years, you don't know how proud I am to be a part of this. We sometimes lose touch, but we're all connected by this. I mean you're taking me back. Did you know that we all went to Santa Maria? Me, Ollie, Vass. Bobby Ferness. We all hung around on Glover Street and played stickball together. We all grew up together you know. Remember Jimmy Bodkin? He was in the neighborhood. He played with us. When I played, he was our center. I was the right guard. John Juliano or John Paul as we used to call him, he passed away when he was forty-one. Yes, those were great days, those were special times.

It may have been a good three weeks after I placed that call and sent an email to Dr. Dennis Kent. I did not expect a return response as, I told Biff, Dennis is a dean at Rutgers University. He is one busy man functioning not only as the dean in the Department of Earth and Planetary Sciences but also as an active professor of geological sciences. His primary research relates to paleomagnetism, geomagnetism and rock magnetism, and their application to geologic problems. His current research interests also include Cenozoic and Mesozoic magnetostratigraphy and geomagnetic polarity time scales; paleogeography, paleoclimatology, and the long-term carbon cycle; paleointensity of the ancient geomagnetic field; magnetic recording properties of sediments, oceanic basalts, and polar ice. Other than Henry Helenek, does anyone understand what Dennis does? Can anyone possibly explain this to me? And lord knows where he would find the time to have ten recent publications. I'm certain that these are all an easy read.

Needless to say, I did get that return call from Dennis. Let's go to school and listen to Dr. Kent's lecture. "Bob, it was probably about sixty-two, sixty-three, so I would have been sixteen when I joined the Warriors. They were around the neighborhood and that was really the connection, Vastola, Biff, and the rest of them. So, we were at the junior high school 127 playground a lot. We were playing touch football and baseball and that sort of thing. I played probably about three or four years. I was mainly a running back. That was more or less my position. I never played quarterback. That was Vastola's position. Jimmy Oliveto, I think, he was mainly a defensive end, that was his usual position. There was another guy there, a big guy, he was a good runner, Bobby Ferness. I played in high school at Stuyvesant and then a year or two when I was at the City College of New York, but then I sort of tapered off. With school you somewhat drift apart from the guys. But I have fond memories of all of them, certainly many of them. There were some of them that didn't play but hung around. They were part of it, they really were part of the team. The social aspects were such a big thing. There was the neighborhood, so you had more contact with these people, the coach, than just from the field. I lost contact with all of them. Things intrude in life, a career, age. I haven't been in contact with anyone there. But I had an outlet. The high schools and the colleges were looking at me for athletics. The high school that I went to, Stuyvesant in lower Manhattan was a commuting school. I never saw anyone after school. It was an all-boys school down on Fifteenth Street. I was on the subway every day back then, back and forth. The coaching there was more structured, more formal because there was more time. We did it every day, whereas Jerry had, what did he have? Once or twice a week, tops. That was the constraint for him. So, it was athletics as well the social aspects in my life that was a nice balance for me. Now with my connection to Jerry, other than playing, was in another group as we got a little older. Towards our drinking age. He was ten years older than us but once we hit eighteen, he was twenty-eight, twenty-seven, not a big deal. It's almost as if the age difference shrinks, you know what I mean. We would go to Emerald Isle or the Bronx Irish Center. The Bronx Irish Center was a bar type of place on Tremont Avenue. We weren't hopping around bars or nothing like that. We were socializing in that way, so he had an important effect on me certainly. It was a structured socialization. Plus of course the athletic component."

I stopped Dennis with a little history of my own. "Do you know what the Emerald Isle is today. It's McNulty's Funeral Home."

"Are you kidding me?"

"Yeah, Pat McNulty is the funeral director. He's now fifty-two, big strapping guy. He played for the Warriors in the mid-seventies as a tight end. His sons played for the Warriors."

"Thinking back Jerry was not the obvious player let's say. He was a diminutive man. You know he quarterbacked in touch-football, he knew the game."

Dennis and I continued on, me catching him up on current affairs. I mentioned the death of Eddie Stack.

"He was a coach. I'm sorry to hear that", Dennis said with condolence. "I remember, he was a big, burly guy. The Archer Street Rams. They were a big rival. I know Ed and Jerry were close friends. But In retrospect, Jerry was special, putting that kind of effort into a team. And he did sort of threaded the needle of being a mentor. Kind of father figure because of the ages, but also a coach, mentor, father and a friend. He became a very positive part of a mentor and a role model. He wasn't a disciplinarian but on the other hand, I never remember him letting us stray into bad things. I think over all my time, I can't think of anyone who comes to mind that ever got into a bad situation. Partly it's selection. People that do this may be predisposed to do that, we all need a little guidance at that time. He provided that. Yeah, he was a straight shooter and he had a sense of humor. He had to, to be dealing with sixteen and seventeen-year-olds."

As a scholar would, Dennis seemed to search every corner of his mind's eye. He resumed upon finding something in that corner. "And his brother, Frank was, for me at least, kind of an interesting dimension on Jerry, although Frank didn't play, as was the experience of the neighborhood. There are other paths that as an individual, you could accrue and that was that you could be an academic. I don't know how big a role it (academics) played in, but it kind of gave you just an existence there. You know that you can do it. Whether you do it or not depends on your initial convictions."

I interjected, "Many of us, talk about how 'Jay taught me this, he taught me that'. And we apply it to our lives, our jobs, the way we go about things."

"That's why I brought up Frank. You know where I ended up and I was kind of drifting at that time. I was wondering what to do with my life. Do something in academia, was a thought. It was kind of a recurring theme, it would come up every now and then. Knowing somebody that I respected, Jerry's brother did that as a professor. He was a pretty solid individual, and a launching board, a model. Let's put it that way. The other thing with Jerry was him not getting too carried away in quests for victories. Most of us walked out of that thing without serious injury. There was the level of being competitive. It was competitive but not cut throat. That's the best way that I look back at that. I enjoyed the competition, but you know it stayed at a reasonable level. You know it wasn't win at all cost. It was play a good game at all costs. You didn't have to necessarily win. He did all the right things. That's exactly who he is, and it was done honestly and when no one was looking so to speak.

I mentioned to Dennis that Frank had recently passed.

"I'm sorry to hear about Frank. I liked him."

Chapter 4

P.S. 106 – The Sixties – The Second Half

P.S. 106 Schoolyard, Bronx, N.Y.

By 1965, P.S. 106 was thriving. It was teeming with athletic talent, producing champion after champion all led by one coach who was walking the path of a legend.

Over time, my dad came to be good friends with Jerry as my father became enamored with our team. It didn't take long for my dad to realize that we had a special group and it didn't hurt that we were winning every week. Before long, he would be at every game. With his sideline presence evident, the guys took to calling him our number one fan. I contended that the number one fan had to be Ann Brady-Simmons, a good friend of Matty Dowling, Kevin Burke, and John and Mike Fallon, as she had been watching our games a good year before. There was a third person who would be at every game. A solitary figure, always in the distance, always in a beige trench coat. We didn't know who he was. It wasn't until several months ago that I had come to learn that this was our running back, Tommy Pryor's, dad, Robert Pryor. It seemed that there was a toss-up as to who the Warriors number one fan was. I voted for Ann as she is a lot better looking than dad. Also, as my father played fast-pitch softball in a league, he was a pitcher, and Jerry being an umpire, it wasn't uncommon to see Jay behind home plate calling balls and strikes. Many years later, he revealed to me that he didn't like when Jerry was behind the plate. I had asked him why he would say that, and his response was that with all the respect he had for Jerry, he found that he couldn't argue a bad call with him. But it was a conversation they had on a particularly hot August afternoon during one of our workout/practices at Rice Stadium. My dad, who was still playing softball, was also on a touch football team in a league and playing ice hockey out in Commack, Long Island with thirty-year old's, while he's about to enter his sixties, enjoyed the company of the younger guys who played ball and he was a good athlete. He admired Jerry who was eleven years the younger for his involvement with "the kids". Jerry explained his start as a Parkie and how he would create these "leagues" in the playground and how he would also participate. "What the kids didn't realize", he told my father, "was that I had the whistle. This carries more weight than the guy that came into the schoolyard with the ball. I had the whistle, I had control." The did develop quite a relationship over the years.

***

The night at Westchester Manor, back in April 2012, to reiterate, was an incredible affair. Lots of food, drink, but most significant, there were lots of us. Initially, upon entry, we cued up in single file to check in and to receive a CD which was a video history of the Warriors touch tackle teams and the tackle team. The tackle team also were given a replica of our jerseys from our playing days, a simple white jersey with red tackle twill numbers and two red stripes over the shoulders. Within no time a log jam formed as we all just started shaking hands and hugging one another, be it a close friend or a good friend not seen over the years. We took to our tables and settled in for a grand evening. Joe Regina, our defensive tackle, took to the podium and in his usual way, in a professional and sophisticated manner, emceed the presentations. Hence the name Paparazzi. Jeff Ortiz of the P.S. 106 group and a member on the 1967 touch tackle team kicked off the ceremonies by introducing his entire 1967 New York City championship team. He then called Jackie Kaufman, who was the team captain and together, they presented the coach with a memorial to Kenny Aronoff, the center on that team. It was his original jersey which was put in a glass frame. A standing ovation honored a very touching moment. Kenny Aronoff passed away from a severe bout of pneumonia, he was forty-three. Jeff was followed by speakers paying tribute to Jerry with remembrances and anecdotes. Frank Demers, Councilman Jimmy Vacca, Danny Miller, Jackie Cawley, our quarterback and captain, Joey Reich, our defensive captain, John Macchiaroli, our center and another captain, and Ollie, Jimmy Oliveto, who delivered a fiery, passionate speech, all came to the podium. Dr. Arthur "Artie" Langer, now a professor at Columbia University, presented the coach with a pencil sketched portrait of Jerry wearing his familiar white ball cap with the big red "W" and his Warrior jacket. It was the beginning of an amazing night.

The buffet table became the next presenter with the bar as its co-host. After a short while, the crowd began to circulate amongst themselves for chit-chat, catching up on old times and new times. Five particular Warriors, of P.S. 106 prominence, sat at an table to share a beer and reminisce the good days. They were Jack Kaufman, Eric Wulf, Jeff Ortiz, Lew Lubarsky and Neil Altabet, all of the 1967 City Championship team. Someone posed the question as to if they remembered first going into that playground.

Eric Wulf, as a good quarterback (he also played outside linebacker), took the lead. "I think the year was around 1962, I want to say, 1963, somewhere in there, I was about twelve or thirteen when I was first coming around the park."

Jeff Ortiz, who also played at the quarterback position and linebacker on defense, took the second rep. "It all began for me in 1961 when my parents moved from the Parkchester North Quadrant, then to the East Quadrant and I transferred schools from P.S.102 to P.S.106…I was now in the fifth grade and started making new friends, friends that to this day I am still in contact with. For me, sports were always the way I made friendships either in Little League or playing ball at lunchtime in P.S. 106 or after school in the P.S. 106 schoolyard or the Park, as it came to be known."

"I was probably about ten years old." Lew "The Spleen" Lubarsky added. Lew played flanker, defensive back and ran back kicks.

Jeff continued, "I could remember the three o'clock school bell would ring, and I would run home, change and run back to the park because the first ones to get back would be able to play football, basketball, whatever... If you were late you would have to wait to play the next game or maybe not be able to play at all because it would get dark or it was your suppertime."

Neil jumped in, "Unless you were the best player. Then you would get in. The best player always could get in. Or if you brought the Spaldeen down for the punch ball game. Then you could get in. You always needed the ball to get in."

"All in all, there were about forty, fifty kids that would "hang out in the schoolyard and about ninety percent of us would always be playing some kind of ball. So eventually this Parkie who we all called Jay would form schoolyard leagues in football, hockey, wiffleball, and soccer. It should be noted that Jay would make sure that these leagues would be maintained by age groups, so no one would have an unfair advantage. The result was that we would always have two divisions, juniors, and seniors. The juniors were ages thirteen and under and the seniors would be fourteen and over. Sometimes some of the juniors were allowed to be brought up as replacements in case someone in the senior division couldn't be there and some of these juniors were as good as or even better than some of the seniors.

Eric went on, "You were there to compete. You were there to see your friends. You were there too, you know, to have a good time, and you know, it was one of these things. I can remember, on a hot summer's day, somebody would volunteer to go to the store and pick up snacks or a cold drink. I would always end up getting a club soda. The reason I got club soda was, first of all, it was refreshing on a hot day. Plus, the fact that nobody else wanted to drink the stuff. It was about twenty-five cents for the quart bottle."

"And there were two candy stores, one on each corner and a deli in between", Lew added. "One was called Jack's and the other we called the Spas, on Starling Avenue. Odell Street cut in the middle of Starling and stopped at the playground."

"You could get egg creams from Jack's store", Neil laughed. "A nickel for a small Coke and a dime for a large. The owner of the candy store's name was Jack, of course, and his wife was Mal. Remember? You know when Jack was working, we used to go in there and get these half pints of ice cream. Jack would have to pack the ice cream into this plastic cardboard container, which was in this metal thing and then he'd put the ice cream in you know? He'd stuff it in. Now, Jack, he used to stuff in a ton of ice cream, but his wife, she used to just push it a little and say, "Okay, that's enough." Neil couldn't hold back his laughter but somehow talked through it. "You'd get the same ice cream from them but from Jack, it was like twice as much as what Mal gave us."

Lew carried on after they all stopped laughing. "Then we'd go across Odell Street to the other corner and that's where the Spot was. That's where we get our Spaldeens, the pink rubber ball, that's where we would buy those. They always kept a stock of those. And we were also into Whiffle ball. It was a solid Whiffle ball, no holes in it. A store on Castle Hill Avenue, a little toy store, had a stock of them. They'd come in a sleeve of three in a plastic bag. Jerry would tape the seam with an adhesive tape which gave it a little more weight. We had people who could throw any pitch a major leaguer could throw. We had people who could throw pitches that didn't exist in the major leagues. Eric, you would throw this fastball that would almost hit the ground and then start coming up. It was unhittable. Jackie, you were virtually unhittable. Remember when we played stickball. The school was a U-shaped building. If you hit it off the wall and it came back and didn't hit the other wall it was a single. If it hit both walls it was a double. If you hit it above a certain window it was a triple, up on the roof was a home run and if you hit the ball on the roof a certain way, we called it an eight ball, it would hit the roof and spin back. If you caught it off the roof it was an out. We actually played a game that we called it Sockee. Jerry got us to play that. It was soccer with hockey rules in the handball court. We played with a volleyball. And you had to kick the ball, the goal was one of the sections of the fence, but you played with body checking. Jerry was always worried about kicking the ball over the fence, hitting the building next door and breaking somebody's window. So, if you kicked into the third section of the fence that was high kicking as Jerry would call it and that was a five-minute penalty. And there was a two-minute penalty for roughing or whatever. Well, one day Jerry says I need eight of you, I need four on a team. We're going to demonstrate Sockee for the Department of Parks. So, we play this little game and these guys are watching us. Two weeks later, rules come out for mini soccer and how to play it in the handball court for all the playgrounds in New York. When we played punch ball it got to the point where it was easy to hit the ball over the fence so if you hit it over where the park house was that was an out. The next section, where the kid swings were, was a double, a home run was into the handball court, it had the high fence, that was a shot. I think I hit two in my life. But way down one side was a manhole that was first base. You couldn't hit to the right of the basketball court because that was a short fence. But you had to run fifty percent further than to any other base to get to first base, so it was tough to get on. You hit a ground ball you're going to get thrown out. We used to play ball by the hour in there. But one day it snowed, and it wasn't enough to play tackle, it got slushy, so we went into the park house and got the shovels. We pulled that manhole cover up and shoveled the field, putting all the snow down the manhole so we could use the field."

Neil entered the discussion with his memories. "When we first started going to the park, when six o'clock came, Jerry would leave to go home, and everybody would have to leave the park. He would close the gate, put on a chain and lock it up. They didn't want people in the park at night. But then what would happen was, we would just climb the fence. And if Jerry should come back around and see us back in there, he would yell at us. But he had rules and you couldn't break the rules. If you broke the rules, you got punished for breaking the rules. The punishment was not being able to play in games the next day."

Eric continued. "And one of the biggest reasons I kept coming to the park was Jerry. At that time, we just seem to migrate into the park not really knowing what to expect nor the person who was running the park, Jerry Demers. We initially began playing pickup games whether it was football, basketball, stickball, etc. We really only started to get an idea of the intricacies and nuances of football with Jerry's guiding hand, literally. He would start drawing up plays using his chest as a blackboard and giving names to the different patterns and responsibilities that each player had. From that point on, say 1963 is when the basis for our team actually began."

Jack Kaufman, was unanimously acknowledged as the best athlete on that team (tight end and middle linebacker) I had a conversation with Eric Wulf who detailed Jack's essence.

"I would have to say that the leader of our team, whether it is softball or football, would be Jackie Kaufman. Jackie was a leader on and off the field. A strong personality and an excellent athlete. From his position at middle linebacker, he dominated and held the defense together. When guys got to the huddle, Jackie on defense, and I on offense, we really didn't tolerate much in the way of kibitzing about the last play or what they did. We were too busy preparing for the next play.in the huddle."

Naturally, the Captain, Jack, took the floor. "For as long as I can remember, Jerry has always been a part of my life, yet I can't remember exactly when I first met him. As a young teenager, I hung out with my friends at the P.S. 106 schoolyard just outside of Parkchester. There was a park house where the Parkie would give out balls, board games, jump ropes and anything else that young kids needed to play with. The Parkie was an older guy (who must have been 21 years old) ...that guy was Jay. But Jay was not just some guy giving out toys while biding his time sitting in the park house. He got involved. If there were more than two kids in the playground, he created "teams". If there were more than two teams, he created "leagues". Winners would get trophies and the losers would learn that they had to try harder."

Jeff chimed in, "Looking back I maintain that in the early 60's Jay came up with the format that is now used for all fantasy sports leagues. For instance, in football there were forty kids who played all the time, so Jay divided the players by age and named the four best quarterbacks of each division as the captains of a team, then he let them pick a team name, and let them "draft " all the remaining kids using a pre-determined draft order. The result was there would be four teams per division consisting of five players per team. I was lucky enough to be one of the quarterbacks on the seniors and I named my team the Giants. Jay would then draw up a schedule for the teams to play and he would post the results, standings, and statistics on the bulletin board outside of the park house on the wall. At the end of the season, there would be playoffs and trophies were handed out to the winners. This draft procedure and scheduling would also include leagues for hockey, whiffle ball, and soccer and once again standings statistics and scheduling would be posted on the wall. These leagues ran from 1965-1968 and to me were some of the best times of my life. To this day I am in contact with over fifty of these former teammates and friends."

Jack continued on. "Jay saw to it that every inch of that schoolyard was utilized. The handball courts were the home of our four-man soccer games, and our two-man wiffleball and stickball games. I cannot remember ever playing handball in the handball courts. At the far end of the schoolyard was an open field where punch ball games were played either the "long way" if there were enough players to cover the field, or the "short way" if we only had a couple of kids on each team. The "short way" was also the home of our touch football and field hockey games. Only the basketball courts were used for its intended purpose. There were four half-courts which could also be used as two full-courts, but only one of the half courts were generally used. The winning team stayed on the court to play the other challengers. And yeah Jeff, you're right. The park was home to a multitude of kids usually divided up by age. The "older" guys, Danny Miller, Jimmy Oliveto, Tony Vastola, Biff was one group, our age group was us, Spencer Blank, Jeff Gold, Lauren Zeltner, Eric Wulf, Tony LaMagna and the "younger" kids Joey Reich, Neil Altabet, Artie Langer, Ron Watson, Mike Pisaniello. Usually, the younger guys didn't play on teams with us and we didn't play with the older guys unless the older group needed another guy, or the younger guy was a good player. The younger guys looked up to us, we looked up to the older guys, and we all, in turn, looked up to Jay." Jack leaned back in his chair and took a pause. "You know, Jay related to each group differently. I think he was a father figure to the youngest, an older brother to us and a friend to the older guys, but to all of us, he was a leader. And, his leadership extended well beyond the fenced-in boundaries of the schoolyard. Asking me about my remembrances of Jay is a little like asking me about my remembrances of my father. I always felt I had a special bond with Jay and Geri, his wife. I'm sure he gave the same attention to the other guys, but that was the magic of Jay, he could always make you feel you were special."

Neal Altabet rejoined the commentary. Neal was one of those "junior" players that was called up to the "bigs", the senior team in 1967, playing defensive back and returning kicks alongside Lew. "Jerry you know just did so much for the kids. For everybody and you know I used to go to school there by 106. It was cool. There was always a punch ball game. At lunchtime, everybody ran home to eat lunch and you'd get back to the park as soon as you could, so you could get a punch ball game. Then when it was three o'clock and school was out, everyone would run home and run to the park so that they could get in on a punch ball game or a football game. Then Jerry started making leagues. We had a hockey league, a wiffleball league, like Jack said. We used to play wiffleball on the handball courts. We would put up like a strike zone and draw it on the wall, remember? And a guy would pitch from the fence and we were back over by the wall. If you'd hit it over the fence it was a home run. If you hit it in the upper level of the fence, it was a triple and the middle was a double and anything that got past the fielder was a single. And, I had my partner on the team. It was Ricky Slatin, from Starling Gardens. We were always the underdogs, but we won the championship there two times in a row. I was about fifteen, sixteen years old. But he used to make all of these leagues for us. And yeah Jack, we had a hockey league. We had like a little football league with drafts. There were four teams and each one had a quarterback and there was the first-round draft and the second-round draft and the third-round draft. And we played against each other. It was two-hand touch. It was probably like five players played at the same time. There was a quarterback and four receivers. And the touchdown was down by the shuffleboard courts. The basketball court would be a first down. There wasn't like a yardage for a first down but there was a designated marker for a first down. If you got past there, it would be a first down. We played all the games and it was great. You know, it was very competitive, and it was good. We'd play a lot of punch ball games and Jerry would be the catcher and the umpire. We would have basketball and each season it would be a different kind of a league. There was a basketball season and a hockey season and there was football. There were a lot of things going on. Then once a year, Jerry used to take us out to Palisades Park. Remember Palisades Park?"

"Jay kept us focused", recalled Jack. "He kept us busy, not only with athletics but with social activities as well. He knew the greatest enemy to youngsters was boredom, and he saw to it that we were never bored. He would arrange trips to Rye Playland, like you said Palisades Park, swimming at local pools, have parties for our teams. My favorite was his New Year's Eve parties where he would dress up as an "Old Man" of the years gone by. And Jay was not just a "fair weather" friend. When the weather was inclement, he always arranged for us to have indoor activities, whether it was in the park house or an outing to the movies or to go bowling."

Lew: "Yeah, we would go there, and we would go to other places, or we would have a barbeque. He kept us busy, he kept us off the streets. I remember, 1966-67, Jerry took us down to Madison Square Garden to see the Knicks and Celtics play. I remember that the Celtics had a forward by the name of Toby Kimball. Jerry kept commenting that Kimball looked like a giant flightless bird trying to take off. That's how bad this guy played."

Everybody was now into the discussion as the conversation drifted into as to whether or not their parents knew who Jerry was or if they had ever met the man.

"They probably knew of him, but my parents never really came down to the park. They knew we were safe because there was somebody at the park. And things were different then too. You know, think of today and if you have a twelve-year-old son that says, "Hey Dad, I'm going to Palisades Park with this man." You would be concerned...like, "Who is this guy?"

"My parents knew him vaguely by name and who he was. They knew he was the park keeper. I remember going for ice cream...Jahn's Ice Cream parlor on Kingsbridge Road, remember Jahn's, they had the kitchen sink" [Note: The Kitchen Sink was a monstrous concoction comprising as many as thirty scoops of ice cream and nearly as many toppings that helped make the chain a local legend[24].] We didn't have cars at that point, so we hopped into

---

[24] The City, Urban Studies, Jackson Height, Douglas Quenqua, The Last One Standing, March 20, 2009

cars...it was probably Danny Miller and Vastola driving. But I remember going to Jahn's, we all had spoons digging into this kitchen sink. We had a whole table. I remember we would all go to the beach. Things like that."

Cathy Ackerman, a known associate of the all-girls 106 crew, wandered by. "What are you boys up to?"

"Just remembering the good old days in 106, what Jerry did for us guys."

"I guess you would say me and the other gals were on the sidelines. We would go onto the basketball court and play but there were no leagues for the girls. But we loved Jerry. He was just such a nice guy. He always gave us a hello along with a great beautiful smile that he still has today. I do remember one time I was standing on the swings and pumping myself up real high... and I fell. No rubber mats at that time. I scraped my knees really bad. I just remember Jerry helping me to his office and taking care of my knees. I cannot tell you how bad the cuts were. But anyway, he calmed me down and he was just so sweet to me I will never forget that time with him. I don't know if you know what Jerry did after our last reunion three years ago. He sent all the girls a letter apologizing to us that he didn't focus on us as much as the boys. I wrote back to him and said that we loved the sidelines. We were just so happy seeing the "boys." Like, Armand, Tony LaMagna, and Meatball [Richie Ruggiero] . Great times for sure."

Cathy went on her way leaving the fabled five horsemen of the Bronx to recall their glory year of 1967.

Lew took over. "At the end of 1965 the guys were gone for two years, Tony, Ollie, Danny, and Bill, along with others. In that period, we had a touch football team from the playground which also won a City Championship in touch football in 1967 so that was very rewarding. We played a team from Staten Island at a neutral field in Manhattan and won six nothing when Neil Altabet scored on a long pass from Eric Wolf. It was very gratifying. Of all the playgrounds in the five boroughs, our guys were the best. That was one of the highlights of my Warriors career."

Once again, the captain began the exchange. "Remember Jay would enroll us in Bronx-wide and Citywide tournaments which took us to the other boroughs to play against other kids of our age. In 1967, when we won the NYC Touch-Tackle championship. That is an experience I will never forget."

On December 14th, 1967 the Bronx Press Review, in their sports section, announced "Warriors 11 Set for Title Game. The eleven were actually twelve. In addition to Jack, Eric, Jeff, Lew, and Neil was the three-man offensive line of Kenny Aronoff at center, Spencer Blank and Neil Rabinowitz at the guard positions. Lauren Zeltner was the blocking back. Lauren was also an outside linebacker. Tony LaMagna was at defensive end, Sammy Scicolone was the other defensive end and Jeffery Solomon was the defensive tackle. The article read as follows: *The P.S. Warriors seniors will meet a team from Staten Island in Central Park, on Saturday, for the City championship in the Park Department-AMF eight-man football tournament after beating the Queens champs, 27-0 on Williamsbridge Oval, Sunday. The Warriors wasted no time. Captain Jack Kaufman carried the opening kickoff eighty yards for a touchdown. In the second period, quarterback Eric Wulf scored twice on sweeps, and Hips Lubarsky tallied later on a pass.* Lew would come to be called Hips, as he was tagged by Jerry with that nickname in a Bronx Press Review article, because of his running style. A hip fake going one way and a hip shake going the other. The team has been undefeated and unscored upon.

On that Saturday, December 16, 1967, the Warriors took to a sloppy, muddy turf. The temperature hovered around thirty-five degrees with a wind that whipped up to fifteen to twenty miles an hour. Scoring would be the exception this day.

Eric recalled his early days, 1962, 1963 learning football from Jerry. "I never knew what a pass pattern was before Jerry came into the picture. And one of the biggest things that I found while being in the park was getting to understand the underlying concept of what we were doing. It was the structure that Jerry brought to what we were doing. I mean, he would just stand there with his back to the defense, and he would say, "Okay, you do a square out." And he drew it on his chest. "You do a V pattern, or a nowadays called a flag pattern or, a post pattern, a hook…whatever the case may be…and he brought that to life. You know, I love football. Always had, you know, growing up in the days of Charlie Connolly."

Lew added, "Jerry taught me football. When we first started going down there (106), I was probably ten and he would play football with us. We would play four on four and I remember that first, we would huddle up and he taught us how to huddle up. You didn't just take a place anywhere in the huddle. If you were the end on that side, you would stand here and if you're the end on the other side you stood there, if you're in the middle you stand here in the middle. Then he would tell us, here's a down and out we're going to run. You do this and then you cut out and I'll tell you how far to go before you cut out. He was very detailed on every pattern, every play. I played intramurals in college and we were running Warrior plays. Unfortunately, we didn't have a quarterback, like Eric or Jeff."

"We would always go to his house for meetings, skull sessions, review the audibles, work out plays on the blackboard and the practices. I was maybe fifteen years old," Jeff added

The discussion turned to that fateful day.

Neil started the dialogue. "I can remember that we came on the field and they were warming up on the side. There was some exercising and we were getting psyched out because these guys looked good. It was a scary situation, at least for me."

Lew shook Neil off like a receiver shredding a tackle. "We weren't intimated by nobody. You couldn't score on us."

"Tony Vastola, Ollie, and Danny Miller were there as support. All of those guys were there. Tony lined us up and we did some exercises. We got pumped." Neil said.

Eric returned. "Yeah Tony led us in warm-ups, he almost wore us out. The field was a mess, it was muddy, and it was windy. Our offensive game was the long pass. I would get behind somebody that day, but all the passes, they were all incomplete. The wind blew that much."

Lew went back to evoking the playoffs leading up to the championship game. "The first game we were going to play was somewhere in The Bronx, I don't remember. We had to play three games. We had to scrimmage them the week before. So, Jerry says, "We show them nothing". So instead of me being the flanker, I'm the tight end. Jerry Guerra is the quarterback and he wasn't even on the team. And the entire game Jerry runs right, Jerry runs left, maybe he throws a little dinky pass here and there. Then we come out the next week and we've got wide receivers, Eric is the quarterback, somebody they never saw. We had the west coast offense before the west coast offense existed. We're throwing the ball all over the place. I think we beat them forty to nothing. Actually, nobody scored on us the entire year. We had to go undefeated because if you lost you were out. But we played, I guess, the three games for the district and then we had a bye. Manhattan was playing Queens, we were going to get the winner of that game, Brooklyn was playing Staten Island. So, we went wherever that game was, and we scouted them.

Queens physically beat the heck out of Manhattan. We told the kids from Manhattan that we were going to take care of them for you next week. So, Jerry devises this play, the first play of the game on offense, I'm not going to start. Eric, you were going to start at flanker, Jeff, you started at quarterback. Eric is going to line up on the left side and do an end around. We get the opening kickoff and the kick was a little short and it comes to you, Jackie. You took off up the middle, nobody touches you and we score a touchdown. Jerry was brilliant offensively. He had a play where we'd come out and it looked like we had a center, two wideouts, and a tight end but we'd come out with what looks like an unbalanced line. We got a center, both linemen on the right and actually, the tight end is split. The wide receiver is our tight end on the left. They didn't realize that. We'd hit the receiver on the left side and scored every time."

Eric took over. "What can one say, it was a great year. I don't think any of us really knew how much it would mean to be champions of New York City. Except for the championship touchdown pass, I really don't remember any single play. Without sounding obnoxious, we were so well trained and organized that no team could even touch us. In the entire year, I got knocked down only twice and that's because I had sent Jackie out on a pattern and the linebacker came. That was my fault because I should have picked up on the blitz. But only twice. We were that strong offensively. And defensively, I'm telling you, the pressure that those three guys on the defensive line would put on the quarterback was remarkable. Then to add to it, having Jack, or myself, or Lauren going in on a blitz, that was just…" Eric couldn't finish his thought as he chuckled himself down memory lane. "I hate to say it, but we were unstoppable. And the greatest play that I can think of. I'm not really sure at what point in the game the play occurred. Neil Altabet came in with a play from Jerry. It was a chair pattern down the left sideline. The ball was hiked, the protection was outstanding, and the pattern that Neil ran was absolutely perfect. The ball reached Neil in midstride, probably the most perfect spiral I ever threw, and Neil ran past the safety for the score. I would say that the entire play probably covered about 60 yards. Then we let the defense do its thing."

Neil corrected Eric as to who called the play. "I was the wide receiver, split left end and this guy was guarding me on the line of scrimmage, trying to do a bump and run kind of thing. When I came off the field, I told Jerry, "Coach, listen, this guy is guarding me tight. I could do what we used to call a chair pattern. So, he sent me back into the game with the stop and go pattern. I went out about ten yards and Eric pumped the ball and faked it. Then I turned around and then flew alright? Then I caught the ball. It was a perfect pass. I caught the ball on the dead run like Willie Mays making that catch off Vic Wertz in the World Series. I caught it just like that. On a dead run on the forty-yard line, with the defender five yards behind me. That's the greatest play of my whole career. Eric, you had a great arm. You could get it to anybody if they were open. But at every position, we had the best players. Real great players, you know except for me." Neil paused in laughter. I mean I was good but not as good as you guys. We had such a great team."

Lew went back in time. "There was a Sunday in October 1965. I was down at the park, I was fifteen years old, and we were playing catch with a football. Eric Wulf throws me a pass, I was running a little square in, and I reached with my left arm and caught the ball. The force of the ball, that pass pushed my ribs through my spleen. It punctured my spleen. That night I had surgery at St. Francis Hospital in The Bronx. I was in the hospital for about a week. A couple of days into that Jerry shows up. Now we jump ahead forty years. I decided to Google Jerry. Was he still alive? I see a few articles, I see where he's retired from the Parks Department, I also see a Warriors' website. Which I didn't know existed. He was mentioned in there but there were no links, no contact information, no email other than some guy's email, so I send him an email. "Hey, I played for the Warriors in the mid-sixties and I would like to speak with Jerry, do you have an email address? About three days go by and I get an email from his son, Ricky. He said my dad doesn't have email but I'm sure he would love to talk to you, here's his phone number. So, a couple of days go by, it was probably in the afternoon, I called, and I got his answering machine. I left him a message, "Hello this is Lew Lubarsky from P.S. 106 back in the sixties and this is my phone number". Twenty minutes later the phone rings. I said "Hello" and the voice says "Hello, did your spleen grow back yet". We laughed so hard."

Eric brought the talk back to "that game" and supported Neil with some comfort. "Yeah, that was a hell of a play. Jerry Guerra was our end, but he aged out at some point and couldn't play. Anyway, the long and short of it is, he was replaced by you. I mean, to be honest with you, for whatever reason, you were virtually ignored for the good part of the season, and that was my bad…and it wasn't that I didn't trust you to catch the ball or anything, but for some reason I was always going to my three other receivers, and that was always towards the right side or the middle. It was a comfort zone for me. And, you know, it wasn't done intentionally. So, Jerry sent in the play. I got in the huddle and said, "chair pattern", to Neil on the left side. I get the snap, you do your out route, I fake it to you, and this guy, the cornerback, was so faked out, that he fell and laid flat on the ground. I threw it to Neil and it was possibly the best pass I ever threw because I got him in between the safety and the quarterback, and the rest of the way he just took it himself. Yeah, perfect spiral. Perfect, you know, just get it to you in between the linebacker and the safety, and then you took it all the way. I mean, I swear to God, I've never seen you run that fast. I mean, Lauren was quite possibly the fastest guy on the squad, but on that play, it was you. God, Lauren had the worst hands I have ever seen. I mean, I would worry about giving him a handoff. It was, you know, it was one of these things where nothing could get by Loren, nothing, except he just couldn't catch the damn ball. You know, and I always was afraid to throw to him because I figured, he's going to drop it. Hey Lew, didn't you intercept a couple of passes?"

"I intercepted three passes that day. I said to myself if I have the ball when we win this game, I'm going to throw it as far as I can, not that I can throw that far. What turned out to be the last play of the game was when I intercepted Staten Island's pass in the end zone and I remember just being mobbed. I couldn't move my arms, everybody had me in a bear hug so I couldn't heave the ball. So, we go over to the sidelines all jumping around, and Jerry has the film of it, he's got a bottle of champagne and he pops the cork. You probably couldn't do that today. Kenny Aronoff comes over to me with the football and he says, "it's not official but here's the game ball". He gave me the game ball. Neil caught the touchdown and that might be the only one he caught all year, but I got that ball."

Eric brought up one more team memory. "No one on the team liked losing but to my knowledge there was no finger-pointing after a blown play. I think everyone knew that everybody was responsible, and we would need to work harder to get a win. When we won, we felt great, but Jerry always knew there was still work to be done."

Neil, in excitement, jumped in. "And another great part of that game is that Jerry had his 1966 Mustang convertible. I think it was a sixty-six convertible. But we were so high from that game, we went home from Central Park with the top down. It was a cold winter day. It was freezing but we didn't feel a thing. It was really, really, really great."

Eric nodded in agreement. "The mustang…yeah."

"Lew leaped in. "Hey Eric, remember that time we had to get Jerry's brother Frank out of the airport. We go to JFK in the Mustang. We drive to arrivals, but Frank isn't there, so Jerry tells us to go into the terminal and find his brother while he circles around. We don't know what Frank looks like, but Jay tells us he looks like him. So, we go in and wander about calling out "Frank, Frank Demers". Some guy comes up to us and says, "I'm Frank Demers". We tell him who we are and that we'll bring him to his brother. Frank looks nothing like Jay."

Jack, who seemingly was sitting on the sideline, just soaking it all up, during the whole conversation, spoke up. "To this day, whenever I see a green Mustang convertible, my thoughts immediately return to P.S. 106 and a smile comes to my face."

"Oh and, then a continuation of this story is a week or two weeks later, we had a party at Jerry's, Neil enthusiastically said. "I think he was recently married at this point. I was never a big drinker. I didn't even like beer, but I started drinking beer that night. I got so sick that I fell asleep on his bed. In the morning I wake up and there was Geri introducing herself to me. It was a crazy situation and I just drank too much but hey, those were good times."

Lew one-upped Neil. "About a month and a half after they had given us our trophies. We got a small trophy for winning the district, the bigger one for winning The Bronx, and we got a bigger one for winning the City. So, we have this party and all of a sudden Jerry kind of disappears and he comes out of a room. He was wearing a referee's uniform and this Santa Claus beard and a cane. And he's hobbling out and he's an old referee and it's fifty years later and it's "whatever happened to" and he would create a story about different guys. We had this one guy, passed away now, you would have called him a hood. He was into drugs. So, the skit goes on, "What happened to so and so" and Jay says "Oh, he became a priest". Well at that time you may remember Dr. Christian Bernard pioneered the open-heart transplant in South Africa. Well, they said whatever ever happened to Lew? Jerry says "Oh, he moved to South Africa to have a spleen transplant". Everybody lost it. It was so funny. Jerry has quite a sense of humor. And the Warrior Jackets. It was a wool, heavy coat. You didn't have to be one of the twelve on the team. Anybody in the park, anyone who wanted it could buy it. Jackie, your father was in the business in some way, so we ordered it through him. It had your number on it, it said Warriors on the back with a football and your name stitched on the side. When I got mine, my mother says that I can't wear that to school because it looks like you're in a gang. Eventually, my mother relented, and I

74

wore it to Monroe. I walked into homeroom, nobody ever talked to me in homeroom and nobody knew who I was. With the Warrior jacket on, some guy comes over to me and says, "You play for the Warriors?". I said yeah. He says, "With Spencer Blank and Jackie Kaufman". I said yeah. He says, "What position do you play?" I said flanker, defensive back, run back kickoffs and punts. He said, "Wow". From then on, he talked to me. I was somebody all of a sudden."

Erich changed the tone of the roundtable. "Jerry impacted my life on so many different levels. Honesty, integrity and a drive to succeed. It would be difficult for me to comprehend what my life would have been without him. As I said earlier, Jerry became a surrogate father for someone who didn't have one, me. It's so much of a life that was, you know, my life. Probably the happiest time of my life, and I mean, with the exception of getting married and the birth of my children."

Lew agreed. "Of all the adults in my life other than my parents, Jerry had the biggest influence. For some guys, like yourself Eric, guys that didn't have a dad, Jerry was a surrogate father to them. In my case, he's like a big brother. You could talk to him about anything. My first drink or two was at his house. He was always at the park organizing stuff. We weren't out there running around the streets. It was the park whether it was basketball, football, whiffle ball, a little soccer league…whatever it was we always had a game to play. I coached my kids in all different sports using Jerry's techniques. It's the only way I know how to coach. I didn't scream at kids, just like Jay didn't."

"He gave me a sense of purpose and accomplishment", Eric stated. "In 1968 I ended up having to work full time and go to school at night which kind of limited my time at the park. Then by 1969, I had a prior engagement in the U.S. Army and Vietnam. By 1971, I was going to school and met my future wife. And I think that Jerry taught us something that would become one of our strengths. We never forgot who we were, and we could count on a fellow Warrior to have your back if needed. I don't think I felt as close to any other group of people, even to this day than I had with you guys. The one thing that I never forgot was what it means to be a Warrior."

Jack, once again engaged his teammates. "Jay did one other thing for all of us. Something that we would not appreciate until decades later. He documented our childhoods both in photographs and film. I know I speak for many others when I say that he had more pictures of us as young teens than our parents had. I always looked forward to these Warrior reunions because I know that for a few hours I would be reliving my childhood through those pictures and through the group"

Neil took over. "I'll tell you guys how Jerry affected my life. You know, Jerry did all of these leagues, working with us kids. Later on, in my career, I became a teacher, and, in the summer, I used to work at this place called Stevenson Commons. It was a housing project in the Bronx on White Plains Road and Lafayette Avenue. And they hired me to run an athletic program. Like a day camp during the summer. What's so outrageous is, I did the same thing as Jay only with another generation. I did it for maybe seven or eight years. I kept these kids off the streets. Learning from Jerry, I did the same thing that he did for me and the people I was growing up with. I made a little league during the summer. We had a basketball league and at the end of the year, I would have an Olympic Day. Then I would have a paddle ball tournament and a tennis tournament for the older people. I used to take the kids, at the end of the year, on a trip. We would usually go to Rye Playland or Mohansic State Park. I'd do the barbeque and the pool thing. Get the kids out and have some fun. And these kids…this is outrageous, and this is a long time ago, it was about twenty-five years ago. Now, these kids are grown up, and they got together and had a reunion, of all the Stevenson Commons kids. And we're having the reunion and they honored me. They got me this trophy that was maybe …I've never gotten one like this in my life, it was three to four feet high. They said, "Thanks to you, a lot of us are here." They said, "If it wasn't for you keeping us busy, we would have been on the streets doing the wrong thing. I felt like a little Jerry because that's what he did for us."

They sat back with a gleam in their eyes and a grin across their faces. The affair did, sadly enough, come to a conclusion. But it was a wonderful, unforgettable night on every level.

The P.S. 106 crew, as interesting as they were all so very successful. Eric Wulf was with the Armed Forces for eight years. Two on active duty in Vietnam as an Army Ranger, trained by the Green Berets. His mission was long range reconnaissance patrol. He gave two more years on active reserve followed by two years as an inactive reserve and concluding with a two-year stint in the National Guard. He is a graduate of Southern Connecticut University with a degree in history. As a post graduate, he gave lectures on civil war topics, the merits of military weaponry, and then some. He also had a career as a medical life disability claims examiner. Jack Kaufman is Dr. Jack Kaufman, D.D.S. a dentist specializing in oral and maxillofacial surgery. He is a graduate of the school of dentistry at the State University of New York at Buffalo who did his residency and internship out of Albert Einstein Hospital/Bronx Municipal Hospital Center. Sports was something that Jeff took very faithfully. He had a passion and love of the games unlike very few I've ever met. When Jeff wasn't at Jerry's side assisting the organization for many years, when he wasn't attending over a thousand concerts in his life, he did find the time to work for the phone company. He started with the old New York Telephone which became NYNEX which became Bell Atlantic which became Verizon Communications. Jeff worked on the technical side of the business as a "trunk" assigner. He was the guy on a computer placing his field techs to a particular hot spot on the street to repair problem cable lines which in turn provided for network access for customers. Lew Lubarsky is your typical, "what did you do for a living" person. He started out with a company called Logistics Speed and was there for five years. Someone who worked with him, left the job but five years later he called Lew out of the blue. He told him that he's with a company out in Washington D.C. that builds railroad cars. They needed someone with a steel background in the purchasing department. Lew went down to Washington, interviewed and got the job. They were the biggest manufacturer of railcars in the world. This was Fruit Growers Express specializing in refrigerated railcars which was very important in the transportation of perishable food. Today they are part of CSX Transportation, the largest railroad east of the Mississippi. Working for them for thirty-six years, Lew performed a number of functions from purchasing and materials, to the finance department to operations. Yes, we shop for tires for our car and Lew purchased wheels for a rail car, and every car part known to the railroad industry. Strange sidebar to this story was Lew explaining to me that his son and daughter worked on the family's genealogy. Long story short, it turns out that there is a history of railroaders in Lew's family tree starting with his grandfather, back in 1855, who came to America and worked for the Iron Horse amongst others. As Lew told me, "Turns out it's the family business and we didn't know that". Me being me, my mind dashed back in time fantasizing about the old railroad days and hobos. I asked him if he had a good hobo story. He did.

"Bob, do you know what kudzu is?"

"Not really."

"Ok, well that vine. That vine that ate the south. I've had rail cars covered in kudzu that we've had to cut out in order to move them. We were getting rid of some cars. I was also responsible for scrapping rail cars and uh, we were getting rid of a car. Well actually I think it was a line of cars but anyway, so I sent my guy to go make sure the break lines were up and everything. He gets to this one car and there's electric wire running to it. The car has carpeting, a washer and dryer. People were living in it. Well he tells them, 'Look you gotta get your stuff out. We're moving this train tomorrow'. So, they cleared out and off they went. So, you know, crazy things like that were happening all the time. We got a car in once. A refrigerated car. We got it in our shop in Alexandria. They come in to get repaired. We get this one in because it's under temperature and it reads zero degrees. We open it up and there's twelve tons of hamburger in it. We closed it up and called the people who owned the meat. They said, 'Oh, my God. If administration finds out we'll never hear the end. Get rid of it, just get rid of it'. So, we all took home hamburger that night."

Not being in a rush to get back to Florida, my wife Carmen and I stayed an extra few nights at a nearby Marriott Courtyard motel. The very next morning, in the breakfast area, I ran into Mike Pisaniello, a renowned member of the P.S. 106 1967 Junior team. Mike has had an interesting background. He is a retired U.S. Postal Service worker, currently serving as the Director of Operations for the Highlander Training Academy in the Bronx. He joined the Lehman College baseball staff prior to the 2015 season. Dedicated to the sport of baseball, Mike also runs the Tri State Prospect Report, a database of the area's top high school baseball prospects. Mike administers the College Baseball Prep, a self-help program that aids High School athletes find their way into a college baseball program. In addition, he serves as a New York Area Scout for the Global Scouting Bureau, and is a member of The New York Professional Baseball Scouts Association. In those roles, he has facilitated signing players to independent, affiliated, and foreign baseball programs in the United States and abroad. As a member of the Advisory Board of the Service Alliance for Youth, he fosters the growth of boys and girls through sports activities and educational excellence for the community-based organization. He also holds a certification from the National Alliance for Youth Sports. Additionally, Michael acts as an advisor and administrator for College Baseball PREP, a Service

Alliance for Youth program, which assists high school student-athletes with the college recruiting process. Mike is everything baseball in the Bronx[25].

We exchanged hugs and talked about what an incredible evening we had.

"Hey Bob, Jerry tells me that you're writing a book about the Warriors."

"Well, I'm attempting to write a book", I responded with a chuckle.

"Would you like to hear my part of the history?"

"Absolutely, do you have time now or do you want to do it at another time?"

"No, now is good. Let's get some coffee."

I pulled out my trusty digital recorder and we went to work.

"I was a precursor to what you call the TEAM, the tackle team. I arrived at 106 Park when I was about 12, around 1965-66. Of course, I didn't come alone. My little crew, Joey Reich, Hank Mager, Matty Totero and Jerry Maringione arrived as a group and it was a smooth transition from the confines of Parkchester. I guess it was because we all had the common bond of the love of sports and competition. Lots of the other kids hanging in the park lived in Parkchester too. It was like we all escaped a place where everyone knew your parents and now, we could have some real fun without getting in trouble. Trouble wasn't a big thing, but it wasn't easy being an energetic kid and having to deal with the Parkchester rules. No playing or walking on the grass, no bike riding or playing ball outside the designated areas. No roller skating, except on Sundays around the Big Oval. No playing in the carriage rooms or hallways, which was always tempting on those cold winter days. Lots and lots of rules that resulted in lots of write-ups from those pesky Parkchester patrolmen. Don't get me wrong it was a great place to grow up in the early years. A truly self-contained community where at eight years old your mom wouldn't have a problem sending you to the store or not feeling you were safe out playing all day long. Anyway, we wind up in 106 and we discovered that there were two different age groups. The seniors and the juniors, but there were no hard and fast rules to age group. It was kind of who you gravitated to. And, who you played with. Some of the younger kids played with the older

---

[25] highlandertrainingacademy.com/staff/

79

group. Some of the not so older guys, the guys who couldn't play as well played with the younger group and there was no problem with that. It was all about making it even. Trying to even things out. A lot of those guys came from the outside because they heard there was something really crazy going on in that park, "We gotta get involved." So, a lot of guys from surrounding areas would come in. But they all became part of us because, not only did the Parkie organize the football, the four-man football, we also had four-man hockey in there. And then, we had four-man soccer in the handball court and we had four-man punch ball. Every part of that park was utilized for something. There were always teams coming in. Kids would come in and you were put on a team and then you became a Warrior. Not necessarily a football player but, you became part of the Warriors where everybody knew everybody. There was a buzz about what was going on in our park too. People would just come from the outside, other neighborhoods, and they were just amazed at the activity. You know, compared to other playgrounds around the city, like 127 or 119, we had a lot of organized activities going on. Jay was the ultimate organizer. What Jay used to do was, he had a tendency to kind of weed out the smart kids. Not necessarily the best athletes. We all were all athletic and everybody could do something. But what he did was make those guys captains and he told us that we're going start a football league in the park. In-house you know. Maybe, I think we had about six teams in the junior division and six in the senior division. I was one of the captains. I think Paul Hanson was another captain. [Paul Hanson later went on to play quarterback for Mount St. Michael High School where they won the 1969 Catholic High School Football League city championship. We went on to attend the University of Massachusetts where he played defensive back] He picked twelve of us to choose up sides. I'll take him. I'll take him. Well, we did it like a fantasy football setting. We sat in the park. Everybody's names were on a board and we would pick somebody, and he would put them on your team. Each team had five guys, I think. It was four-man football. And usually the captain was like me, it was the quarterback. So, after we all picked our teams, and everybody had their guys, then we started making trades. Ok, well, I need a wide receiver. I need a guy that's fast. I need a guy that can play defense. So, it was the forerunner of fantasy football, only with real people. It was pretty interesting. We didn't know what we were doing. Jay just had a way of organizing things that made it interesting you know. Now we all had our teams. Now these guys, they were going to stay with this team for the whole summer and into the winter. And Jay would set up schedules. When we weren't playing our games, we were playing each other in pick-up games. Whoever was there, we would pick up and just play, but every Saturday and Sunday there was a schedule to play and guys were there, and we took it seriously, and it was really good. Each team would have their own little practices. Away from the other teams so they wouldn't know what was going on. It was really fascinating how Jay used to motivate us to be interested in things. Not just play them but, to really get focused in on them. That's what he was good at that. He was good at motivating and organizing and letting us run with it. He would have a bulletin board inside the Parkhouse with every team's standings and how many points everyone scored. And there were never any fights in our park. It's was amazing. You would think with everyone being so competitive with each other that there would be fisticuffs going on but as soon as something was going to blow up, everyone would calm it down. And, it was always Jay's influence because he would say, "I'm a kicker, I can kick," because, he would always kick kids out of the park for doing something they shouldn't be doing. You know, you weren't allowed in the park for three days, seven days, whatever your sentence was, you just couldn't risk that. That was the death sentence. Getting banned from the park, where you couldn't play with your team, where you couldn't play with your friends, you didn't want that. And if it got really bad, let's say and argument between two guys, we would have a boxing match. Two combatants in the sandbox, gloves and all. It hardly ever came to that cause, someone was going to get embarrassed. It amazed me how few fights there was amongst anybody. And there were thirty to fifty kids hanging out at one time. You would think that with all us kids, something was going to happen. But it never got to that point. Like I said, you always had Jerry in the back of your mind and that you didn't want to get banned from the park. And Jay used to do strange things too, at least we thought so. We had one Chinese kid who never played football in his life, never watched a football game, David Wong. His parents owned the "hand wash" laundry store on Purdy Street. And you know, Jay made him the head referee in our football games. And this kid, he hardly spoke English, Jay gave him a yellow hanky and he tells him, "Anything you see that doesn't look right, just throw the hanky and just mark off some yardage." And he would throw the flag and we'd say, "Hey Wong, what'd we do?" and he says, "Don't know. Don't look right." And you know, Jerry made him the head referee in our football games. And this kid, he'd throw that hanky and just mark off some yardage. If he would see two guys pushing or shoving each other, yeah, he'd throw the flag and he was usually right. You'd see the guy going out for a pass and you'd maul him, he'd throw a flag. I guess it was all common sense to him, but nobody argued with him because Jay appointed him as the referee. And it made things pretty, pretty interesting. You really had to be smarter. You had to out-smart the referee to make things look legal. It was funny."

Carmen and I were hysterical listening to Mike and Carmen really doesn't know a thing about football, but this was one humorous story, from sandbox fighting to an Asian referee.

"And he kept track of every single thing that happened in the park.

You would run out there in the morning, look at the board that he would put it up every morning, to see who did what. It was pretty cool, and everything was fair. That's for sure."

"But in 1967, you guys almost went all the way, the same year the senior team won the City."

"Yeah, but it was not to be. We came close. We lost in the semi-finals to Queens. We had me, Joey Reich, Ron Watson, Paul Hansen, Tony Bosco, Jimmy Ackerman, Jerry Maringionne, Matt Todero, Donald Swick, Kenny Schneider, Robert Stein, and Robert Ferrito."

At that moment, Joe Reich was spotted on the coffee line. Mike called him over to our table. "Hey Joe, come here. We're talking about the '67 Junior championship year when we lost in the finals."

Joe acknowledge us and joined the conversation. He had a look of disgust on his face from the mention of that loss. "Beating the other boroughs in touch tackle that was quite an accomplishment. We had a basic game plan offensively and defensively and we came that close to almost winning the city championship. I was very proud of that. We came in second and weren't at our best. I remember that look that Jay gave us that day. 'Hey guys you did your best'. He realized that we were decimated. Half the team had the flu that we caught from the week before watching the Senior team win their championship and other guys had injuries but still, we could have won this game. Here's another thing. I think we played Brooklyn and I remember that we were talking about the ages of these kids. Half of these kids had beards and moustaches."

"We were good but, on that day...it wasn't meant to be." Mike took a pause, perhaps to consider that game but as a true captain and quarterback could, he recovered quickly.

Ron Watson, another member of the 1967 Junior City Championship runner-up team, joined us. Ron was another individual in a long list of impressive Warriors. He retired from the

US Marine Corp as a Lieutenant Colonel, after over twenty-two years of service to our country. He then became a Business Development Principal in working for the Lockheed Martin corporation. It was an honor to have him sit with us. We exchanged good morning pleasantries and I introduced him to my wife.

"Ron, when did you wander into P.S. 106 and what was that experience all about for you?" Gives us a little of your background and thoughts on Jerry."

"I was born in '53. I probably met Jerry in 1964 so I would have been eleven or twelve years old. I attended P.S. 106 and Junior High School 127 and then DeWitt Clinton High School. I was always a public-school guy. I grew up in Parkchester. I used to walk to 127 every day and on the way home from school, I saw some guys that I played little league baseball with playing at 106. There were guys I knew from Parkchester, guys I went to school with. I was a pretty decent athlete but I needed some direction to let out some aggression that I really wasn't getting from the Parkchester Recreation you know. The Parkchester was mainly basketball and I was not a basketball player. I needed to be in a sport that required some physical contact, some hitting, some blocking, and tackling. Sports that would test your manhood, you know what I mean? Sports that require a lot of thought, a lot of strategies, a lot of teamwork. Sports that build comradery. I found that going to the P.S. 106 schoolyard, with Jerry, particularly with hockey and touch tackle football which led into tackle football filled my need. Jerry, of course, was the Parkie then. People's impression of Parkies was the guy that worked at the park, and all they did was, you'd go to the park office, and maybe you'd sign out a football. You give the Parkie a library card and they would give you the ping pong ball and the paddles. But with Jerry it was different. Jerry was truly an athletic director. He planned the sports out. There would be multiple sports activities during each season. He recruited kids into the park, from the neighborhood to play these sports. And some of them were very, very good and some of them were not so good, but even the ones that were not so good, they became part of a team. And as you can see when we go to some of these reunions, people talk about football games and this and that but whether you were a starter or whether you were the last man on the bench, you were just as much a part of the team as everyone else. And at these get-togethers, everyone breaks your horns and that's a sign of affection, that's comradery. That sense of belonging that Jerry instilled in all the guys that came to the park. Whether they became part of the formal team that would compete with the other parks or teams from other boroughs or you played community sports such as hockey or punch ball or stickball. Jerry was good at that. I can remember he never really cared about our performance. I mean, I wouldn't say that winning was our main purpose. Our main purpose was learning how to play the game. He taught us good sportsmanship, being a good teammate, how you need to rely on your teammates in order to succeed. But he would go the extra mile to teach us. He would teach us on defense, coverages such as blitz packages and on offense, he showed us various formations and the passing tree [the NFL route tree is a numbering system used by both the offensive and defensive side of the ball to identify specific stems/breaks/directions that receivers run on passing plays[26]]. You know we had never heard of that before, a passing tree, and we're learning like they do in the NFL. He showed us how to block, step up with your inside leg. For the quarterback, he taught them how to step up into the inside pocket, things like that. We would watch, we would go to his house and we would look at films of different teams that he may have taped, or something from the television or maybe films of us when we played a game and he would critique us. Jerry would have team practices where the senior team would practice, then the junior team would practice, and we would have collective practices. This is where we would practice together. That way the junior players were getting better practicing with the senior guys. Then you would go into a league and play against other parks in the Bronx and then throughout the city. The borough games would establish who would make the playoffs. You played in the playoffs and you kept advancing until you were the last team standing. Now the senior team won the championship. The junior team, we lost it in the city championship actually. Which was a little disappointing but you know, you've got to learn how to win and you've got to learn how to recover from a loss. While he was not ahead of his time in terms of technology but bringing that technology to the schoolyard was something that was never done. That really opened our eyes as to how much better we could be. And he did it in such a way that it was a critique and not criticism. Nobody likes criticism. It was done deliberately in such a manner that it would become more accepted. You accepted it more and then you would practice it. Then the next time you were out there on the field you were doing it correctly. We took a lot of pride in getting better. For years with Jerry, there was no tackle team but the touch tackle team became the nucleus for the tackle team. I think it was my last year in junior high school that would have

---

[26] Bleacher Report; Matt Bowen, April 4, 2014; *NFL National Lead Writer for Bleacher Report*

been 1968 when I played on the tackle team ok. But then once I got to high school, they had a rule. If you were going to play high school football, you couldn't play sandlot so that kind of ended my warrior football days. But I still kept up with the hockey. The hockey was neat. There was a park that had pebble concrete so you couldn't wear skates on it. We used to play with our sneakers and we would use a roll of electrical tape as the puck. We used to go up to, Castle Hill Avenue to this little toy store in the middle of the block. We would buy hockey sticks and we would tape them up so they wouldn't break. We were poor kids. We didn't have hockey equipment. We would wear a set of street gloves or snow gloves, and high-top Converse sneakers and that was our equipment. The goalie had a goalie stick and he might be wearing a catcher's mask or a softball mask and for knee pads, he was wearing some form of cushions with a rope tied around it. It's almost like the "Little Rascals" when you think about it. When you think about sports today, mom and pop are going to pay this amount of money to get you into hockey and the only thing we had to do was buy the hockey stick. It really was like the "Little Rascal" inventing things. We didn't have a lot of money but we all thought we were rich because our environment was rich. We had sports, we had friends, we had leaders and adults that cared about us. Whether it was Jerry at 106 or coaches from little league, they cared about us. So last night, Joe Regina was asking people if they want to speak, I got up there. I talked more about the meaning that Jerry's coaching, teaching, and leadership had on us then. But more importantly how as we have gone on to our own careers, how we raised our own families, how we fall upon those wisdoms that he imparted on us many, many years ago. We've all had some adversity in our lives. We're all a product of our environment, of our experiences. You can almost apply a mathematical formula to it. And that formula is a + b = me. My experience with Jerry and the leadership he imparted upon me. Then I become, that experience which is "b" and that equals a new me. And it's always building. From every day that you walk into the park. From every day that you're competing and you're playing a sport. Just hanging around with people and friends that are on the team, it's just interaction with those people. People like Jerry taught us to be nice, to treat people the way you expect to be treated. It adds to your personality. That continues on in life and these are the things that you draw upon. To suck it up and work hard. You're going to do that later in life because the foundation was already built and a big part of building that foundation was your experiences with Jerry. Some of the guys went on to be union workers like sanitation, cops, and postal workers. Good lives. Good careers. Our careers kind of range from

A-Z and everything in between. But the one common bond, that rite of passage that we all had was going through P.S. 106 park and Warriors football and Jerry Demers was a big part of that."

Mike Pisaniello returned to the fold. "I believe 1968 was the re-start for the tackle team. It was actually not something that Jay wanted to do. He said it took too much hard work to make it work. It was Joey and Tony Vastola that nudged Jerry to reformulate the touch tackle team. I believe you, Joey, convinced him to start again. I say start again because there were many incarnations of the team. My first recollection was in the early 60's when my older sister had a crush on William "Biff" Bafundo. My sister Nancy hung out with that team. I was in awe of their maroon parkas with the name Warriors on the back. Those guys looked like Gods to a ten-year-old. Little did I know that the coach, Jay, would be a big part of my life a few years later. I remember the team coming to our Parkchester apartment for parties and how cool they all seemed. Biff, Ollie, and Vas, they all seemed to have each other's backs. Maybe that was something Jay instilled in all his kids because it seems to be a running theme right up to this day. I only played the first year with some of my 106 friends. We only played a few pickup games until it morphed into the Jackie Cawley era."

"Okay, that makes sense. I joined the team in 1970 and it was Jackie's team, offensively. We missed each other by a year."

Mike continued. "And above everything else, I think there was always that underlying pull to come back to normalcy, that was all from Jay. Jay was only there during the daytime. As we were getting older, we would all go out and start experimenting with all kinds of crazy stuff. Drink our wine or beer, maybe some guys do other things, you know. I'll give you an example. There was a whole other group of kids that hung out in the park that we were all friends with. They were junkies. They were hardcore junkies but, they used to kind of separate themselves. We used to get them involved in playing touch football. We could have gone in that direction. All of us, after Jay would leave the park, all hell would break loose, but we always came back the next day to get into our organized sports. That kinda kept you on your path to not go too far off the edge. When we got older and Jay left the park, we kind of went our own way and not until we got married and a lot of us started having kids, did we start going back to Jay because of the football program that he ran. My son played for Jay. I coached for Jay. A lot of my baseball career is due to watching and learning from Jerry. I was old enough to understand what was going on and what he was doing for us. There was always that loyalty thing. And that was the theme throughout all of this. Even being loyal to your little four or five-man football team. You were much more loyal to them than any of the other age groups or kids in the park. Jay always had a way of creating. Then there was the bigger picture. He always used to say, no matter what age group, he used to say that we were all Warriors. "I don't care if the name of your team was the Jets or the Steelers or if you're the Packers. Remember one thing. When we are all in this park, we are all Warriors." And he would always instill that in you know. No matter who you were playing against, they were still a Warrior. You know, in that park we always had each other's backs. Back then, you're looking at it from the perspective of your specific age group, your age, but Jay manifested this thing for years and years and years with all different age groups. And with Jay, he knew everybody. We were his kids. I remember telling him that a certain kid passed away that we hadn't seen in thirty years and he just broke down in tears, he just left the room. You know, kids, his kids we are his kids forever."

WARRIORS
CITY CHAMPIONS 1967-68

1967 Senior Team – N.Y.C. Championship Team
Top row – Jack Kaufman, Jeff Solomon, Neil Altabet, Eric Wulf, Jeff Ortiz, Sam Scicolone,
Bottom Row – Lew Lubarsky, Spencer Blank, Neal Rabinowitz, Ken Aronoff, Tony Lamagna, Loren Zeltner

NYC Runner Ups ....

1967 Junior Team – City Champ Runner Up
(l to r) Mike Pisaniello, Robert Stein, Tony Bosco, Joey Reich, Matt Totero, Don Swick, Kenny Synder, Ron Watson, Paul Hanson, Jimmy Ackerman, Robert Ferrito, Jerry Maringionne (not in picture)

Ice Time at P.S. 106 - Kneeling – Joe Reich (middle). Standing – Unknown, Joe Scioto, Jeff Ortiz, Ron Watson, Unknown

The Crew - 1967

P.S. 106. Senior Touch Tackle Team 1967 – Trophy Day at Central Park

P.S. 106 Junior Touch Tackle Team 1967 – Kneeling – Unknown, Joe Reich, Donald Swick, Ron Watson, Jim Ackerman, George Nardone. Standing – Robert Stein Gerry Maringione, Mike Pisaniello, Paul Hanson, Tony Bosco, Matt Totero

Chapter 5
Umpires & Referees

Stock Photo – Referees at a New York City High School game

The world of an umpire, a referee is, as we all know, a thankless one. A great official is the one that goes unnoticed. The goal is to be part of the game and not become the game. I know because I used to umpire for the Castle Hill Little League and the West Pasco Little League in Florida. I also refereed ice hockey, pick-up games, out in Commack, Long Island. For me, it was a great way to stay connected to the games, especially when you realized that as a player, you're just not as good as the other guys.

Jerry was a football ref, working sandlot leagues, and a softball ump doing schoolyard games. There was a game at J.H.S. 127, off Castle Hill Avenue just a few blocks from 106. I'm pitching softball in the Castle Hill Softball League for a team called the Knights. As I'm warming up who should walk behind home plate in umpire gear but none other than Jerry. Well, as the game progresses, I'm finding that Jay is squeezing the strike zone on me. In my frustration, rather than argue with him I turn to our dugout and starting yelling at Frankie. Frank

Botti was my closest friend and manager of the team. He was also the "Commissioner" of the league which ran from 1976 to 1984. Anyhow, I'm whining to Frank that Jerry ain't calling strikes for me that's he's calling for the other pitcher. The conversation gets heated between the two of us, me being the emotional one and Frank always level-headed and calm. It gets to the point where I wear him out. Frank throws out his arm, raising his voice and asks "Why are you yelling at me. Talk to the umpire". I respond in utter defeat, now screaming, "I can't yell at him. He's my coach". I resumed my position on the mound only to see a grin on Jerry's face. Game, set, match Jay Demers.

Frank Botti was our power fullback from 1970 to 1973. Once we were inside the five-yard line, a handoff would go to Frank on a dive play, a run between tackle and guard, and he would always take it into the end zone. He not only started and ran the Castle Hill Softball League he did the same thing for The Castle Hill Girls Softball League and the Castle Hill Football League, touch football. Let's give Frank a listen.

"The Castle Hill Softball League had a shelf life from 1976-1984. Jay was with me from the start and was really like my partner because I let him work as much as he wanted, along with Stu Liebowitz, I was blessed with two very loyal and attentive umpires and that helped make my league a great success. I started a girls' softball league in 1977 and ran it for 4 yrs. Castle Hill Girls Softball. The reason why I mentioned this is because Ollie worked that league two years, Jay only did the men's league. This league lasted five years past my involvement. Finally, my biggest endeavor was The Castle Hill Football League which ran from 1975-1985. In '75 I tried to go without refs, a big failure, but in 1976, I brought in Jay, Ollie, and Vas, they brought me instant credibility. Danny Miller worked a few games. Vas and Danny didn't return the next year, Ollie worked two seasons and another referee, Stewie, Liebowitz, picked up from the second season, nice guy, God rest his soul. Because of The Warrior connection and Jay, I was a very successful Commissioner. Bob, your father gave me that title, he would always call me the 'Commissioner', as kind of a respectful tribute, and that stuck."

As a side note to the above, not only were Frank and I best friends, he was best man at my wedding. His dad and my dad both attended Samuel J. Gompers High School in the Bronx. His dad, Ralph, a mechanic for Pan Am airlines, signed my dad's yearbook. I still have that yearbook

During this period, two gentlemen come into play in Jerry's world that would impact them profoundly. Danny Miller did play for Jay on the famed team out of 106 in the early sixties and would become our defensive coach from 1968 through 1974. Danny and I sat one night at Jimmy Ryan's.

"Bobby, I got out of high school in 1962 so I was sixteen, seventeen in 1961 when I first met Jerry. I worked with him during the summers in the parks department. He got me to work twenty-four hours a week during the school year of college and during the summer full time. I worked with him in P.S. 106 and then I went to J.H.S. 127, around the corner, and then I left. So, I got out of college in 1966, tried the business world and didn't really like it. I worked for two major companies, Standard Oil of New Jersey and I worked for Proctor and Gamble. It wasn't my thing. Jerry had called me and said that they were hiring in the Parks Department. I think I had to take a test or something. So, I started in 1969 with the Parks Department."

"But in 1961 you were a player."

"I played with the Blue Devils with Marty Kelly, a wide receiver, and we joined up with Tony Vastola who had a team called the Vikings. Then I came to play with Jerry, I'm not sure of the date. I remember that Tony went to Jerry and says that we would like you to coach our team. And very shortly thereafter, he recruited guys from other areas. Marty Kelly and I were the only guys from the Blue Devils that came over. But you had Vas, Ollie, Billie Bafundo, John Paul Giuliano they were all guys from Castle Hill, 127 area. I'm trying to think of guys, Frankie Calvanta and a whole group of those guys. We also got guys from the City Island Giants. We had Billie Birmingham, a running back, #22, Bobby Baker came who later coached college football. Who else came from City Island?" He paused and thought for a moment. "Walter Kretzer, his father owned a big boat yard up there, Bobby Lutz, a very good linebacker. I remember coaching you guys more than I do playing. The guy who quarterbacked us was Mike Yurcik and they had two great linemen. Kenny Carpenny and the other guy was Gilbert, a really good player, a guard. Spencer Blank, he was a lineman, he was a big guy. Altabet had good hands. Lauren Zeltner was a fast guy, but he had no hands. We were a tackle team back then. When we originally played, we had a lot of guys from Yorkville. I guess Jerry brought them when he moved up here. Some of them were from the end of Jerry's playing down there. They were tough guys. We had some good players. And Eddie Stack was always around us back then. Jerry and Eddie had a really good relationship. They were the same kind of guy. We never played against his team, the Archer Street Rams. I don't know if that was done on purpose. We used to scrimmage against them before the season. I think maybe one year we played against them in touch tackle. We used to practice at the Santa Maria gym on Zerega Avenue, every Thursday night and after we would play basketball and that went on for forty years, beginning in 1966. We stopped playing in 2006. But it was always competitive. And after basketball, we'd go somewhere to eat. It would be 10:00 on a Thursday night. Certain places on Crosby and Buhre Avenue would keep the kitchen open for us. Another place we'd go to was Joe & Joe's on Castle Hill Avenue. We'd come in, seven, eight, ten guys. And then me, Ollie, Tony Vastola, Bobby Ferness we all went into the Marine reserve unit up in Fort Schuyler from 1966 – 1972. It was funny, all of us guys, Vas, Ollie, Biff, Jim Aris, we all signed up." Danny leaned back into the wooden seat at the booth and continued. "I started working in the Parks Department in 1969. Jerry had gotten promoted and I got the job at P.S. 107, Seward Avenue in the Soundview section in the Bronx. That's when Jerry went out to Queens and then he got me out to Queens."

And then there's the tale of Jimmy Sherry, "Froggy", our offensive line coach. Jimmy wasn't out of 106 nor did he play with that group. At that reunion at Westchester Manor, that night I inquired as to why Jimmy wasn't with us. Ollie and Jerry told me that he was now living in Venice Beach, Florida. Venice Beach sits on the west coast, up against the shore of the Gulf of Mexico. Fourteen miles of white sandy beaches, a beautiful part of the world, the city on the Gulf. Hearing this, as I now lived on the Gulf Coast of Florida, I grabbed an extra Warriors CD knowing that I would call Jimmy and present him with it. A week after our shindig in Westchester, my wife Carmen and I made a four-hour drive due south to his home and sat with him and his lovely wife Bernadette, Bernie. It had been about forty years since I had seen the Frog. Upon pulling up onto his driveway he was out there waiting for me. We embraced long and hard. Froggy was my coach. Yes, I was the kicker and he was the line coach. Memories raced through my mind. I remember my second game as a Warrior. It was a Sunday in October of 1970 and we were playing the Pelham Bay Spartans, my ex-team, at Bronx Park East. The field was a disaster as a driving rain was pushed so hard by the wind that it was coming at us sideways. A miserable day to say the least. As the game unfolded it was apparent that scoring would be at a premium as neither team could move the ball in the muck. As the first half was winding down, we recovered a fumble on the Spartan's twenty- five-yard line. The offense ran out onto the field. We picked up some yardage on first down. I paced the sidelines knowing that if we didn't get a first down, I would be called upon for a field goal. I had something to prove not only to the Spartans but also to my new teammates. Watching this unfold from the moment of that fumble and with the conditions prohibiting all offense for both teams, I had the sense that I might come out for a field goal that could be the only score of the day. I paced about the sidelines. I guess my teammates held the same thought. One by one they came to me with a slap on my shoulder pads or a pat on my butt giving me words of encouragement. "Be ready, we might need you." Jimmy Sherry, Froggy, our offensive line coach came up to me. "Are you loose Weasel?" I was in the zone, my eyes glazed as they stared out towards where I would kick. "Yeah Froggy, I'm loose". With that Jimmy hit me in the gut with an uppercut doubling me over. I could hear him as he walked away, "Now you're loose". Jimmy had knocked the air out of me. Suddenly, the impending possible field goal was not of importance. Trying to breathe was the priority. I couldn't stand up straight, let alone try to go out there and kick. Luckily, there were two more downs to go. We picked up some yardage on second and third down but not enough for the first down. Somehow, after the third-down play, I was able to stand up as I had shaken off the effect of Froggy's blow. It was fourth and two and Jerry called out, "Kicking team, let's go." Putting on my single bar helmet I trotted out still feeling a hole in my belly but I was ready. I wanted this kick against the team that never gave me a chance. We lined up for the kick at the seventeen yard line. I took a one-step approach hoping to maintain any sort of traction, praying that I wouldn't slip in the sludge. The rain and that strong, stiff wind were pushing directly towards me. Match hiked perfectly, Mike Fallon gave me a good hold and I kicked. A line drive of a kick which moved like a knuckleball, through the elements, barely cleared the crossbar inside the left upright. I was mobbed by my teammates as if we had just won the Super Bowl. As we ran off the field I ran right to Jimmy and with a big smile on my face I quietly told him to please not do that again. Jimmy with a huge grin said, "I had to loosen you up, mo. You looked tight". We won that game 3 – 0.

Many years later, Tommy McGurl recalled that moment. "Bobby, when you kicked the ball it started out to the right and came back to the left. But you had enough on it that you could have kicked it from another ten yards. Prior to the kick, you were on the sidelines. I'll tell you what happened on the field. I remember because we were moving the ball a little bit and when you started to come in, a couple of guys were going "ah f**k" and were looking "this is pretty

95

far out". And then I remember, I don't know who said it, maybe it was Jackie, 'yeah but if he makes it, that could be the game because nobody is moving the ball today". And we all said okay let's go, let's see what he can do. And when you put it through, I think we all knew that was going to be it. That's all we needed to win this game. I remember the footing was horrible and I told you "just get the hell into it". It was like a knuckleball but as soon as you made that kick, we knew that we were going to get every extra point which was a big thing back then. Now we figured, we get inside the thirty we've got a guy that can score. And three points in the BUA League was as good as a touchdown because nobody else had a kicker. Once you hit that field goal, we all knew we had something special. We said "man, these guys don't know what they're up against. We didn't have to score touchdowns. We could score every time we have the ball. All we have to do is get this guy in range."

Thank you, Tommy, thank you offensive line, thank you, Jimmy Sherry. Over the years I would always hear the accolades for my kicking, but my response over the years was always the same. "I'm as good as my offensive line. They give me the time to make my kicks. They make me look good". I believed that so much so that I would attend the offensive linemen meetings at Jimmy's house, on Archer Street. About ten guys would go into his living room and he would go over strategy for the upcoming week, highlighting our opponent's strengths and weaknesses, all the while that Bernie would bring out snacks and beverages for us boys.

Froggy and I sat at Sharkey's on the Pier, a wonderful beach, restaurant and tiki hut bar. Its pier stretches out over seven hundred feet, twenty feet about crystal clear water, a true-blue beach. After dining for lunch in the restaurant with Bernie and Carmen, and my daughter Lyndsy, Jimmy and I snuck off to the picnic table area to "tawk" Warrior stuff.

"Jimmy, when did you start with the Warriors?"

"Maybe sixty-nine. It was a long time ago. It could have been the early part of seventy. I think I had come right before you."

"I joined in seventy and you were there."

"I met Jerry though Danny Salomini's umpire's league. And we worked a couple of games together. Then he asked me, "Would you enjoy coaching some games?" and I said, 'Yeah, I think I would'. So, I got involved and one thing led to another. He already had his team established when I got there. It wasn't like I was there from the beginning of the team's start-up. It was already established. But he needed a line coach and he thought I could handle it. I played ball when I was younger, but I had never coached. And Jay wanted me to be the offensive line coach. I knew nothing about the line. When I played ball, I was a receiver. I knew nothing about blocking schemes or techniques. I had to read a book to catch up on it. Well, I would ask the other coaches, Vas, Ollie, Miller, questions about, a particular technique that I read in a book. And they would say to me, 'That's good but this is not good'. You know, I would get pointers from Jerry about what is and what isn't. All I read and thought about was blocking assignments."

"You know Jimmy, I was just the kicker, but I would go to your house, on Archer Street and Leland Avenue, with the guys for linemen's meeting. What was that? Tuesday night Thursday nights?"

"We had all different nights. It depended on when everyone could get together."

"And we'd watch film."

"No, we never ran the film. Jerry would do that at the team meetings. We never ran film at my house. But we sat down and went over tactics. A lot of the times, when we were in the park, we would have our meetings right there. It was a tight-knit thing. The guys were ready for it. Everybody was open to it and everybody wanted to do it. The kids wanted to play, and we wanted to coach. We had a good thing. It was a partnership. There was a lot of guys interested in doing what we wanted to do. And we all seemed to get along. There was no animosity. No, I'm better than you or I don't like what you said. It all went smoothly. No deep seeded problems. It worked well. We had very good players, a lot of outstanding athletes. I mean, look at Match. Johnny was our center, but he also was our backup quarterback. Look at Denis Waldron. Originally, he was our tight end. We could use him at guard, on any side and Dennis wasn't a big guy, but he had a thick body. Dennis would get the job done. However, he had to do it. He would get the job done. He was a tough kid. To be the smallest guy on the line, he certainly wasn't the easiest guy for the other team to take on. The unit worked well together as a team. You know, they got together as a line and said, "We can do anything we want." And they proved it. They'd open up any hole, any place, any time. There was a feeling of mutual understanding. If you needed help, one of the other guys would give you help. There were no stars. They were all stars, but they didn't walk around with fat heads. They were an all-star line. Whatever they had to do to win the game, they did as a team. I was exceptionally proud of that. That's why we kept screaming, "The line, the line, the line!"

"I loved that. I would be part of that, me the kicker."

"Everybody was part of that. There was no saying, "Okay, that's the line and we're the defense. You could hear Jackie scream as loud as I was screaming and he's the quarterback. You don't have a play until the offensive line makes you one. You can design any play in the world but if you don't have that blocking, if you don't have that line up front, it isn't going to work. It's the same as the defensive line. They did the same thing. You know, they accepted the job they had to do, even though it's a thankless job, but they realized it was important enough to get it done right. Even Tommy McGurl, even though he was a tight end. Tommy was a part of that line. And that's what made the team. They were one. Whether you were on the line or on the backfield, we were one. And when I first got involved, I found that Jerry as the head coach was different. Nobody ever thought about outranking him or saying, "No Jerry, you can't do that." But if you felt like something was wrong, you could go to Jerry and say, "Listen, Jerry, not today. Not with this." He would listen and if you gave a logical reason then he would do it. There was nobody unapproachable. If Ollie had something to say, Ollie would say it. Danny had something to say, Danny would say it. Tony would say it. Everybody had an equal share in what we were doing. Never once did we get into an argument with another coach. There were no heroes. There was a team. There was no instance where I wouldn't hesitate to use a backup. Actually, I never used the word backup. And I never had a problem taking someone out of a game. If I saw that we needed help at a particular position I would bring that player out and say, 'Listen, I don't think you're doing it right'. I could send anybody in that I thought was capable of handling the job and whoever came come out would not question the move. Well, there was one guy. My brother's the only one that ever gave me a hard time about it. And I would tell him to go take an 'effing walk'. Other than that, nobody ever gave me a hard time." Jimmy took a moment to gather his thoughts and continued on. "But that is how I met Jay. I was working at General Motors at the time. I started in sixty-one at General Motors. A friend of mine who was an inspector said to me, 'You played a lot of ball. You might want to work with me'. I said, 'Doing what'? He says, 'I'm refereeing football'. So, I asked, 'What the hell do I get paid'? He replies, 'We'll talk about that but you got to go to school first'. So, I went to a referee school and I wound up making a big fifteen dollars a game. I said to my friend, 'Hey Mike, what's this'? He goes, 'It's alright. What's going to happen is, now that you're doing good, Danny's (Salomini) is going to give us three more games. So, it wound up being forty-five dollars for the day. And, forty-five dollars a day back in that time was good. Danny Salomini got used to us working together. Eventually, me and Jerry got to working together because Mike left. But that was my start with Danny Salomini which led me to meet Jerry. My first reaction when I met him was, he's kinda small to be doing this job. I watched him work that first game and I'll tell you, there's nothing small about the way he moved, and his calls and his plays were right. I worked games with him and Bobby Baker. We probably worked five, six years together. We also worked up in White Plains at night. Danny Miller became the director of sports up in White Plains. We worked the White Plains two-hand touch league for about six years."

I moved the conversation in another direction. "Jim do you think with the Warrior teams that you coach, you talk about how we always got along, and we did. You can't beat that comradery and to this day we still have a brotherhood."

"Exactly. Where do you find that lasting for sixty years?"

"What do you think might have happened if we weren't winning all the time? Do you think that togetherness might have been diluted just a bit? I wondered about that in the end, when we weren't winning in 1975."

"I want to say to you yes. I would think it would be affected but I look at the other end of that and you guys haven't played ball in how long and you're still together. So, there's something more to it than just sports. And you guys were unique. I know with my linemen the guys were quite capable of handling anything that I threw at them. And that was the whole key to everything that we did. You guys were capable. We could make changes. We could make differences on the line. We could swing this around. We could swing players around and make it work. You had talent and we could use it. I thought some of the guys had enough brains to do the different things we threw at you (laughing). My biggest moment was not a game that we played in the league. It was the game that we played for Joey Reich after he had the accident and wound up a paraplegic. It was an exhibition game to raise money to buy him a hand-controlled car. That game was so emotional. We played that at German Stadium in Throggs Neck against the Archer Street Rams. That was probably the best game I have ever seen. And I'll tell you something. It wasn't just me. Where I work at General Motors up in Tarrytown, the next day when I went back to work, I had four guys, that came to me and they told me, 'We've never seen a better game in our lives'. What happened was, that game started off so good that by halftime, we had double the amount of ticket sales than what we expected because everyone was spreading the word. Guys were coming out of their houses and the woodwork to see that game. It was amazing. It was absolutely amazing. That game was played with nothing but heart."

"Were you at the dinner for Joey Reich?"

"Probably so. I don't remember off hand, but probably so."

"Ollie talks about that night at length. He told me that we had a charity dinner to raise funds for Joe, again for the car. It was a nighttime affair on Morris Park Avenue at the Knights of Columbus, and we raised a lot of money. That night, late in the night, unbeknownst to anyone, the Rams had had a similar charitable party to raise funds for Joey Reich and later on that evening, they came over and presented us with a check."

Jimmy did remember. "They did. You're right. I was there. They did give Joey a check."

"Ollie couldn't remember the exact amount, it might have been two thousand, three thousand dollars but they came over and gave us that check. Eddie Stack and a couple of other guys they came over with the money and it was just an astounding night. Ollie said that when he was younger, the Archer Street Rams were our arch rivals but that the whole of bunch of them were really great guys."

"Yeah, I remember that night. We, the other coaches, believed that this was done because of the relationship between Jerry and Eddie and because of the camaraderie of the guys at that time. Amazing stuff. It was a lot of good years that I remember. Never regretted one moment with the guys. Because not only did we have the team, but we had a social thing going with ourselves. Between doing the football and refereeing and up in White Plains. We spent many, many hours together. But then the team went away. There were a lot of new people too. That's when I started to leave."

We sat back, enjoyed the view, and order another round of drinks. Jimmy was either deep in thought or far down memory lane.

"To me, that's what makes Jerry so good. He would never under any circumstances, not coach. And he would never, ever, ever contradict another coach. He may pull him over later and say, 'Listen, what I'm looking at is not what you're looking at'. You know what I'm saying? And that's the things that brings a team together. I never hear Jerry say one thing to a coach in front of a player. He would discuss it later. I don't mean that he would tell another coach what to do. He would discuss it to see what would be best for the team to do. Not for the coach. And that's what Jerry had as a head coach. He had the ability to keep a team together. That's Jay. He had a personality. Don't get me wrong, Jerry got hot. He would blow. I've seen him blow but never at a coach."

Jimmy jogged my memory. "I've seen that look in his eye. I only got it once because I would never make that mistake again."

"What did you do?"

"I called an onside kick."

"You called an onside kick, not Bob Alfieri (special teams' coach) or Jay?"

"Yeah I called it."

Jim let out a hard laugh. "I can imagine what Jay said to you."

"Jerry was a special man, I learned a lot from him and not just sports."

***

It just not fair when a head coach is in cahoots with a referee on the field, ask Joe DeSimone. Joe was coaching one of the youth football teams going against Jerry's team. One of Joe's running backs breaks loose and runs it down the sideline for a touchdown. While the kids are celebrating, Jerry walks over to the referee and points to the sideline. The ref blows his whistle and indicates that the runner stepped on the chalk ruling him out of bounds. Joe debated the call only to hear the referee tell him, 'I saw the chalk kick up'. With a big smile, Joe tells the ref, 'Terry, there is no chalk, this field is painted', and walks away.

Chapter 6
The Tackle Team – The First Half

Rice Stadium, Pelham Bay Park, Bronx, NY, circa 1968

1968 was a tumultuous year politically and culturally, highlighted by the bloody Democratic National Convention. What started out with the debut of Rowan & Martin's Laugh-In, became a year of violence, political turmoil, civil unrest, rioting throughout the nation, stressed by the assassinations of Martin Luther King, Jr. and Robert F. Kennedy. President Richard Nixon was sworn into office after defeating Hubert H. Humphrey in a tightly contested election, winning the popular vote by less than five-hundred-thousand[27]. Nixon ran on a campaign that promised the American public to "bring us together again" who were tiring of civil rights and antiwar protests. He also promised "to bring an honorable end to the war in Vietnam"[28]. As President, he introduced an eight-point peace plan for Vietnam and withdrew twenty-five-thousand troops. He would subsequently establish the draft lottery. During the

---

[27] The Washington Post; November 7, 1968; David S. Broder; Page A01
[28] www.history.com

Summer Olympics in Mexico City, U.S. athletes Tommie Smith and John Carlos who had won gold and bronze medals respectively in the two-hundred meter running event, bowed their heads and raised their black-gloved fists in a recognized salute to the Black Power movement during the playing of "The Star-Spangled Banner". The tumultuous year ended on a positive note, at least, as three astronauts aboard Apollo 8—Jim Lovell, Bill Anders and Frank Borman—became the first humans to orbit the moon.[29],[30]

1969 would follow commencing with the Beatles last public performance which they conducted on the roof of Apple Records office in central London [31]. Muhammad Ali is convicted of evading the draft after he refused to be inducted into the U.S. Army two years earlier. He applied for an exemption as a conscientious objector but was denied and he was stripped of his boxing license and title. Charles Manson and his cult-crew would go on a wild rampage in a night of helter-skelter and murdered actress Sharon Tate. Woodstock, a free concert, was held at Max Yasgur's farm in Bethel, N.Y. which drew 350,000 rock-n-roll fans, during the Age of Aquarius' summer of love[32]. The only non-controversial, non-confrontation entry into the year was the introduction of the Pontiac Firebird Trans Am, the essence of the American muscle car, available for only thirty-five-hundred and seventy-five dollars[33].

***

If 1961 was magical for the Bronx with the adventures of Maris and Mantle and another World Series victory, then 1969 was miraculous. The New York Jets sent the NFL topsy-turvy, shaking up the old-guard establishment, by pulling off one of the most incredible upsets in football history by defeating the Baltimore Colts 16-7 in Super Bowl III. What was anticipated to

---

[29] *https://www.history.com/topics/1960s/1968-events - Mark Kurlansky, 1968: The Year That Rocked the World, (New York: Random House, 2003); & 1968: Timeline, The Whole World was Watching: An Oral History of 1968. & "Eight Unforgettable Ways 1968 Made History", CNN, July 21, 2014Made 20 - History"*

[30] *Smithsonian Magazine, January 2018; A Timeline of 1968: The Year That Shattered America by Matthew Twombly, researched by Kendrick McDonald*

[31] *Lewisohn, Mark (1992). The Complete Beatles Chronicle: The Definitive Day-By-Day Guide to the Beatles' Entire Career (2010 ed.). Chicago Review Press.*

[32] *cnn.com/2009/US/08/09/summer.1969.timeline/index.html*

[33] *www.nadaguides.com/Cars/1969/pontiac/firebird/trans-am-2-door-coupe/values*

be another ho-hum Super Bowl was enflamed by Joe Namath's guarantee of victory. The conservative diehards were licking their chops in the expectation of some long hair, hippie-playboy quarterback getting his ass handed to him. Joe Willie "fixed" them. The image of Namath walking off the field wagging his index finger to signal "we're number one" is eternal. The woe of the defeated bookie went unnoticed.

Not to be outdone, the New York Metropolitans created in 1962, yes, those Mets, who had been until this year, the laughing stock, known for their ineptitude, the lovable losers of all of baseball turned the sports world on its head by winning the 1969 World Series. They were so "amazin'", that the New York Times declared them "Baseball's Wunderkinder" and put them on the cover as they played the Braves in the NLCS. The whole nation, other than Baltimore of course, was rooting for the ultimate underdog. They beat a strong Baltimore Oriole team, led by Brooks and Frank Robinson, who were no match for the vaunted pitching of Seaver, Koosman, and a rookie fireballer, Nolan Ryan. Assisted by a bunch of kids and castoffs, under the steady, quiet hand of Gil Hodges, the Mets took the Series four games to one. In a frenzy, people throughout the City went ballistic, getting into their cars and driving around in celebration. Two guys were so fueled up, they got into a vehicle and went to the moon. Neil Armstrong and "Buzz" Aldrin actually had to take a walk on the moon to regain their composure.

***

1968 or perhaps 1969 as you come to see, was the re-start for the tackle team. It was actually not something that Jay wanted to do. While Jerry was somewhat reluctant to start the tackle team, he was encouraged by the enthusiasm of Joey Reich. That convinced him to start again. I say start again because there were many incarnations of the team. There was also the Tommy McGurl version of how the tackle team came into being. Forty years later from when I last played, 1974, I had met up with Tommy at one of our "huddles" at the Crosstown Diner. Tom was now retired after nineteen years with the New York Police Department, starting as a Transit Police officer and rising to Detective in the Major Case squad.

"Hey Weasel, I hear from Tom Piccininni that you write books. He told me that you're going to write about us, The Warrior story."

"I'm thinking about it, Tom. I don't know. I don't do non-fiction but then again, what do I have to lose in trying."

Before this story continues, I will tell you that I was as I am today and always will be The Weasel, A true alter ego. I wasn't always The Weasel, I was originally the Wheeze. I was born a severe asthmatic hence the Wheeze. At age twelve, living in a new high rise on Pugsley Avenue in the Bronx, Chatterton Terrace, I was walking through the lobby to go across the street to play ball in P.S. 119. At that moment, John Fallon, who was easily six feet tall and would be one of our defensive ends on the Warriors, got off the elevator with his little brother, Patty. Patty might have been all of five years old. John greeted me.

"Hey, John, who's the little guy," I asked.

"That's my brother Patty. I'm taking him across the street. He's never been in a schoolyard so this could be interesting." John looked down at his brother. "Hey Patty, look who's here. It's the Wheeze."

Little Patty looked up at me with the most quizzical look and these words came out of his mouth, forever who I would become. "The Weasel?"

John and I laughed and the name…well to this day it has never left me. I am The Weasel!

Little would I know at that time but I would be well served and protected by Patty Fallon. Patrick Fallon grew up to be an officer with the New York Police Department, recently retired after thirty-two years in the South Bronx. John served thirty-seven years with the Nassau County Police Department retiring as a Lieutenant. Mike Fallon, my favorite holder albeit for only a few games started with the Port Authority Police Department and went into the FBI where he retired, somewhat. Currently he is working in New Jersey doing criminal investigations for the state.

***

Tommy McGurl waltzed me out of the diner. "Listen, this is how we started, it was 1968, I'm pretty sure of that. I remember the first day that I ever met Jay; I had only seen Jay from the park by St. Raymond's. I could see him in the park playing with the kids. And what happened was, the guy who ran the Mister Softie truck, Steve, with, my brother Jimmy, Dougie Williams and Denis Waldron were on the Softie truck. Steve stopped the truck at P.S. 106 and started a conversation with Jay. Jay said that he had a football team and Steve said, 'I've got two ballplayers here and a kid that could throw a ball seventy yards. And Jay said, 'Really, so why don't you come to practice'. It was a Wednesday, in the summer, I would say July, and so we went to Rice Stadium, me, Dennis, and Dougie. Jay was there with another player, Jackie Cawley. I didn't know this guy; he was from another neighborhood, Country Club near Throggs Neck. Tony Lombardi who ended up going to the Kiwanis Saints, his first year he played with us, and I think Artie Langer was there and one other guy from Country Club who practiced with us but never played. There was only like six or seven of us. I remember Jay said let me see you throw a pass and I threw a couple of passes. Denis Waldron went long and I threw a bomb to him and he caught it. Jay said come here and then he called Jackie over and he told Jackie to throw a few passes. I told Jerry that could I run a pattern. He asked me if I knew how to do a down and out and I said yeah. He said to do a down and out and go. Jackie hit me on the full run, three times. I came back and said he's the quarterback and I'm the receiver. Jay smiled and he goes, you're reading my mind. Jackie had a bullet arm. And the funny thing was I think that day, honestly, Jay thought of the flanker reverse pass, because he had seen that I could throw the ball a long way and pretty accurately."

At this point, my mind flashed back to something Jerry had told me in a previous conversation we had. *You could use that play (the hook and lateral) for both positions, tight end or flanker if you have the right guy. For the most part, Tommy McGurl played flanker but was an incredible tight end, he was that right guy. Most of our offense was centered around not only Jackie, but also Tommy and his ability to not only block, but perform multiple functions, and of course we had a quarterback (Jackie) who was as talented as any quarterback I've ever coached or seen. We did the hook and lateral with Tommy because he was a tall receiver. I wanted that position to be able to catch the ball, that's the first part of the whole procedure, is to catch the ball. But he also developed a very good ability to go to the middle which is the second part of the play, which would draw the guy covering him to the middle. Tom was great at this. He would be able to catch the ball in the middle of the field, take a hit and still be able to lateral it to the wide receiver running an underneath crossing pattern. That's what you needed. If you have a weak flanker, he catches the ball, he gets hit, it (the ball) goes up in the air and that's it. The flanker reverse was where Tommy lined up as a flanker, came off the line of scrimmage into the backfield, and received a pitch-toss from Jackie. The play looked like a sweep but Tommy would pull up and throw a bomb downfield, always executed perfectly, it rarely failed. Both plays, the hook and lateral and the flanker reverse pass, were a thing of beauty. That's the whole secret to offensive plays. Condition the opposition for something and then do something else. That was my byline as a coach (laughing).*

Tommy continued, "We went back home (Zerega Avenue) and told the guys, listen we're going to have a team that's going to be good. We told Macchiaroli, Gary Cosentino, Teddy McGarrigle, Tommy Piccininni and we brought those guys to the next practice. This was in 1968. I remember the first year that we played, not sure if we were in a league or not. Let me try to remember the first year. We were in the BUA League. We had our first game against the Van Cortlandt Titans at Rice Stadium (Pelham Bay Park) and we tied them. We could have beaten them. The last play of the game, Jackie threw a pass to me, I ran a chair pattern. (A chair pattern is a square out, the quarterback pump fakes and the receiver goes up the field for the pass). I dove for it in the end zone. I probably should have caught it and I would have if I dove a little better but it was just a little too far for me. It hit my fingertips but I couldn't hold on to it. I didn't dive long enough for the catch. We tied that game. We didn't win much in our first year. I can't remember who we played the next week but we won that game. It was a team that was very disorganized. It might have been Mt. Carmel, the guys from Harlem. We went in against the Pelham Spartans in the third game of the year. We scored, they scored, we scored, and they scored. Then I caught a touchdown and they called it back. It was like a seventy-yard pass play. I got the banana of the year for it. It was 14 – 14. I got the touchdown, they called it back. They got the ball and they scored every time they got the ball."

I stopped Tom. "Why did they call your touchdown back?"

Tommy gave me an embarrassed look. "Because I went offside." He took a moment to regain his recollection. "That's why I got the banana of the year. The Spartans were big. Compared to them we were small. There were a dozen guys bigger than me. The kid I beat for the touchdown was Little Sallie. They had a kid, Bobby who played linebacker. He crushed me one time. He was a big friggin' guy; he was the biggest guy on the team. He wasn't fat. The guy was built like a brick shithouse. He tackled me and broke me in half. The Pelham Spartans won the league that year. I know we beat the Bronx Spartans. They were from the Williamsbridge Oval section of the Bronx. They wore green uniforms. We beat them at Harris field. We didn't make the top four teams in the league but we did beat some teams in our first year. Then the next year we [the Warriors] went to the Queens League. We started to solidify. We got guys coming

107

onto the team that played defense. Every year we seemed to pick up a couple of players from other teams that we really needed. Like our second year we got John Fallon at defensive end, his brother Mike at wide receiver, Kevin Burke, Matty Dowling and Tommy Garrett on defense, Mike Hume and Jimmy Quick…I can't remember all the names. The third year we were in the Metropolitan League, and that's when we had the undefeated season. Our offense was now on par with our defense. We had picked up Curtis Elston and Frank Botti at the running back positions. Heck, we picked you up and we needed that because against the Titans we didn't score any extra points. If we had you, we would've won that game. Waldron was the long snapper for you. Waldron started out as the tight end for the team because we didn't have Nardone until four games into the first year. Gorgeous George, he was like a Lance Alworth. Once we got Georgie as a receiver, Dennis moved over to left offensive tackle next to Dougie. He as big as our other linemen but he was as tenacious as a pit bull. I remember that year, '69, the coach of the Spartans had asked me if I would play for them but after watching them play a game, I told him no. He asked me why and I told him you don't pass the ball. The coach replied that they were a running team. And as soon as I went to Jay and seen what Jay was doing, I said this guy (Jerry)…let me tell you, he was light years ahead of all the coaches in the BUA. The biggest advantage we had, besides the fact that I really think as a team, we had a connection. There were guys we might not have got along with but for all intents and purposes there were guys on that team that would die for each other and a lot of teams don't have that. But I think what we had that made us better than all the other teams was that we were far more superior with our coaching than any other team in the league. Bobby if we had third and twenty-four, Jay had a play that would get us twenty-four. The hook and lateral was a touchdown play, if we did that play right it was a touchdown. You know who came in and made us a team, a couple of them didn't stay, but when the guys from your neighborhood, the K brothers, Cutty, Larry Munoz, Louie Cavalieri, Paulie Bakousa, Gary Ruffino, and you, but also, when we got a lot of good players from City Island that helped a lot. We got a lot of good ballplayers from City Island, the Andersons, Schaeffer, and Cupie. So, as I was saying, in 1969, our second year, we went out to the Queens league. I remember that we played the Woodside Warriors, the Tiremen, and the Lions. As a matter of fact, the Lions were all ringers (over aged players). Half of their guys were Vietnam vets. As a matter of fact, when we played them in a playoff game, Jimmy Oliveto and Vastola, our coaches, suited up. Oliveto could play. Joey Reich did really good. Other than Gary Cosentino and Cutty, the Waterbury Avenue Javelins had the best halfback I had ever seen, Louie Botticelli. Louie was some running back. You know what, that was a good team too. Then we got Frank Ninivaggi, the Schnoz, he came over from the Throggs Neck Navajos. We got Mike Hume, he came over from the Titans, Gary K who came over from the Bears who played out of the Belmont neighborhood. Golio brought Victor Fernandez from the Javelins. The first full practice we had with pads on, we did the nutcracker. Danny Miller put me up against Joey Reich and whoever was blocking for Joey Reich, I threw him out of the way and Joey Reich put his helmet right into my solar plexus, he knocked the shit out of me. The reason why we are the way we are and we care about each other comes from Jay, Danny, Ollie, Froggy and the rest of them. When we ran out there, there were a handful of guys you had to watch every game. If those guys showed up, we didn't care who else showed up, we could win. Jackie, Match, Joey Reich and you…we needed the core guys. And you were definitely one of them. Without you…you don't know how much confidence we had because we knew you were the kicker. Every time we scored you were going to make the extra point. There were no other kickers in the league."

I responded humbly, "I had no choice but to make my kicks, I couldn't let my brothers down."

Tommy went on. "Dougie Williams, there wasn't a lot of guys that Dougie liked. And he might have broken your balls. I remember against the Saints, a night game, I believe it was 1971. It was the final game of the regular season and we were tied with the Saints for first place. The winner of that game would be league champs and face the fourth-place team in the playoffs. We were on the one-yard line (end of the game; we're losing 6-0). They stopped us on our first two plays. It was third and one from the one-yard line. Me and Dougie went into the huddle, we looked at Jackie and I said "Jackie, take the f#*$@%g ball, me and Dougie are going to blow these guys to the back of the end zone, walk it in and let's get f#*$@%g Bobby out here to fucking cap it off. And Dougie looked right at Jackie and said, "Let's get f#*$@%g Weasel out here. Come on, just walk in behind us and get f#*$@%g Weasel out here and win this f#*$@%g game". Dougie and I blasted away, Jackie took the ball and ran behind us and scored without being touched. After the game, Jackie told us that 'I could have read a book and walked in behind you'. But that's the way Dougie was. Do your job, lunch pail guy. When he pulled out on the flanker screen for me, when we timed it right, Dougie would blast his guy and I'd have an open field. That's how we came back against the Crusaders when they were beating us, the year we lost in the playoffs to the Javelins, 1970. We did the flanker reverse and I fell. I got the ball on the reverse and I went to stop to throw it, it was frigging muddy and I went down for a fifteen-yard loss. The next play Jay calls a flanker screen. I'm thinking 'give me a frigging break'. My frigging shoes were full of mud. On that play, Dougie's late coming out so the defensive guy comes and grabs me, I'm trying to get away from him because now everybody is running at me, I'm going to get hit by five guys. Dougie came over and blew him into the sidelines. I broke down the sidelines but I didn't score. After the play, I came to the sidelines and there was Jay breaking my balls. He said, 'I've never seen you run so fast McGurl, you actually outran somebody you slow bastard'. I started laughing because they got me down around the twenty and then the next play, we gave the ball to Curtis and Curtis brought it in on the sweep."

At that moment, Jackie came out of the diner. "Head Lad and the Weasel, what are you two characters up to? Probably up to no good."

Jackie has been employed with Amtrak for forty-seven years, rising up the ranks to locomotive engineer/local chairman. Currently, he is on Amtrak's National Committee, appointed to serve on the Bylaws & Finance Committee which takes him all over the world for such conferences. There is an article titled "Abandoned Amtrak Train: Who is Jack Cawley?" This has to do with the writer of the story being notified by a friend of an "abandoned train, seven or eight cars but no engine, in New Jersey. The train was old, rust worn, weather beaten, and striped down, with a small amount of vandalism, no empty bottles of beer of liquor. What the writer found were pay stubs littering the floor, all from a Mr. Jack Cawley, who has resided in multiple locations in the Bronx. But who is Jack Cawley? Was this his train car? Did he make repairs at the work bench? Was that his pillow on the middle of the floor? Why didn't he take his pay stubs with him? The writer had more questions than answers and attempted a search for Mr. Jack Cawley, only to exhaust her quest as she found multiple Jack Cawley's in the Bronx. The article basically ended in the writer's call for the real Jack Cawley to respond to her[34]. Searching for Jackie Cawley, indeed.

"Hey Jack, when did you come onto the team", I asked.

---

[34] *Bernadette Moke, November 29, 2011; Untapped Cities, Around NYC Arts & Culture, Events, New York Transit.*

"It's so long ago, I'm not sure but I can tell you the how and why I became a Warrior. The reason that I played ball was that Ricky Bull played for the old Saints in my neighborhood. Actually, Ricky started with a team called the Allies. I don't even know where they were from. They used to play at Pelham Bay, they played at Rice Stadium. My friend's father also used to follow them and he would drive us to Williamsbridge Oval and Harris Field to watch them play. I used to go to Macombs Dam Park, by Yankee Stadium, which was like a road trip back then. So that's how I grew up. I would go to these games in the cold, steam coming out of our mouths, woman in fur coats, it was like real football. My mother would give me a quarter because the hot dogs were fifteen cents. So, I used to get a hot dog, in the cold, and that was like a meal for the day and I would have ten cents left over. It was a nickel for a Yoo-Hoo and I would come home with a nickel and I was large. Ricky was a big lineman and I used to play football with him. So, I was going to play for the Allies, they were five, six years older than me. Ricky's best friend was Joey the flea. He wasn't a big guy. He only ran back punts. So, I go to this particular game and they punted to him. They broke both of his legs. That's the end of that crap, I can't play this game, I'm only eighty pounds, and I was a scant kid. I'm thinking that I don't need to be playing with these older guys. 'Cause I wanted to play with them, but they were so much bigger and older than me. I remember coming home and telling my mother about the game. My mother said, "What are you crazy? You want to play this game. I don't want you to play football. In eighth grade, we had a neighborhood team, we were nothing. There was a weight limit, eighty-five to one-hundred-fifteen pounds. I was eighty pounds. If they would have weighed me in, they would have caught me and I wouldn't have been able to play. But I was a pretty good receiver. I would actually dive for balls. Nobody in the eighth-grade dove for balls. At the end of the year, I was told by one of the coaches, Bob Walpole that they were having this thing with Dick Lynch and Joe Walton from the New York Giants, an award thing at Glen Island Casino, in New Rochelle on the Long Island Sound. They started with the league awards. You know the MVP of the league, the best this, the best that. So, they get through all of the best and they have this last award. 'The Little All-American Award goes to Jack Cawley'. I was like, 'What'? What I didn't know was that my father was there. He was very sick at the time. He wound up having ten heart attacks in his life. He shouldn't have been there. He was that sick, but he told me later on that the coaches had told him he should be there 'because I was going get an award. You should have seen the look on my dad's face when they gave me that award. He showed up to the dinner straight out of the hospital. I believe my daughter has the trophy in her apartment. That was my first year playing football and it was great but having my father who very sick was hard. The heart attacks kept coming so there was no money coming in. My mother, typical Irish Catholic, was a stubborn woman. She refused to take welfare. My mother never accepted welfare because back then if you were on welfare you were scum. She was too proud. That was the mentality back then especially with the hard Irish. So, I became the breadwinner. I'm thirteen years old at this time and one of six boys supporting my family. I started working at Buhre Avenue Deli. Ron Watson also worked there at that time. I'll never forget it. That actually, believe it or not, was to help feed my family. It was Ricky Bull who pulled me into the job. I was making a dollar twenty-five an hour and that was big for us. I was the sole supporter of my family. Here I had won this best of player the year award at South Park. They had a scholarship to Cardinal Hayes High School for me but I couldn't play ball for Hayes 'cause I had to work. I was one of the best football players in the Bronx and I couldn't play ball cause I had to work. My father had passed when I was sixteen. I'm still working at the Buhre Avenue Deli now making six twenty-five an hour. I had told Ricky Bull that I want to play but with guys my age. Ricky says to me, 'we've got this guy Jay who lives around the corner on Hobart Avenue and he's starting a football team'. I used to deliver food to his brother, Frank, and Jay lived around the corner from the deli so that's how I got to know Jay. This was in probably 1967. Ricky must have mentioned this to Jay because Jay comes into the deli. I'm working behind the counter. He introduces himself and tells me that he's starting a team. I told him, yeah, I'll play because they don't have a younger Saints. I was going to their games every single week. Wherever the Saints were playing, I would go because they were in my neighborhood. The only reason I played for the Warriors was that there was no Saints team for my age back then, they didn't have a younger team. Anyway, we try out. I wanted to be the receiver. We had Mike Hume who came over from the Titans who could throw the ball a mile. He wound up getting an offer from some team in the Canadian Football League. The funny thing about it was when we started the Warriors. They wanted me to play quarterback. I didn't want to play quarterback, I was a receiver. After my first tryout, they told me to throw at the next practice, you throw the ball. I don't want to throw the ball I want to catch the ball. The irony of this whole thing was I don't want to play quarterback. And now we have a couple of practices and we sit down at Rice Stadium and we get numbers for our jerseys. So, I told them I want number twenty-four. Ollie (Jimmy Oliveto, coach) said to me 'no, you're the quarterback'. Ollie and Danny (Danny Miller, coach) come over, everybody is on the outside, I don't know anybody, except Limbo. Limbo wanted double zero and he got it. They told me no, you're the quarterback and you're not going to get number twenty-four. So, I said I'm a receiver. Give me the ball, I'll catch the ball and I'll run. Danny and Ollie yelled at me 'no, you're the quarterback'. Then Ollie says to me, 'what quarterbacks do you like?' I said I don't know…I like Sonny Jurgensen. They said, 'that's it, your number nine'. That's the only reason I'm number nine, I would've never picked number nine. But they gave me number nine, I played quarterback and then I became captain. The next year, they start a young Saints from my neighborhood. Limbo says to me that he's going back to the Saints 'cause that's where he's from. That's where we both came from. I was the water boy for the Saints at one time. They wanted to make me the quarterback of the Saints but I'm a loyal guy. I'm not gonna quit Jay. I stayed loyal and that's where the big rivalry with the Saints and us came from. The first thing I noticed about Jay was that he would take a special interest in you. I would see him off to the side with his arm around somebody and he would be talking to them going over whatever problem they were having. He used to pick me up at my house to get to a game. He would always start by going over offensive strategy but without me realizing it, he would shift to family and life issues pertaining to me, my loss of my dad, me working to support a large family, things like that. He became a father to me. But it wasn't just me that he did this with. Jay was just a great guy to all of the players. He didn't want anyone to fail. He saw it as a family thing. It didn't matter who you were. Poor or rich, black or white, it didn't matter. That's who Jay is. Jay wanted to help all of us beyond football. And he did. Without a thank you ever, he didn't care about that. That is just him. His influence on people… I don't know how else to describe him. He is a teacher, a mentor, such a great guy. You could not hate Jay Demers. You could not dislike the guy. I don't care how much you hated the Warriors. You couldn't hate the coach. It's impossible."

We went back inside. There were sixteen of us, including the coach, that early evening at this huddle. Food and drink were about the table as we were served and managed by Lulu who as always did a masterful job. Jerry loved these get-togethers, even at the age of seventy-four.

"What were you guys doing out there, plotting to destroy the world?" Joey Reich called out.

"Those three, they couldn't find a plot if you dug one up in front of them," Match replied.

113

One thing about us as a group, if one guy wasn't squeezing 'em on you another one was.

Jackie answered for Tommy and me. "We were just talking about how we started with the Warriors."

Joey Reich, as a captain would, took charge. "The team actually started in 1968 believe it or not. I can confirm this because I got evidence. I got the coaches award that year, it's sitting in my garage. That's the year we got our Warrior jackets. I remember walking home with Jerry Maringione, it was snowing out, badly. It was icy and I tripped, I slipped on the ice. I got my jacket all muddy but I hung onto the trophy. We had a couple of cocktails or two at the same time. I'm sure that had something to do with my fall."

I stopped Joey as I questioned Jerry. "There seems to be a little confusion as to when the tackle team started and who got you to put together a team."

Without hesitation, Jerry recalled. "Joey was one of several people that wanted to us to form a tackle team. But the beginning of the tackle team was in 1968 but that first year we weren't in a league. We didn't play league ball in '68. We played other neighborhood teams from the Bronx, just like we did in '52 and when I went up to the Bronx, we would play neighborhood teams, that was in '57. We did play as the Warrior team in 1968, but these were not league sanctioned games."

Tommy jumped in with all excitement. "You know, my mother says the same thing. That we did not play in a league in 1968 but Jay, with all due respect I beg to differ. I remember our first year was in the BUA and that was 1968. We went to Queens in 1969 and came back to the Bronx in 1970."

I decided to add my three cents. "Jerry, my first year on the team was 1970, my first year of college. I only know this because my first trophy, and I have all of the trophies from 1970 to 1973, which says Metropolitan Football Conference League Champions."

Jerry was quick to reply. "Bobby, the Metropolitan League was in Queens."

"I don't remember ever playing in Queens until 1974", I rebutted. "I remember all of our games were in the Bronx in my first year."

Jerry shot me a look as our past history from over forty years ago was wreaking havoc amongst all of us. The one thing I have come to know, it is almost never that the Coach is wrong. Perhaps this is why he is the coach.

Jerry moved on. "I'm telling you guys that it was 1969 because in that year, our guys who had played on the '63, '64 and '65 teams were out of the service and we started another team and of course that was the greatest team of all, you guys, because forty years later we still get together for a Huddle once a month. We didn't know that in 1969 we had an advantage of having all these former players back as coaches. We picked up one other coach, Jimmy Sherry, who I worked with as a referee in touch football. So, Jimmy was added to the staff of Biff Bifundo, Tony Vastola, Danny Miller and Jimmy Oliveto and with their discipline from the Marines and their knowledge from the history of the Warriors in the past we were able to put together quite a good team. At the same time, we were very fortunate in having another great quarterback to match Bernie Lyons who was our original great quarterback from my playing days and his name was Jackie Cawley. He had the same leadership qualities as Bernie, the same great arm and as I've always been a passing quarterback, I was delighted to see the young man play. We were a young team in '69. Everyone had the jump on us but that was the last year they would have the jump on us. We went into the Queens League which was the Warner Conference. It wasn't Pop Warner, but was the Warner Conference run by a gentleman named Mr. Nick Mitsokus. He was a tough buzzard but he ran a good program. We played teams like Jerry's Tiremen, there was another Warriors team, the Crusaders, the Ramblers and such. We realized that the ages weren't right, some of the players we faced were overaged so we went to the Metropolitan League in 1970."

Tommy McGurl again interrupted Jerry. "Hey Jay, I can remember a game where we ended up beating the Lions who were all ringers. They had guys who were a lot older than us. So Vastola and Jimmy Oliveto dressed for that game. Jimmy played middle linebacker. We won that game because I had a touchdown and Joey Reich intercepted a pass for a touchdown. We beat them 18 to 7. Out of six teams we ended up in fourth place but we lost our first playoff game. I don't remember who we played."

I jumped into the fray. "You know in trying to write this book…in obtaining everybody's memories from 1948, I gotta tell you, some of these stories are like episodes out of the Little Rascals."

Joe supported me. "Well that's the whole thing. In fact, the first year that we did play it was like the Little Rascals. We were borrowing equipment from the older guys. I remember I had these thigh pads that were twice the size of my leg and they were floating on me. They were made out of turtle shell, I don't know, they were like from the 1930's. We had to borrow all the stuff…we had some equipment, a few of us, but we had but there was a lot of the stuff we didn't have. We looked like a rag-tag team. We all had the same jerseys, white jerseys with red numbers but with the stripes down our sides. God knows what other equipment we had. Really bad helmets, concussion helmets that's for sure. We'd hit somebody and the helmet would crack. They were the cheap helmets like the $5.99 helmets at E.J. Korvettes." He paused as he gave Jackie a funny look. "I'll tell you guys something about Jackie, he was so anxious to get things going in the huddle. His huddle was like controlled chaos however Jay made sure that Jackie was the only one to speak. The huddle smelled like Hall's cherry liquor menthol eucalyptus because Jackie was always sucking on them. It was the best smelling offensive huddle I've ever been in. What strikes me most in my mind was that he was always anxious. I remember one day I just looked at him and I used my hands, 'calm down'. 'You've got plenty of time to call the play, it's going to work'. And sure enough, he called the play, it was probably a tight end square out delay, but it worked very well but he was just so anxious. We got close to the end zone and we're not going to run the ball because of his passing. He passes brilliantly as you all know. I'll tell you one thing that hurts me to this day and I'll leave it at that. It was our first or second year probably 1969 we played I think the name of the team was the Titans. Jay didn't like this team because he didn't like the coaches. He didn't like the coaches because the coaches were brutal to their kids and there was a question as to how old these kids were too. Jay wasn't the type to say 'show me their birth certificates' but we were down by four points and they put me in at left end so it had to be 1969 early on. I said to Jackie, I think I can beat this guy. Even though they were in a zone if I could make this guy turn one time, I could go to the corner of the end zone. It was a very friggin' cold day. I mean it was freezing cold at Bronx Park East, and we were on probably the twenty-five, thirty- yard line. I said I can pull a zig-zag on this guy. I can just do a head fake and run a post pattern. Once I raise my arm, I'll be looking at his foot. If his foot turns towards the

116

post I'm zigging out and I did. He turned and I zigged out and Jackie had thrown a beautiful spiral. It went right through my friggin' hands. My father was there, my Uncle Smitty was there and that was it after that. We had one play left. Jay, the next year, summertime, we're playing around in J.H.S. 127 probably eight against eight and I'm left end again doing a post pattern or a square in and the ball was thrown an inch and a half above the asphalt and I caught it. Well I got back to the huddle Jay says 'oh you found your hands this year'. To this day I'm still sorry for dropping that ball."

Artie Langer, our defensive end and outside linebacker entered the debate. Artie Langer is Dr. Arthur M. Langer, Professor of Professional Practice in the Faculty of Professional Studies, Academic Director of the Programs in Technology Management, and the Director of the Center for Technology Management at Columbia University. But wait, there's more. In addition, he is Vice Chair of Faculty and Executive Advisor to the Dean at Columbia's School of Professional Studies. He serves on the faculty of the Department of Organization and Leadership at the Graduate School of Education (Teachers College) and is an elected member of the Columbia University Faculty Senate. He has published numerous text books, articles, and papers relating to service learning for underserved populations, IT organizational integration, mentoring, and staff development. Dr. Langer consults with corporations and universities worldwide on information technology, staff development, management transformation, and curriculum development. But that's not all. Artie is also the Chairman and Founder of Workforce Opportunity Services, a nonprofit social venture that provides scholarships and careers to underserved populations around the world. He does this work face to face traveling around the world[35]. This program also helps empower military veterans and young adults with unique, innovative work-study programs. The WOS works with academic partners (including Rutgers, Penn State, Georgia Tech, University of Texas at El Paso, University of North Carolina at Charlotte, and others) to create company-appropriate academic curriculums. Carefully-selected students are then trained to fill roles in IT services, programming and design, cybersecurity, finance & accounting, customer services, operations, and other areas requested by the companies. Program graduates are now working with Johnson & Johnson, Prudential, ADP,

---

[35] *http://sps.columbia.edu/technology-management/faculty/arthur-langer-academic-director*

HBO, Hewlett Packard, Merck, Panasonic, and other global and national organizations[36]. I'm certain that Dr. Artie could hold quite the conversation with Dr. Dennis Kent.

Artie had the floor. "The first year that we played, that the team was formed, I got hurt. I had to rest y arm for six months so I didn't play and that was the year when we had the stripes on the sides. That was the year that I don't think we won a game and it was definitely BUA. We played the Spartans and we got killed. We were a new team, we didn't do very well. The second year, I came back we went to the Queens League. Jerry, you didn't think we were ready for a second year in the BUA so we went out to Queens. We play a team called the Queens Warriors and the Tiremen. That's the year when the guys from City Island, the Giants, came in. Vic and Mark Anderson and all those guys. One guy played middle linebacker, he was very tall and another guy who was very fast played tight end. So, we went out to Queens, we had a great season but there was a team called the Queens Warriors and we just couldn't beat them. We had a playoff game against the Lions. They had ringers and that's when Ollie and Vastola played. We beat those guys in that game, the first playoff and then in the final game we played against the Queens Warrior under the 59th Street Bridge and we lost. So, we weren't the best team but we were very, very competitive."

Jerry laughed and continued his history lesson. "I may have a bad memory but I know when we played. At the end of our first year another team formed in our neighborhood, and Jackie was very close to a lot of the players on the other team. So, somebody told me Jackie's going to go play for the Saints. I said 'oh boy that would be rotten' but as a leader and a loyal person that he is, he stayed with the Warriors and that's the beginning of a great story as you know. 1969, our first year in a league, was a building year. We were putting our team together getting our coaching straight and we did not finish in first place that year. We had some good players, of course Jackie, Gary Cosentino, who was our star running back, and Joey on defense. We certainly enjoyed ourselves after each game and we'd go back to the Leonardi's to have a drink or two and to talk about the game and other things that were important to the guys at the time. By 1970 we had an excellent team defeating our primary rivals, The Saints, The Navajos and Javelins. I recalled one of the best games that sticks out in my memory was in '70 or '71 against the Javelins at Rodman's Neck by City Island where we held them on eight consecutive

---

[36] *http://www.alanger.com/workforce-development-mentoring.html*

118

plays from the one-yard line. We wound up winning that game and went on to future success after that."

Joey took over the conversation. "P.S. 106, 1967, that team had a lot of the guys that you know, Artie Langer, Ron Watson, Jeff Ortiz, George Nardone and those guys. We approached Jerry because we won the touch tackle league, we came in second place in New York City as the junior team, the guys above us, the older guys…Jeff Ortiz was on that team, the senior team, they won the entire championship, the New York City Championship which was sponsored by AMF, the bowling company. It was a big deal. We all got jerseys for that tournament. Jerry let us know that he was proud of us but he spent a lot of special attention to the big guys because they did it. So, it made us feel like if you're going to do something you've got to go all the way with it. And after that, the next year we asked Jerry if we could start a tackle league. He was very reluctant. So, he gave it a one-year test. All the people that showed up for practice were from St. Helena's, Parkchester, P.S. 106, and Castle Hill Avenue. That was the core of the original team in 1968. As I said, we had to borrow equipment, shoulder pads, thigh pads, the whole nine yards and the old Warriors were willing to give it to us. I think these things were made in 1933. In 1968 Jay gave us a chance to play organized tackle. We weren't in an organized league like The Bronx Umpires Alliance or the Queens Umpires Association but he would set up games with different people that he knew from other neighborhoods. Teams that were clean, not over age or play dirty football. And that's how we kind of cut our teeth on that. And after that first season with practices and actually working out, a lot of people quit. But the beginning of The Warriors, to me, is 1969. That was our first year as an organized team out in Queens. I tried out for the Spartans in 1968 and they said I was too small for their team. Come back next year. I remember being rejected and saying 'no, I'm going to show you some day. I'll come back and maybe be on the other side of the ball'. Back then parents were allowed to smack a kid. Your parents smacked you, the teachers whacked us, coaches could get physical and usually verbally abusive. However, our coaches never did any of that. Jerry would look at you one time and you felt like you got smacked with an anvil. Our coaches, Ollie, Miller, Froggy, Vas, and Bif, were all outstanding people. As a matter of fact, almost all of our coaches were ex-Marines. Are you going to act out in front of ex-Marines? "Whatever they said, you just did it. You didn't have to be asked twice. I tell you one thing really quick. After that year in 1968, before we went into the BUA, some of the 106 guys felt a little betrayed because once our season ended, Jay started recruiting people during the offseason. I think Jackie was the first one that Jay recruited because he lived near him. Match came along that early. We got Vic and Mark Anderson from City Island, Bobby Lutz, Mike Hume and Jimmy Quick from the Titans. All of a sudden there was a big influx of new guys. There were a lot of guys from 106 who were definitely less talented than what Jay recruited. After that first year, 1968, a lot of players dropped out. They felt a little like...why are you going outside to get players...it was a 'we're not good enough' type of thing. Guess what, it came down to no you weren't good enough because the guys Jay recruited were outstanding. Outstanding in their positions and they made a big difference."

Tommy McGurl chimed in. "I always thought the two best athletes were you, Joey, and this guy, Jackie, without a doubt."

Jerry jumped in. "You know, when Joey was in the playground before he was a Warrior football player, he was one of my kids in 106. Skinny little rail. Jeff Ortiz has the pictures and I probably still have the picture too. Used to play whiffle ball in the handball courts and I have a picture of him, he's getting up to bat left handed and my comment under that picture, I used to make labels for each picture, is a future star, that's what is under his picture. He was a terrific football player. He gave everything out of his body. Pound for pound, he was the toughest, that's the kind of guy he was on the field. It's amazing how some guys have that mentality of being completely different off the field and on the field they're just wild, two different people. On the field, he was vociferous. Jackie on the other hand, he was reluctant to be a quarterback, hesitant to become a leader but he did and I think you guys would tell me that he was a great one. Two guys that I knew from different neighborhoods, very unlike in the way they led, one vocal and the other soft-spoken. Both led by their performance on the field. Sorry to interrupt you Tommy but please continue. I'm enjoying the memories."

Tommy chuckled, "No need to apologize to me coach. Joey in the defensive backfield was all over the field at the point of attack whether it was a run or pass or a blitz and Jackie at quarterback who could throw a bullet, throw the soft pass, run like a halfback or scramble like Russell Wilson of the Seattle Seahawks, were on a level all of their own as far as talent. Nobody who played during that time was on that level except those two guys. Joey could've played pro ball probably Jackie too. You know who was a good athlete, not that level, but he was good ballplayer too was Sully. Sully was a monster at middle linebacker. Running backs, quarterbacks feared him. Heck, receivers wouldn't go over the middle on him. He was fast and strong and played with a rage. And another guy was Gary K at defensive back. Gary made up for what he lacked in size by being smart and being out of his mind too. I forgot about a guy. The best two athletes we had from the original Warriors were Joey Reich and 'Buck', Gary Cosentino. Gary Cosentino as a running back was on that level too. Gary, he left the team to play minor league ball (Cardinals). Yeah, when we first started Gary and Joey were on a level nobody was close to. I would say that those three guys were the best athletes that ever played for the Warriors. Gary the Buck, when we first started, he was our weapon. We had a good passing attack but Gary, if you gave him an inch he was gone. He could fly."

Match laughed. "Yeah, he ran like that because he was scared. He didn't want to be tackled. He ran out of fear."

Tommy went on. "Of all the running backs we had, Gary was the best. I would say second would be Cutty."

I moved in with my commentary. "I've known Cutty, along with Gary K since we were kids, maybe twelve, thirteen years old. Cutty was Barry Sanders before Barry Sanders. Gary, well Gary was always a winner, very confident, and he would let you know about it throughout the game. He was trash talking before Ali was doing it."

Tommy went on. "And then Curtis Elston would be third best running back, he was so quick and dependable to pick up five, six years. Of course, Frank Botti at fullback was Curtis' escort. He was a bull. It was like having another lineman in the backfield. And anytime we were inside the five-yard line, Frankie was money in the bank. He would blast up the middle on a scissor or dive play. I can't remember him not scoring. He wasn't fancy, he was brute strength through the line and Curtis, he was smooth as a runner, very quick. And with those two in the backfield as blocking backs, Jackie almost never got that outside pressure when he went back to pass. Back when we started, we had 'Gorgeous' George Nardone and Gary Ruffino at the receiver position. George was like Buck in that he didn't want to get hit either. Hell, he didn't even want his uniform to get dirty. Remember the time he ran around the puddle. He was gorgeous. Gary Ruffino could motor. Once he was in the open field there was no catching him. He had great hands. He would run the hook and lateral with me to perfection. Once those two, George and Gary left the team we picked up Joe Golio and Victor Fernandez from the Javelins. I remember when Joey Golio came to our team. He quit the Javelins and my friend told me the story. We were playing at Williamsbridge Oval and we did the flanker reverse pass and I hit Gary Ruffino for a touchdown. I threw a bullet. What happened was their safety; he stayed back so Gary cut in front of him. I actually couldn't lob the ball. I fired it. I threw a frozen rope and it hit him perfect and he scored. The safety came up and couldn't catch him. Gary was like lightning. And Joey Golio ran over and told Eddie Esposito, his coach, 'their receivers throw better than our quarterback'.

"There also may have been an incident in the end zone," I interjected. "The Pinto (Joe Golio) told me that he didn't like his introduction to you, Joey. It was that game in 1970, that damn game that we lost to the Javelins. Golio caught a pass on a fly pattern and as he entered the end zone for the touchdown, he also entered the world of one, Joey Reich. He says that you presented yourself to him by tackling him as he scored. I mean you nailed him. He said that you rang his bell and that he didn't ever want to be hit like that ever again."

Tommy resumed. "Joe could fly, probably faster than Ruffino, and he was a showman, he was Hollywood but he also didn't like to be hit either. Victor was skinny but he could take a hit. He would run those routes over the middle and never dropped a ball. I wonder how many guys we picked up because they got tired of losing to us. But I'll tell you, we had nothing but good guys on the Warriors. The guys that were screwed up, couldn't get along with the others, guys that wanted to inflate their ego and be the star, they didn't stay. They came and left quickly, you know. Jay never cut a single player. They just knew that they didn't fit in."

"Match took over. "We weren't the biggest or the fastest. Hell, half of our defense was undersized. Artie, Matty Dowling, Kevin Burke, Tony Volgere, Gary K…I can't remember them all but somehow, they all fit into what Miller and Ollie were trying to do. They would rotate them in and out, four-man fronts, five-man fronts, guys stunting from defensive end into the linebacker area. But despite our lack of size and speed, we played well together and we had great schemes from the coaches."

Perhaps the quietest Warrior of them all, Tony Arroyo, spoke up. "I came to the Warriors in 1972. I played with the Morris Park Lions and Ed Maddalena played for the Crusaders but was now on the Warriors, that's how we first met. We interacted a lot on Morris Park Avenue, where I grew up. Eddie always said to me, 'Get away from that team. Come to the Warriors. Meet me at Rice Stadium and bring your equipment, we got practice on Sunday'. I was introduced to Mr. Miller (Danny) and the next thing I know I saw Mr. Miller take Eddie to the side and go, 'Where'd you get him from? Get more like him'. At that time, I was weighing close to 255 and I was working out. The next thing I know is that we did some hard hitting with full pads. Mr. Miller put me as defensive tackle and middle guard on a five-man front with Mark Anderson, John Fallon, Jimmy Quick and someone else, I can't remember. I wanted to impress the coaches so on the very first play I broke through the line and sacked Jackie. Everybody is looking at me. Eddie comes over to me and says, "Buddy, you hit Jackie. Did you know that'? and I told him 'Yeah, what was I supposed to do not hit him'? Eddie further explained, 'You don't hit Jackie, he's our bread and butter'. The next play he came up with something to get back at me. It was a pick play and Dougie Williams really put me down. I mean he buried me. What was different about the Warriors was that they were all team players. If you were having difficulty or there was something you couldn't do, a team player would come up to you and help you, 'No, you go to the left on that play. You don't go to the right. That way, you loop around'. They all came up to me, the coaches and players and they would go over the play with me step by step. Remember, I was new to the game of football and I didn't know the rules and regulations. This was a team, a team that cared for his teammate so that he knew what he was doing as opposed to sitting him on the bench. Everybody would look out for each other. I found a place that I knew that I was going to get experience and understand the game. Knowing what you can or can't do or what to or not to do and if you do it, don't get caught. And the best of all with playing for the Warriors was after we would play a game, it was over, I loved going to the Well and downing a couple of beers."

"Yes, The Well was a great place to go after the game and drink to either celebrate after a win or drown your sorrows after a loss," Jerry stated. "Originally it was Leonardi's. So, it was always good to go back to the Well. We had our first team party in the back room and that was fun to put together because we had so many guys in the room and the room was not that big. That was the tackle team that Ollie, Vas, Miller, and Biff played on, '63 to '65. We gave out jackets that night, we performed skits that night, and we gave out trophies for the MVP, outstanding player and best lineman. We had the banana of the year award. One year my brother in law, Geri's brother, played for the Warriors, he played for one or two years. That one year he won the Banana of the Year award by going out to the wrong huddle when I sent him into the game. Automatic banana of the year hands down. I wonder if he still has that."

***

I had joined the team in 1970. It was a mid-August Saturday where I was on my way

towards the Hugh J. Grant Circle to catch the #42 bus up Westchester Avenue to a grass patch between Calvary Hospital and Westchester Ave off the Hutchinson River Parkway. I was going for a workout with a football team, The Javelins, a team from Waterbury Avenue. It seemed that their head coach, Eddie Esposito saw something in me that he wanted to add to his team. It felt good to be courted. I was a place-kicker in a sandlot league that didn't have place-kickers. The year before, I had played for the Pelham Bay Spartans, a highly successful, disciplined team, a good team with a long tradition. They never used me other than kickoffs and punts as they preferred to run in the extra point and never once had me attempt a field goal. As a kicker, other than winning, camaraderie was important to me. I had found that after practice and games everyone went their separate ways. There was something missing for me on the Spartans. I wanted to be part of something more.

On that August day, three of my buddies, Gary Ruffino, Neil Balzano, and Pauley Bakousa had jumped out of a car, put a burlap bag over my head and shoved me into the back seat. I was taken captive on Virginia Avenue

"You're not goin' to the Javelins, you're comin' with us."

Neil and Gary held me in that back seat like I was a hostage. They removed the bag when we got to Rice Stadium at Pelham Bay Park. I had never been there before. My eyes opened as wide as saucers. It was enormous, it was a sports haven. It had a football field with actual goal posts (a lot of fields didn't have goal posts), surrounded by a quarter mile track. This was heaven, a park that held a football field, a baseball field, a running track, and a picnic area. There were tennis courts, exercise stations and a playground for young children. An enormous limestone sculpted statue stood atop the concrete bleacher steps, the statue of *American Boy,* a fifteen-foot partially clad figure almost like a Greek Olympian, on his pedestal, watched over all of us. *American Boy* was built to exemplify the spirit of American youth and serve as a representation of healthful recreation[37]. In that summer of 1970, I had no idea that joining a football team at age eighteen would have an impact on the rest of my life.

On that Saturday as we arrived at Rice Stadium, I crawled out of a sunbaked vinyl covered back seat of Pauley's 1966 Pontiac Tempest. Like a shy boy entering his first day at school, I wandered away from the car a little intimidated by about forty-five guys sitting on the concrete steps of the stands. I didn't know a single person. I followed Gary, Neil, and Paulie into the stands as a coach flanked by other coaches was in the middle of his welcome speech. I assumed he was the head coach. He was the only one with a whistle around his neck. He spoke with a softness to his speech, one could say that he probably would make a good Irish tenor. There was none of the fire and brimstone and cursing that I had become accustomed to from past coaches from other teams. That was my introduction to Jerry. He continued with his orientation and instructions to us. Upon concluding his welcome speech, he blew his whistle.

"Gimme a mile around the track and then fall out for calisthenics."

Gary led me over to introduce me.

"Jerry, this is the guy I was telling you about. He's the kicker."

Jerry extended his hand.

"Hi, I'm Jay."

"I'm Bob."

"Bob, I will tell you that if you don't hit the track, you'll have a lot of catching up to do. We don't like stragglers," he said again with that soft chuckling tone.

I was thrown by Jerry's casual greeting like I was just another face. This was in stark contrast to Eddie Esposito who treated me like I was a superstar. I thought that he might take me aside and discuss kicking duties being most teams didn't have a kicker for extra points and field goals. I assumed he would have me take a few kicks so he could see what I had. Of course, this assumption was predicated on not having to run a mile under a scorching sun and work out. Don't get me wrong. I enjoy a good work out just not in that kind of heat. I realized that my best course of action was to run the mile. As I ran the track, I thought to myself that there was

---

[37] https://www.nycgovparks.org/parks/pelham-bay-park/monuments/21

something somewhat both unusual and intriguing about Jerry. This diminutive man was unlike any coach, Little League baseball or sandlot football, I had ever encountered. He spoke like a priest holding mass at St. Raymond's. Facially, at least to me, he resembled Don Shula a little bit, the Miami Dolphin head coach. I would learn that his name was Jerry but most of the guys referred to him as Jay.

The veterans knew the routine. Rookies became victims to leg cramping and vomiting. Quitting was not an option. All had to complete the run regardless of how long it took. I had finished somewhere behind the middle of the pack. I knew that we had a long day ahead of us. A hot Saturday afternoon would only grow hotter, unbearable in its humidity, intensified by a full two-and-a-half-hour workout. Once done, I raced off the track onto the dirt portion of a baseball diamond that was one end of a football field and joined the group partaking in calisthenics. The whistle was figuratively handed over to Tony Vastola as he took over calisthenics. Tony Vastola gave no quarter, he worked us hard. There seemed to be a glee in his eyes as he dispatched his cruelty. I quickly learned that I hated rockers. Rockers is an exercise where one lays down belly to the ground clasping both hands behind the small of the back, arching the body and proceeding to slowly rock back and forth from chest region to thigh gaining speed with the drill sergeant's cadence I soon learned that this was a work out that demanded a jock strap because if there was but a pebble under your groin there was no negotiating the dire pain, understanding that you needed permission from the drill master to shift position. If you were new to the team, Tony didn't recognize your request. I would come to associate pain with Tony. I would also come to learn that he trained us well. He had that look, tough, and no-nonsense. Tony had a glee and a snarl in his eyes. I swear he looked straight at me as he called out, 'okay, let's pick up the pace'. I figured I was in for it because it wasn't only that I was a rookie, but I was the 'keeka', not a real football player. Over a half hour of exercise mercilessly came to an end and we were separated by defense and offense, but the drills were basically similar for each unit. We commenced with hitting drills first, with tackling dummies and then amongst each other in various forms. From three and four-point stances, we'd go at each other from whistle to whistle, hands clapping all around with encouragement from the others and the coaches. This had become a spirited workout. We didn't want to hurt each other, that was our code of conduct amongst ourselves, but we wanted to show the coaches what we had. The established players didn't want to lose their position to the new guy wanting to make an impression. A hot Saturday afternoon got hotter. Eventually the offense went against the defense in walk through running and passing drills. At this point I just stood on the sidelines and watched. I figured that at some point they would have me take some kicks with the offensive line. The session ended with sprints. We had been at it for a good three hours, exhausted as we were, but feeling good from the gained pain, three sharp toots of Jerry's whistle signaled the end.

Jay yelled above the moaning and chatter of a hard first practice, "Same time next Saturday. Special teams give me five kicks. I need a center and a holder."

Even though he didn't acknowledge me, I knew that this would be my moment to make an impression. But deep disappointment set in as I watched Jerry, all the other coaches and the rest of the team walk out to their cars in the parking lot. John Macchiaroli, our center, came up to me. He looked drained of all energy, dripping with sweat.

John "Match" Macchiaroli approached me along with "Gorgeous" George Nardone, and Tom, "Pich" Piccininni. The look of disappointment was all over my face as I watched the entire team make their exit to their air-conditioned cars. Not one coach stayed behind to decipher if they wanted me on the team. Johnny Match barked at me. "Hey, let's get this done it's hot out here. Take your kicks. I wanna get out of here," he said in exhaustion. My exasperation grew. Not only did the entire team leave. The one guy entrusted with giving me a few kicks really didn't want to be out here. At that time, I didn't know that John was one of our captains and he would report back to Jerry. Match snapped the hike to George, my holder, and Tom Piccininni, retrieved my kicks in the end zone. I proceeded to kick the ball from the thirty-five-yard line. One kick, two kicks, and a third kick. Tom, in the end zone shagging the kicks, threw the ball back to George who tossed it back to John. After the third kick, Match reared up from his stance putting the ball into a large equipment bag. He walked up to me joined by George.

"That's enough for today. See ya next week."

"So, does that mean I'm on the team?"

"Do I look like a coach? You wanna be on the team then come back next Saturday."

The look of disappointment was all over me. I was unfocused and confused by everyone else's exit, particularly the coaches, making me feel like I was insignificant to the team. Match must have noticed this. He continued with a few compliments telling me that I kicked the ball well and that The Warriors never had a kicker. The seemingly gruff person was now complimentary. Unbeknownst to me, Tom took a position directly behind me. As Match kept my attention, Tom depanted me, he pulled down my sweatpants and underwear all in one pull leaving, me, the anxious rookie, in the raw in the middle of Rice Stadium. I just stood there dumbfounded making no attempt to dress myself. At that moment, for some unknown reason, I knew I had found my team. As I headed home, I can remember thinking that we might not win many games because of the laid-back attitude of the workout. Everyone was having fun. Coaches were teasing players and players were giving it back. This was not the Vince Lombardi/Woody Hayes school of football that I was accustomed to. I wasn't used to this as coaches I had played for previously were into berating, yelling, and intimidating. I also didn't think we were big enough in either height or weight or fast enough to compete with the other teams in the league. Heck, we didn't even have a quarterback out there. Seems the quarterback, Jackie Cawley, was a guy who usually worked at Woolworth's in Manhattan during the weekends. But I knew that I liked these guys. What I didn't know was that I would have friends for life.

I played my first game with the Warriors football team, October 10th, 1970. I would be eighteen years old at the end of the month. We had an 11:00 match against the Throggs Neck Navajos at Bronx Park East, A field bordered by the Bronx River Parkway and the Bronx Zoo and White Plains Road. As was our norm, we arrived early, about 10:00, and dressed on a slight rise of a knoll that ran along the east side of the field. A clear blue sky presented a picture-perfect day, sixty-five degrees with a slight breeze blowing across the field from the east. This was ideal conditions for me as a kicker. Our picture-perfect day turned into an impending storm as I watched in awe at the opposition, the Throggs Neck Navajos, as they trudged down the knoll to dress on the other side of the field. They were all huge. In my mind, there was no way we could compete with them. We had a few big guys on our team but we were well stocked with 5'7" to 5'9" guys. I seem to remember that we had a core of players that we referred to as the seven munchkins, mostly on the defense. Be that said, we finished getting dressed and began our pregame workout. The Navajos were still big.

We won the coin toss and received the opening kickoff at the south end of the field. Joey Reich received the ball at around the fifteen-yard line, ran up the gut for five to eight yards and veered left behind a wall of blockers. He was steadily gaining yardage as blocks were made all along the way. There was one man he had to beat, the contain man on the outside. Tommy

McGurl, our big tight end, took care of business. Tom laid him out, decleated him, with a massive hit to the chest region. The cover man's heels kicked up in the air as he landed on his back, a classic, textbook block. He never had a chance. It was off to the races for Joey and just like that, we were up 6-0. I missed my first extra point, but it didn't matter as a charge ran through the entire team. Momentum was instantaneous. We would run roughshod and dominated the Navajos for the rest of the game. The defense took the field and it was a quick four and out. The Navajos couldn't sustain a drive. I would come to quickly learn that our offense was just as proficient. Our quarterback, Jackie Cawley, behind a stonewall of an offensive line, had complete command. His passing was flawless. He had a perfect touch on his passes whether throwing the deep ball, a rope over the middle or with a soft touch on a screen play. When all broke down, which was rare, he could scramble with the best of any collegian, elusive and slippery. The play calling was perfect under Jerry's guidance. Jay was a brilliant offensive tactician, way ahead of his time, and having a passing quarterback, which was uncommon in our league back then, we seemed unstoppable. We were on fire. The very next series of plays, the offense drove down the field and Tommy McGurl scored a touchdown on a flanker screen, one of our staple plays. Tom at six feet four was a threat as a receiver and a blocker. For the rest of the game, our defense stopped the Navajos as they never crossed mid-field. We would go on to score two more times. George Nardone, one of our wide receivers, caught a touchdown pass on a square out. The defender missed the tackle and he went in. Frank Botti scored our final touchdown on a straight dive play which he ran between the right guard and right tackle hole. I finally made an extra point, yes, I missed the first three and never thought that the Coach would send me out there a fourth try but he did. We won 26-0. A strange score one would think for four touchdowns and one extra point. An oddity in the B.U.A. was that as there were no kickers (field goal, extra points) other than me. Teams got one point for running in the extra point and two for kicking it. Once I got untracked, we had a big advantage over the other teams. An exhilarating win in that we dominated the game on both sides of the line of scrimmage. Our defense stonewalled the Navajo offense and our offensive line was knocking their defensive line back about five yards on every play. After that game, I learned two things. Joey Reich and Jackie Cawley were both incredible athletes and leaders. Joey played defensive back, but he was more of a "monster man" allowing him the freedom to defend the pass, play the run, or rush the quarterback. He was spectacular. Constantly making plays all over the field. Jackie, our quarterback, was outstanding. After the game, Tooty Whalen, the Navajo's quarterback, went over to Tommy and told him that 'you guys have some team this year. Your offensive line was knocking our line back about five feet on every play.' Another aspect of the Warriors that I enjoyed was that we seemed to revel in our victories as a group, from stars to backups, we were all one. I immediately sensed a cohesiveness amongst us.

After the game, as would be a Warrior tradition, we all went back to the bar to celebrate. Leonardi's, as I knew it back then, later to be known as the Well, a neighborhood bar, nestled under a two-story walk up. Drinking was legal at age eighteen. For those that might be a little underaged, not there were any, they could get a beer but if they got goofy or obnoxious, they were tossed. The bartender and/or patrons would know your parents and if they didn't approve of your behavior, they would make a call to your house. You didn't want to be banned from the bar. It was a great place to go back to after a game. As we won most of our games over four years, there was a lot of celebrating. It was a small bar, on Zerega Avenue between McClay and Buck Street, about three blocks off of Castle Hill Avenue that normally would host six to ten customers. The crooning melodies of Jerry Vale, Vic Damone, and Andy Williams singing sentimental songs would emanate from a jukebox mounted on a wall on a low volume. The odor of cigars and cigarettes filled the room as the neighborhood gents would peruse the racing form or discuss matters of the day. The bar held a pool table and an old shuffle-bowling table. I can still remember, I believe it was in 1973, when the bowling table, my favorite game, was removed and replaced by something called Pong. It was an electronic table-tennis game with two in-game paddles to hit the ball back and forth. It was black and white with two-dimensional graphics. I didn't know what to make of this and was informed that this was a video game. There was a small back room for meetings and parties with a kitchen off to the side. We would get into Leonardi's and march into the back room, without disturbing the patrons. Usually, someone at the bar would ask how we did. Our smiles said it all. I remember the first time I entered Leonardi's. A few of the guys, one by one, went into the kitchen and grabbed a frosted mug out of the refrigerator. Being a rookie, I was last but I got my mug. I bellied up to the bar awaiting my draught. Life was good…until the bartender leaned over the bar.

"Where'd you get that mug from?"

My new friendly bartender didn't look so friendly and his tone was intimating.

I meekly responded, "I got it from the fridge like all the other guys." I didn't understand what I had done wrong. Maybe because I wasn't from the neighborhood, maybe because he didn't know me."

"Put that mug back. That's Eddie's mug."

Without question or hesitation, I returned the mug to its proper place. I got my short one, a twenty-five cents beer in a pilsner glass. The bartender was now my buddy. I turned to Dougie Williams and asked him who "Eddie" was.

"Eddie is Eddie Egan. I saw what you did, we all did."

"Why didn't you tell me?"

"We wanted to see what would happen. Kind of like a rookie's initiation. You're lucky he wasn't here. Never touch Eddie's mug."

Eddie was Eddie Egan, a New York Police Department detective, credited with more than 8,000 arrests, legendary for busting an organized crime ring in 1961, seizing 97 pounds of heroin, a record amount at that time. This was the basis for a book and a movie called, The French Connection. The character "Popeye" Doyle, portrayed by Gene Hackman in the movie, is based on Eddie Egan's exploits. The character "Buddy" Russo played by Roy Scheider was based on detective Sonny Grosso, Eddie's partner[38]. I was also told that should I see Mr. Egan at the bar, don't talk to him. I did come to see him there, always sitting next to his buddy, I don't know who he was but he was the only person Eddie would talk to. I didn't talk to that guy either. That guy was Sonny Grosso. There was also a man, maybe in his early fifties, Frank the numbers guys. Frank not only knew the number for that particular day, he knew the number for any day. In the side pockets of his jacket he kept a small spiral-bound notebook of the number going back years. He was like the Congress of Numbers. We all wound up in the back room to rehash our victory over beer and Rose's meatball heroes. Rose was Leonardi's wife and made the best meatballs on the planet. Pitchers of beer were on the folding tables where we sat. Of course, there was nothing like watching Louie Cavalieri, one of our defensive ends, chug down an entire pitcher, like a thirsty kid downing a cold glass of milk, as we all chanted "Woodstock". Jerry,

---

[38] New York Times; November 6, 1995, David M. Herszenhorn: Edward R. Egan, Police Officer Who Inspired Movie, Dies at 65

along with the coaches, would congratulate us and highlight certain plays and gaffes. He would conclude our session by announcing the players of the game and give out an adhesive Warrior Head decal that we would place on the back of our helmets. I felt like this was something I could get used to. I remember as I made my way home thinking that nobody was going to beat us. I understood that one game does not a season make but I truly believed that the only team that could beat us was us.

Our second game, as previously mentioned, was the 'monsoon' game against my former team, the Pelham Bay Spartans, the famous Froggy gut-punch game. Winning by the score of 3-0, we were now 2 and 0.

What I had experienced was that being on the Warriors was more than just playing football. There were life lessons being taught by Jerry and the other coaches. Case in point, it was our third game, I can't remember who we were playing but it was at the Williamsbridge Oval. As was our way, we scored on our first possession and quickly took the lead 8-0. I went out onto the field to kick off to our opponent. We huddled on the forty-yard line and I called an onside kick, left. Everyone in the huddle listened to my call...assuming Jay sent in the play. The referee blew his whistle and we executed a perfect onside kick recovering the ball. Everyone was jumping up and down in excitement. I came to the sidelines; a football hero being congratulated by everyone including the coaches. I had shown my coaches that although I was just a kicker, I was good at what I did and that I had a good feel for in-game momentum shifts. If we could score here, we would bury this team early. Yes, the coaches were praising me...all except one. I took a seat on a wooden bench as the commotion died down. I sat there as once again Jackie was methodically leading us downfield. Jerry came up to me and very quietly asked who had called that play. So proud of myself I blurted out that I called the play. Thinking that I would get high praise from the head coach what I got instead was a soft-spoken reprimand, almost like a priest telling me I had done wrong. There was no vitriol, no anger, just a subtle reprimand.

"Bobby, I want you to take off your uniform. You will not play for us and unless you figure it out, you are no longer on this team".

I think I went into shock. I couldn't understand why he wasn't pleased with me. This was like the look you got from a teacher or your parents. The look that was worse than being yelled at or getting a smack to the head. You melted from that look. It was the worst. The guys noticed that I was out of uniform and wanted to know why. I simply told them that I had screwed up. I wanted to cry. I was so humiliated and embarrassed that I didn't tell my dad what had happened when I got home. What I did do, for three full days, was hear Jerry's voice, "you will not play for us unless you figure out why" and tried to get an understanding of what I did wrong. Initially, I thought I called a great play but after only two games with the Warriors, I realized that playing for the team was more important than me. Yes, that was the answer. The team was bigger than me. As an only child, I would always think of myself. We were always taught that there is no "I" in team, but I was the smartass that would answer 'but there is a "me" in team. That past Sunday, I had learned an invaluable lesson. On that Wednesday, I couldn't get out of my college classes fast enough to go to Jerry's house. Unannounced, I rang his doorbell and his wife, Geri who did not know who I was, let me in. She could see my distraught. She led me to a couch in the living room and Jerry soon joined me. Before he could speak, I wildly went into a diatribe about how I now knew and understood what I had done wrong. Jerry couldn't even answer as I broke down, tears and all, telling him, pleading, and begging him to let me be back on the team. Again, with that calm, low tone voice, without emotion, he simply told me to be at practice Thursday evening at Santa Maria. I bought into what Jerry and his coaches were preaching and that was a team concept. I learned the concept of team.

Our final regular season game was against the Crusaders at Van Cortlandt Park. We had already clinched as Divisional Champs, so this game was of no importance to us, other than to finish the season undefeated, but it meant everything to the Crusaders. They needed the win to get into the playoffs. The Crusaders held a 6 – 0 lead going into the end of the game. Jackie called for a flanker screen. Dougie Williams, our left guard, pulled out and the pass went to Tommy McGurl who eluded a tackle and ran it in for the score. We won that game 8 – 6 [a kicked extra point was worth two points]. At the end of the game, Eddie Esposito, hugged Tommy to death and congratulated any Warrior player he could get to. Our winning the game gave the Javelins entry into the playoffs as the number four seed. We would play them next.

My thoughts from game one was prophetic as we did go undefeated in ten games. We were divisional champs. We celebrated like nobody's business at Leonardi's. We were poised for the playoffs. Two games and out and we would be league champs. That following Saturday, we were more than ready to play the Javelins. The team that wanted me, a team we beat handily twice during the season. The game was to be held on Randall's Island, an island in the East

133

River, between East Harlem, the South Bronx, and Astoria, Queens. We were going to play in Downing Stadium, home of the New York Cosmos, a soccer team in the North American Soccer League. This wasn't the home of the New York Yankees but never the less this was the field that the legendary Pelé, Giorgio Chinaglia, Franz Beckenbauer, and Johan Cruyff played on, all eminent international players. The stadium held about twenty-two thousand. We were on an incredible high that morning. For some unknown reason, we were delayed in taking the field. Rearing to go and filled with pent-up energy we began to bang our fists and helmets into the locker stalls as we wildly chanted…Warriors, Warriors, Warriors. The Javelins could hear us. The door to the locker room opened. A man entered and spoke with Jerry. The man quickly left and Jerry announced that there would be no game today. As it had rained that night, more like a drizzle, the field was soft and the Cosmos did not want a couple of sandlot teams "chewing up their field" for their game the next day. We would play this game tomorrow. Tomorrow was Sunday at Bronx Park East. We got dressed on the knoll and went through our pregame drills. One thing I should mention is that as a kicker, I get a lot of sideline time and observation. What I observed was that we definitely did not have the energy we had the day before. We were flat and that was the way we played the entire game. The Javelins scored the first two touchdowns which had not happened to us all season. It didn't rattle us as we were coached with the belief that as we could strike on any one play, as long as there was time on the clock, we could win. We scored a touchdown mid-third quarter, down 13 – 6. Our defense was now locked in and we knew that all it would take would be to score one more. It never happened. Fueled by dropped balls, turnovers and everything we hadn't done all year. Two plays stand out to this day. There was a flare pass into the flats to one of our receivers, Shliskowitz. Shliskowitz was a backup flanker/receiver who didn't get a lot of playing time. He was at every practice and as was the Warriors way, everybody was an important part of the team. Shliskowitz drifted into the left flat, Jackie pumped right pulling the secondary to that side of the field, turned and hit Shliskowitz square in the hands. I was standing right there on the sidelines. He had one defender to beat who was about ten yards off the play. Shliskowitz dropped the ball. Knowing he was wide open with room to ramble, I could see him lift his eyes off the ball before he pulled it in. A collective groan ran through the sidelines. Not a big deal as we had plenty of game to play. The backbreaker occurred in the fourth quarter. We were down on their three-yard line. This was Frank Botti territory. Frank our bull of a running back, nothing fancy, just your typical smash mouth running style. Once we were five yards or less from the end zone it was always the dive play to Frank and a touchdown. One thing to know about our offense, all plays were called by Jerry and delivered to Jackie via substituting players, usually the running backs. On this particular play, second and three, in the excitement of the moment, a backup running back, Joey Longo inserted himself into the game. Frank, believing that Jerry had sent him in with the play, came out. Joey called his own number meaning he told Jackie "right half dive" (this was the right halfback receiving the handoff). Joey got the ball, kind of lunged over the line of scrimmage into the end zone. We went wild at that moment, we thought he scored. Unfortunately, what we saw was the referee blowing his whistle, shuffling his arms like a baseball umpire calling a runner safe and demonstratively signaling that it was Javelin ball. He called the play a fumble. Jerry ran out to debate a lost cause. For anyone who is a football fan, we all know that once the ball crosses the plane of the end zone it is a touchdown. There is no fumble after that point as the play is dead. The referee explained that Joey had to come down into the end zone with possession. We lost the game 13 – 6. We were devastated. An undefeated season in the regular season with a first-round loss to a team we had crushed when we last played them about a month ago. Tommy McGurl, in total frustration and anger, shattered his helmet against the rock at the far end of the field. I guess I was right. The only team that could beat us was ourselves. We beat ourselves that day. The divisional championship meant nothing after experiencing this loss. I felt sick as did most of my teammates. I went home after that game with a bad taste in my mouth. It took a while before my father talked to me. He understood the disappointment as he was quite the athlete and an avid sports fan. He came to every one of our games after he had heard from the neighborhood guys of how his son beat the Spartans and the type of team we had. He would never miss another game for the next four years that I was with the team.

"Kid, I know you don't want to hear this but there came a point towards the end of the season where I thought it would be good if you lost one game. I was actually thinking that you should have lost that last game. Every game seemed so easy and a final game loss, a loss that would take away being undefeated, would have fueled your fire. You had the division and a loss would have taken away your complacency. It's hard to root for a loss in an undefeated season but I really thought you would have been better off with a final game loss."

"Yeah, maybe," I replied staring at the floor.

"And had you played the Javelins that Saturday you would have destroyed them. You were ready that day. I was standing between the lockers. I could hear you guys fired up and there was nothing but silence from their lockers. It was if you had won that game right then and there."

I never believed in what dad said that day but many years later, outside of the Miami Dolphins, I believe he was right.

Enough said. The season was dead. We would get a trophy for Division Champs, but the big trophy would go to someone else. That being said, we had a great awards dinner party attended by parents, girlfriends, family, and former players. We didn't know the former players. As a matter of fact, most of us wondered who the "old" guys were, and it wasn't possible that these geezers were once players. They probably wore leather helmets in their time. They were probably in forties. I can't remember where the award dinner was held, it might have been a Knights of Columbus or VFW hall, but it was a great time. It certainly washed away the sour taste of the final game. Amidst a dinner, and music and dancing were the handing out of our trophies. There were also individual trophies for Most Valuable Player, Defensive Player of the Year, Offensive Player of the Year, Teammate of the Year, Most Improved Player of the Year, etc., there was one particular award that really grabbed my attention, the Banana of the Year. This was the award, presented not with a trophy but with an oversized inflatable banana, that was given to a player or coach, who without question had the goofiest, dumbest moment on the field. Bill "Biff" Bifundo was presented with the Banana as all chanted in unison…banana, banana. I can't remember what it was he did, it might have been during the sky weekend, but he deserved it head and shoulders above all others.

All in all, it was a great season. There were a couple of takeaways from my first year. One was that I had great teammates who truly liked each other. There was a tremendous humility amongst the team. There was no one guy better than another, whether it was a starter or a backup. Everybody contributed, everybody was important. We were a team in the true essence of the word. When situations broke down during a game, there was never finger pointing, no blame, no shouting. Actually, when a play failed, it was common for one of our captains, Jackie, Match or Joey, to shoulder the fault. What you would hear next was a bunch of guys chiming in exclaiming that it was their fault. It would become a chorus of "no it was me, I missed the block/tackle, I ran the wrong hole" It got to the point that the coaches had no clue.

The second take away was that we had incredible coaches, coaches who worked tirelessly and only with the positive. I had noticed that when a unit came off the field, be defensive, offensive, or specialty, there was no barking from the coaches. Normally what we heard from them was calmness. It was not about what went wrong, that was behind us, already done. It was always about moving forward, what we do to correct the mistake. If one of the guys was upset, frustrated, they would take him aside and quietly talk with that player. Said player would come back to the group all in, ready to go. For instance, having that loss to the Javelins didn't wipe away the great year we had. After that defeat, we had a team meeting after the game and rather than wallowing in our loss, Jerry, Vas, Froggy, Danny, and Ollie boasted our morale about our accomplishments during the course of the year and what we would do next year to be better. I think we felt like a million dollars and were raring to go.

***

And in regards as to whether we started the tackle team in 1968 or 1969, I can only add this. I have put in countless hours of pulling microfiche at the Stephen A. Schwarzman Building of the New York City Library and digging out old bounded copies of the Bronx Press Review at the Bronx County Historical Society to find old archives of our games. I will tell you that there is no mention of our team, not a single article in 1968. There are a few in 1969. And much like the conundrum of 1968 vs. 1969, so is 1970 and 1971...and 1972...and so on and so forth up to 1974 or maybe 1975. How is it possible that guys from the late forties, the fifties, the sixties have perfect recall? They all same exactly the same thing, independently. My era, my guys, we're not on point. Joe Regina did point out that it was the '70s, you can fill in the blanks as to what that is referencing. Lots of confusion. The details get foggy with time but to the best of my recollection, and a lot of our recollections, and because there aren't enough articles to define it, this is what it was.

The moral of the story is not to dispute your coach and never, ever, tell your mom, or any mom for that matter, that they are wrong.

Chapter 7

The Tackle Team Part II and New Beginnings

American Boy Statue, Rice Stadium, Pelham Bay Park, Bronx, NY

During the offseason, it was common to find a group of us together doing things that good friends would do. My great teammates were indeed good friends. On almost any Saturday evening we could be found at the Copper Kettle, a pub outside of Parkchester on Unionport Road off of Westchester Avenue. I would be there usually joined by John and Mike Fallon, Matty Dowling, Kevin Burke, Tommy Garrett, Kevin McInerney and on occasion Ann Simmons, our number one fan. During the season, on the sidelines, we had a contingent of followers, friends, family, girlfriends, and adults from the neighborhood. Ann was our number one fan because she was at every game. The Copper Kettle provided good spirits, good companionship, tall tales, pretty lassies and live music. The other popular inn was the Castle Keep. A much bigger venue than the Copper Kettle, a club on Tremont and Bruckner that had a live rock band and young ladies to be chased, none of which were caught.

***

Of course, it would be a dishonor not to mention the fabled ski weekends, the stuff made of debauchery, shenanigans, and pranks. This would occasionally be held after the season, usually in January, February. Certain names are omitted to protect the not-so-innocent.

Tommy McGurl recalls the first ski weekend. "Bobby, it was a cold one, it was held right after the first year we played. It began with my brother, Jimmy, beating everybody for their money in a game of poker on the bus ride up there. He won about three hundred bucks and wiped everybody out. All the guys were almost all broke, but Jimmy had to buy everything for everyone anyway, so it didn't matter that he won." According to Tommy, next on the card was a wrestling match between Denis Waldron and John Macchiaroli in their room. These are no small guys. These two gladiators, being the great warriors that they are, grappled themselves into the paper-thin drywall. Their whole bodies went through the wall, not once but twice. One of the holes was about three feet high and almost two feet wide the other being smaller. The dresser in their room wasn't wide enough to hide the long opening and the armoire wasn't tall enough to cover the large cavity. So again, like a Little Rascals episode, they searched other rooms in an effort to seek out a taller armoire and longer dresser which they did find. They moved the furniture from their bedroom into the others, which required the use of an elevator, in exchange for the proper furnishings that would conceal their mischief. As John Macchiaroli told me, "I don't know how Jerry ever got his deposit back once they discovered what we left behind". The second night they went out to a club and the guys had this idea. They wanted to short-sheet the coaches. Tommy can tell you this one. "We went to this club and when it was time to leave, we had to get back without the coaches knowing. We had to pass them on the road. George Nardone, on this dangerous mountain road at night, shuts off his headlights so we could get back before Danny and Jimmy and without them seeing us. That ride scared the crap out of all of us. When we got back, a select group short-sheeted Danny Miller and Jimmy Oliveto's with shaving cream, toothpaste, salad dressing and whatever was wet and gooey. This did not sit well with

Jimmy and Danny as unfortunately this practical joke was not found funny by their wives. Ollie was so pissed off that he wound up jumping through the window of the culprit and began to beat the life out of him. We had to save him somehow. We had to get him out of there. I think both Jimmy and Danny wanted to kill all of us. There was very little snow that weekend but the lake was frozen, so we played hockey. It was Jackie Cawley's idea to play hockey. Somebody shot the puck, missed the net and it traveled down the lake. I skated down to retrieve it and went right through the ice into the freezing pond. All they could see was my big head bobbing in the water like a buoy. They had to pull me out. There was that one time we were at the Granite Hotel in the Catskills and Chuck Wepner was up there training for the upcoming fight with Mohammed Ali. We watched him work and we were laughing, telling each other how this guy was going to get his butt kicked. There was also a trip to Lake Harmony in the Poconos. It did have a ski run outside but it wasn't operating. We stayed in the hotel and used the pool quite a bit but once again, we created our own good time."

Jimmy Sherry had told me of his first ski weekend experience as a coach. "Bobby, that was a good weekend. I think that trip bonded that team into one. I actually roomed with the players because I came up without Bernadette, my wife. My job was to keep the guys under control." I asked Jimmy as to how did that go. "No such luck, not a prayer of a chance." was his reply. "We were playing cards one night. Just me and the guys. Not the coaches. Before the trip we had told them, no pot, no hash, you can't bring it up there. And they're like, 'okay, okay.' So, we're sitting there playing cards and one of them approached me. I don't remember which one but one of them approached me and asked, 'What do you think? I got a little weed. Can we smoke this once?' I'm like, okay, we're all together here. It's controlled. I don't have a problem. Go ahead. Holy shit they brought out this bag. If any cops had seen this bag, we would have gone to prison for life. They all chipped in. Twenty of them chipped in a bought this bag that was like the biggest thing I had ever seen. Some of the guys were dropping something at dinner time. I don't know what it was, but somebody was dropping something. It had to be a pill, it was a hallucinogenic. [Note - What this was is referred to as blotter acid. It came in the form of candy buttons. These buttons are colorful dots on white of paper that are picked off to be enjoyed. These were always a treat for children who like to play 'doctor and patient'[39]. The ski trip

---

[39] https://www.oldtimecandy.com/collections/walk-the-candy-aisle-candy-buttons-on-paper-tape

version was much different. These were laced with a hallucinogen]. They put it in a bottle of wine and they're tripping. They're having a great time. The young waiter serving them seemed to enjoy this activity, their behavior and had asked Macchiaroli for a sip of their wine. Johnny was obliged. He was into it. He got stoned. He was the happiest waiter in the whole place. They started throwing food and the next thing you know, a whole food fight. All of them. They wanted to get even with the coaches from the night before when they short-sheeted them and took a beating. As a matter of fact, one of the guys leaving the dining area rolled up a flight of stairs. You know when you roll down a flight of stairs. Well, he rolled up a flight of stairs that's how high he was. You heard about the time where the players short-sheeted the coaches? They even jacked up their underwear. It didn't sit well with the coaches, especially Jimmy. They did everything under the sun to give the coaches a hard time. So, when the coaches got back to their rooms you heard all hell breaking loose from them. Jerry went into Denis' room and nailed him to the wall. Right through the wall. Another hole in the wall. We had a hockey game and I was the goalie. I had my ski boots on. My foot got caught in a hole and the ice came out from underneath me. That's how my leg got messed up but I did block the shot. We'd go horse riding in the snow and the guys would start goofing off, going every which way but on the trail. Or the time we're in Jerry's Volkswagen going up this mountain. The car in front of him broke down and Jay goes into the other lane, the oncoming traffic lane and nearly ran another car off the road. Stuff like that was happening but it was a great trip. We had a great time."

I once sat with Jerry asking him about ski weekend memories. He told me that he "organized the ski weekend and that was more of a job than you can imagine because whenever something bad happened and a lot of it did happen you would hear the announcement 'Will Mr. Demers come to the main office' and then I would have to explain away what happened or what I would do about it. One year we went up there. It was in Tony Vastola's' time playing with the team with Danny Miller and Jimmy Oliveto, where one of the players, who will remain nameless, had the State Troopers called in on him for damages. He had to leave his car there as payment, collateral, since he didn't have any money, credit cards or anything else to pay for it. So, there were some rough times. When the younger kids went up the coaches and I would sit outside on the wall as long as we could take it, being it would get late and it was cold, to make sure they didn't get out of their rooms at one in the morning. But they managed to usually counter me on our guidelines sneaking out windows and things like that. But basically, it was a tremendous time especially for the kids and even for the adults. We formed a group of parents who would go every year. We'd play cards and different games at the place and sit around the bar and drink and watch the kids in the pool so it was quite a good experience even though it was a lot of work. If I was to do something like that today, I probably would get arrested. Bobby, I'm sure you've heard lots of stories but you don't want to know the half of it."

***

My second year with the Warriors, 1971, began the same as the first, strenuous workouts at Rice Stadium in the July and August heat. I swear that statue, *American Boy,* was smiling down on us with a look, "better you than me". Summer workouts were not recreational, but they were worth it as proven by the results.

1971 was such a dominating year for us, it didn't matter who we played. I do have six Bronx Press Review articles documenting the second through the seventh games. Going into our seventh game we defeated the Bronx Spartans making us 7-0. We had beaten the Navajos, the Raiders, the Pelham Spartans, the Crusaders, the Javelins, the Saints, and the Bronx Spartans. We were so dominant that year we clinched the division in our sixth game against the Saints beating them 26-12 in a night game at German Stadium in Throggs Neck. In that article, it does state that "the win was the sixth straight for the undefeated Warriors under head Coach Jerry Demers." The article goes on to indicate "the champions have one game left on the schedule before they go into the division's playoffs". With six minutes left in the first half, we broke through on a Jackie Cawley to Tommy McGurl to Gary Ruffino pass-lateral play, the hook, and lateral. The Saints put on a drive at the end of the half but ran out of time on our five-yard line. We went into the half with a 7-0 lead. Early in the third quarter, Jackie teamed up with Gary Ruffino on a fifty-five-yard scoring play. The Saints came back with a forty-six-yard scoring pass. We took the ensuing kickoff to their forty-five-yard line and scored again on a screen pass from Jackie to George Nardone, with Kevin McInerney and Dennis Waldron providing key blocks along the way. Before I continue, understand this, as I repeat previous tales of glory. George Nardone will forever be known as "Gorgeous George". Not that he wasn't a fine-looking young man, it's just that he is the only player I ever saw in the history of any form of football, from high school, college, pro that ran around a puddle. It was a tight end screen left. And after that game, Macchiaroli gave him hell about it. It was like something out of a comedy. The Saints took a kickoff eighty-one yards to bring the score back to 20-12. Things settled down after that when we put on one final drive of sixty-two yards capped by Jackie's ten-yard toss to Tommy. Jackie wound up hitting ten of sixteen passes for two-hundred-seventy yards with John Macchiaroli, Curtis Elston, Joe Reich, Sal Cirillo, and Mark Anderson as standouts of the game[40]. Had the Saints beaten us that night, they would have taken over first place. We were 5-0 entering the game and the Saints were 4-1. A win over us would have given us both 5-1 but the Saints would own the tie-breaker which was a head to head match-up. On November 28th, a Sunday, as all our games were played, we defeated the Bronx Spartans 13-7 to capture our first league championship, the BUA Junior title. In the third quarter, we trailed 7-0 after the Spartans recovered a bad snap inside their own ten-yard line. We came back on a fumble recovery by Kevin Burke and we "marched upfield in a ninety-five-yard, eight-play drive with Curtis Elston scoring on a ten-yard sweep. Later in the fourth quarter, Joe Longo ran for twenty-five yards capping a fifty-yard drive[41]." We ended the season with the most points scored in the league, 147, and what the Bronx Press Review called the "stingiest defense" in the league.

Of course, the victory was taken back to Leonardi's and the celebration was on and ongoing. Louie Cavalieri, in all of the excitement, after emptying a pitcher of beer, reared back in his chair and put his head through the wall. Besides losing only one game in two years we seem to also excel at putting holes in walls. Drinking pitchers of beers into the early evening and not wanting it to end, we made our way to the Castle Keep. For some unknown reason I drove to Rice Stadium, in the dead of the night, 12:30 in the morning, joined by several other teammates in their cars. We ran about the field whopping it up, hollering at the American Boy statue. We just wanted to soak it all in. The celebration was endless, at least for me, but we ran out of gas. We got back into our cars and fell asleep. I think Mike Fallon was in the back seat of my 1965 Ford Falcon. At the break of dawn, from another car, John Fallon, Matty Dowling, Kevin Burke wisely suggested that maybe it was time to head home.

***

Perhaps now is as good a time as any to introduce the legend of Kali (pronounced Kăh-lee). Prior to every game, we had a ritual. Right before we took to the field, someone, usually

---

[40] Bronx Press Review, November 18, 1971
[41] Bronx Press Review, December 2, 1971

143

Ollie, would holler out "huddle up". We would all circle around Jerry. I had experienced Kali from my very first game against the Navajos in 1970. Being the "new" guy and just the kicker, I was always on the fringe of the group, about thirty-five guys. We would all have an arm on whoever was in front of us. We'd hunch slightly forward, almost leaning on each other. From the center of the cluster, you could hear Jerry. "Our Lady of Victory". We would all respond in unison, almost like an amen from a congregation in a church. "Pray for us". With that short and sweet prayer, Jerry would let loose in a shout, "Kali" and we would all answer in kind yelling out Kali. He would repeat this yell two more times, each time with us responding even louder. Me, I thought Kali was some kind of Gaelic spiritual thing, a Celtic holy matter. Or maybe Lassie, a collie dog. Or some Irish name. I had no idea. I wasn't even sure as to what I was hearing. I thought Jerry was invoking the name, Colleen. At some point in the season, it might have been our fourth game, Gary Ruffino turns to me. "You want to see Kali?" Before I could answer he pulled me into the epicenter of the huddle, right next to Jerry. This was an honor, an iconic moment for me. From his Warrior jacket, Jerry pulled out a small white cardboard jewelry box. He opened the box and on a cottoned bed laid a small jade elephant, its trunk curled upward. I thought to myself, "that's Kali. I stared at it astonished. I couldn't fathom that all this time we were praying to an elephant? I went crazy with euphoria. Macchiaroli was standing next to me and he said, "touch it Weasel, touch it". I was fearful to touch a sacred object but I did. I asked no questions but forever would continue to scream Kali to the heavens. I'm sure our opponents had no clue as to what we were bellowing and I'm certain they were scared. About a year ago, I had asked Jerry as to the significance of Kali. Where did this mammal come from?

Jerry gave me the skinny. "Bobby, I would say that this started in the sixties. It probably started when we got into the league in the Bronx, in 1958. It was strictly for football. I got Kali from the picture Gunga Din which was always one of my favorite movies. I have a poster of it in my room, Kali was the evil white elephant that represented the Indian cult that the British fought against, the Thuggees."

I was totally confused by this revelation. I further probed Jay. "But why Kali? What was that…I understand Gunga Din."

"It's just because it's something that I liked. It was my thing."

"Alright, I liked it. I got a feeling that the other team had no clue what we were yelling."

Jerry shook his head and laughed. "No, no they did not."

Being the anal person that I am, I commenced doing a deep dive into exactly what Kali represented. This wasn't just some animal that Rudyard Kipling stuck in a book. I was stunned to learn about Kali. The name Kali comes from the ancient language, Sanskrit literally meaning "she who is black" or "she who is death". Kali is the Hindu goddess of death, time, and doomsday and is often associated with sexuality and violence but is also considered a strong mother-figure and symbolic of motherly-love. Kali's earliest appearance is that of a destroyer of evil forces. She has been worshipped as the Divine Mother and/or Mother of the Universe[42]. So, you mean to tell me that this is what some Jewish guy, me was praying to before every game? This demonic force is what a bunch of eighteen-and nineteen-year-old kids was summoning? This Kali character is some pretty dark and edgy stuff. Maybe that's what we won so many games. She was on our side. I definitely wouldn't mess with this goddess.

Truth be told, it was good to have Kali on our side but I believe what made us a better team than our opponents were two things. One was we had superior coaching both organizationally and in game planning. The other was that we had a unique group of guys in that we were unselfish. A great example of this was the "running back club". This group, comprised of Curtis Elston, Frank Botti, Tommy Pryor, and Billy Coma became best of friend. Not a one of them seemed to care who started and who came off the bench. None of them ever complained about playing time or "touches". They had a true affinity for one another. So was it throughout the team. Our defense was based on a heavy rotation during the course of a game and again, no one protested their time on the field. No player was above the team, no egos and we faithfully wanted the next man to succeed. We sincerely care for each other.

***

1972 was again, another great season. Somehow, we finally lost a regular season game as we finished the season with a 6-2-0 record going against the Archer Street Rams, the Bears, the Ramblers, the Saints, and the Javelins. A failure of memory and a lack of Bronx Press Review articles (we weren't in that newspaper on a week to week basis) leads me as to who we lost to that year. You will come to know that if we didn't win a game, it is as if it didn't happen. I

---

[42] Ancient History Encyclopedia, Mark Cartwright, June 21, 2013

believe this is what is known as selective recall. We did win the conference/division by half a game ahead of the Bears and Saints who both finished 5-2-1. It had gotten to the point where, as a team, we never thought we would lose a game no matter what the situation, no matter how much time was left. With our stout defense and an offense that had the lightning-quick capability to strike on any single play, we felt invulnerable. The only way we could lose, in the words of Vince Lombardi, was if the clock ran out on us. There was one particular game that highlights who we were as a defensive team. It was against the Javelins on a blustery Sunday afternoon. That particular game was moved from a rain-soaked field to Turtle Cove in Rodman's Neck. I can remember kicking an extra-point. As I would, I kicked the ball high and true and jogged off the field knowing it would be good. Halfway off the field, Kevin McInerney stopped me. I turned to him but stood in amazement watching the ball hanging in the air like a hovering UFO. The gusts were so strong, the ball never went over the crossbar. But it is that game where the Javelins had the ball on our one-yard line, first and goal to go. We had stopped them the first three plays but on fourth down, we were called for pass interference. They got another four downs from the one. We stopped them on those four plays. Our defense held the Javelins, on the one-yard line, for eight plays. There was also a game at Williamsbridge Oval against the Archer Street Rams. It was late in the game and we had no time-outs. The clock was ticking. Joe Regina, our defensive tackle, is the culprit in this incident so let's hear it from him.

"We were playing the Archer Rams. We were at the Oval. It was the end of the game, we were losing, we had no timeouts and I think we were getting the ball back with time left on the clock and I don't remember if they were going for it on fourth down or if they were punting. Somebody came into the defensive huddle, they called the set and they said 'Joe, you're getting hurt this play' because we needed a time out. They didn't want the clock to keep going. I went down with a fake knee injury and apparently, the acting was so good everyone thought I was actually hurt. They had to cut my pants open and check my knee, a brand-new pair of pants. I remember it vividly because my friend Mike Pryor, who lived around the corner from me, played for the Rams. After the game, he questioned me as to how my knee was. I laughed and told him my knee is fine. He said 'get the hell out of here'. I said, no, my knee is fine. He was pissed. I don't remember the name of the pants. I was playing with hand-me-down crap my first year (1971) and the beginning of my second year. Finally, I had to get a pair of pants that fit properly and I did. They were nice and they were bright white, like nice stretch nylon/spandex. They were expensive."

We on the sidelines, including some of the coaches, thought Joe was really injured. We could hear him shrieking, "No, no". Joe had told me that he was telling them "don't cut my pants". He also told me that although he wasn't reimbursed for the pants, he did receive a Warrior head decal.

We went on that year to win the divisional title by beating our arch-rivals, the Saints in a 6-3 match at Williamsbridge Oval. In the second quarter, Joe Reich intercepted a pass and ran it back to the Saints' thirty-yard line. We scored the game's only touchdown on a two-yard keeper that Jackie ran in. In that game, we had sacked their quarterback nine times[43]. Their quarterback was Willie Cawley, Jackie's younger brother, who was playing his first year in the league. Willie had quite an arm, stronger than Jackie. One of Jackie's younger brothers, Brian or Biney as he was called, was holding the yardsticks along with some of his younger cousins at the game, Johnny and Peter O'Malley. After they sack Willie, they're all yelling "kill him…kill him". Willie looks up and sees his brother and cousins imploring us to kill him. The Cawley and the O'Malley families were definitely Warrior households. So, the good news was that we had won our third straight divisional/conference title. The bad news was that we would have to play the Saints yet again in a playoff game to decide the League Champs. This game would come to be a classic in that it was one tightly contested bout. This was at German Stadium, under the lights. It made it professional. We had quite a nice crowd, for that game. The field was soft, muddy from previous rain. Scoring was difficult. The Saints had this big tight end, he was like a Gronkowski. Joe Reich had to shadow him the whole game. He didn't have a big play that night but he caught a lot of short passes. "He was tough to play because he was so big it was tough to get the ball from him", as Joey would tell me. We kept Willie Cawley from throwing long but he got us with short quick passes and a lot were going to that tight end. We came off the field at halftime losing 6-0. We walked into the lockers like we were losing 60-0 and we were all despondent. Joe Reich was the last guy into the locker room. He rifled his helmet clear across the locker room, it was a long, narrow locker room. It hit the metal lockers and it woke us up. He started reading us a riot act. He went ballistic on us. I remember sitting by the doorway and I looked to my left. There

---

[43] Bronx Press Review, November 23, 1972

was Miller, Ollie, with Jerry right behind them. They all had a smirk on their faces like "we don't need to say nothing to these guys, Joey's doing it for us". He was on fire. He scolded us like we were bad step-children. I was scared because I was right next to him and I was thinking 'please don't go crazy hitting things… like me'. Joey would later tell me that he knows that this is 1972 only because in 1971 he wore an Ossining High School helmet and that he wouldn't have thrown it because he was responsible for that helmet. He also told me that the reason he was the last man into the lockers was "because Ron Watson, who was at that game, pulled me aside as we were walking off the field and said "what the hell's wrong with you guys. You're not playing very well. You guys look like garbage". Ron had gotten so under Joey's skin that he went into that locker room and took it out on us. I guess it worked. We went back out onto the field with confidence, we were fired up. Yet, we couldn't score. It is in this game that I attempted a short field goal. The ball was hiked and it sailed over my head. This was the only time in my five years that Match would misfire the snap. I scrambled after the ball and realized I had the time, the protection to do something. I certainly wasn't going to run because in my mind's eye those Saints that were coming to get me looked like the tallest beings in the world. To my right, all alone in the end zone was Tommy McGurl jumping up and down so that I could see him. I dropped back, like Joe Namath, and rifled a pass to Tom or at least I thought so. What I actually did was pull a Garo Yepremian pass, frantically throwing the ball like a little sissy, like someone who did not know how to throw. The ball may have gone five yards. Despite that, we did get to the end of the fourth quarter, about three minutes to go and we were on the one-yard line. They stopped us on the first two plays. It was third and one from the one-yard line. Tommy McGurl recalls that third down huddle. "Me and Dougie Williams went into the huddle, we looked at Jackie and said "Jackie, take the ball, me and Dougie are going to blow these guys to the back of the end zone, walk it in and let's get Bobby out here to cap it off. And Dougie looked right at Jackie and said, "let's get Weasel out here and win this game". Me and Dougie blasted away, Jackie took the ball and said 'I could have read a book and walked in behind you'. We won 7-6.

1973 as a season that was marked by changed and marred by tragedy. We would go 7-0-1 during the regular season, clinching the BUA conference title by once again overcoming the Saints 7-6 at Rice Stadium. We had gone through the Redwings, the Crusaders, Bronx Spartans, the Navajos, the Eastchester Ramblers, the Saints, and the Javelins. One of the changes was that Jerry was not our head coach. He did still run the team but from a distance. Tony Vastola was now our head coach which was not a big deal as we were all comfortable with him but it was different somehow. Jerry moved over to a younger Warrior-Rams team. He, at a certain point in our conversations indicated that in 1973 he could see that the team that played together since 1968, which was a long time for a team to stay together, but that "I could see the light at the end of the tunnel where this team maybe breaking up" and that is when he moved on to coach the younger team. I always believed that Jay's strength was working with young players. I felt that he stayed with us this long, we were now in our twenties, because we were a special group for him. He would attend some of our games when his schedule permitted. It was odd to see him there but not directly involved. The other change was that a contingent from Yonkers joined the team. One of the players was a kicker, Mike Cedrone. I had met my replacement. In practice, Mike would hit kicks from the fifty-yard line, clearing the goalposts with distance to spare. He had a pro-leg. There was no way I could compete with this as although I was very good under pressure in any situation, I did not have as strong a leg. Forty yards for me was pushing it to say the least. But for some unknown reason, Mike didn't perform well in a game. I'm not sure if it was the pressure of playing for Tony, who was his uncle, or it may have been the stress of joining a team and taking over the position from the team favorite, me. There was dissension brewing amongst the team or at least the guys were coming to me with it. I never knew if Tony had caught wind of this. In my years with the Warriors, I had never seen this. We accepted everybody onto the team as long as they were one of us meaning that they fit into the Warrior way. Mike was this kind of guy. This conflict bothered me to no end and I came to the decision to leave the team, for the good of the team. I felt that I was causing this dissent. I had called Jerry to advise him of my decision and he understood, not trying to talk me out of it. I hung up the phone, proceed to my bedroom and cried like a baby. My father, hearing me came into the room and I explained to him the situation and my resignation. Trying to console me he told me that football players don't cry. It is the only time in my life that I would curse at my father. "Fuck you, Sam Huff cried when the Giants traded him to the Redskins." Dad, knowing that I was right and not having an answer quietly left me alone. This one hurt badly. Several weeks later I was called back to the team by Jerry and things seem to work out. Where other players thought that maybe there was resentment between myself and Mike, to the contrary, we became buddies by working out together. I always felt that if I could get into his head, he would be our kicker, a great kicker. I remember Jerry telling one of the other coaches that if he could put my head on

Mike's body that we would have the greatest kicker in the history of football. We had a game, it was our second game against the Redwings, where John Macchiaroli quarterbacked us. Yes, Match, our center. He played because Jackie couldn't show up due to his work commitment. Game to game we never knew if Jackie would be playing because of his work schedule and understanding that he was supporting an entire family, we accepted this and supported him. This came first before football. We did win that game 6-0 with John throwing a ten-yard pass to Joe Golio for the lone score. Perhaps now is as good a time as any to explain that we had an overabundance of quarterbacks. Jackie, of course, was the guy. You already know that our tight end, Tommy McGurl could chuck which is why we would run the flanker reverse pass play. You know that our center quarterbacked. But wait there's more. We had at right tackle Mike Hume, a tall one. Mike would check in as a tackle eligible, take a step off the line into the backfield, receive a lateral and let it loose a good fifty yards, cross-field. Mike wound up obtaining a contract from the Canadian Football League, as a quarterback. Our fullback, Frank Botti, had quite an arm and a mind for quarterbacking. He came that close to starting a game for us. But there's one, unbeknownst to me for all these decades that was also one of our many quarterbacks. Thomas R. Pryor. There is now possible way for me to tell this tale so I will leave it to Tommy, #16, to take over.

"In the mid-1970s, I played football in the Bronx for the Warriors. Our home field was Rice Stadium in Pelham Bay Park. I was a running back. In 1974, our starting quarterback, Jackie, sprained his ankle. Our second-string quarterback was our center. The team didn't have a No. 3 quarterback. Jay and Danny, our coaches, knew I threw a solid option pass from the halfback position. They named me second-string quarterback, and I started taking snaps at practice. I lived in Queens then and lugged my 35-pound duffel bag to the Bliss Street station to ride the No. 7 line into Grand Central and then took the No. 6 local twenty-seven stops. I did this three times a week, twice for practice, once for the game. Jackie's prognosis: out at least two to three weeks. After the first practice without him, Jay and Danny saw me walking across the field toward the No. 6 station. 'Hey, come back here', they yelled. 'Let's go'. I followed them to the parking lot and Jay's Oldsmobile Delta 88. They sat in front; I took over the back seat. I was surprised Jay wasn't mad, because I was filthy and so was my bag. They yelled at me, busted my chops. I was having regular conversations with them as if I were one of their pals. They drove me all the way home, 46th Street and Skillman Avenue in Sunnyside. As they pulled away, I felt odd, then I got it: They were making sure their second-string quarterback took it easy. The next week, same ride on Tuesday, Thursday and game day. I didn't miss the subway. For the first game he couldn't play, Jackie showed up on crutches; the next game, he was limping and had a cane. On the third Tuesday, I was late to practice. I looked on the field, and there was Jackie, under center taking snaps. No Delta 88 that night. The No. 3 QB was back on the train[44]."

Tommy Pryor is a writer for the New York Times. His work has appeared in The New York Times, Mr. Beller's Neighborhood a literary website, A Prairie Home Companion a weekly radio show, Our Town an upper East Side newspaper. He has written short stories His blog: "Yorkville: Stoops to Nuts," was chosen by the New York Times. He appeared on PBS's TV series: "Baseball: A New York Love Story," amongst other shows and his memoir, "I Hate the Dallas Cowboys ~ tales of a scrappy New York boyhood," was published October 14, 2014[45]. Tommy comes with a lot of credentials. Two quick thoughts about Tommy. He is the only athlete I have even known or met that showed up pregame with the Sunday Times tucked under his arm and Thomas R. Pryor is a better writer than me.

We had quite an offensive backfield led by Ed "Cutty" Cunningham and Steve Habich. Cutty was as elusive as Gayle Sayers. Once he hit the open field, he was almost impossible to tackle. Steve was a steady strong runner. We would face the Saints in the playoffs only to lose that game 13-0. I can't recall ever being shutout in a game, there may have been one or two but the Saints were the better team that Sunday. We were at 0-0 standoff until a weak punt was returned giving the Saints the lead at halftime. In the second half, Willie Cawley struck with a long pass to his wide receiver[46]. The game was moot.

On November 17, 1973, a Friday, late evening, Joe Reich was heading out to Tommy McGurl from Ossining. Tom had his first apartment and he was having a party. Coming down the Bronx River Parkway on the rain-slicked road, at the big "S" curve by 233rd Street, his Volkswagen beetle hit a deep pothole and spun three times before flipping over. Joe would be a paraplegic. This was devastating and struck us all intensely. Thanksgiving Day, for me, was

---

[44] The New York Times, Metropolitan Diary (Reader tales from the city.); Thomas R. Pryor, September 18, 2016

[45] http://www.askanewyorker.com/author/thomas-pryor/

[46] Bronx Press Review, December 20, 1973

always spent at my aunt's apartment in Jackson Heights. There was no way that we would not be with Aunt Evelyn and the rest of the family. It was always the one day out of the year that the Nieder family would be together. That morning, I approached my father and told him that today was the first day the non-family could visit Joey. I expected dad to give me the lecture about how we have to all be together on this day and that I could visit Joe tomorrow. What I got shook me. His voice thundered as he leaned right up to my face, "Yes, yes, you go see Joey today…I don't care if I don't see you all day. You see Joey". Early that morning, I hopped the six train down to Rusk Institute-N.Y.U. Medical Center which was housed on First Avenue off of 32nd Street. I entered his room as if I was attending a funeral. I'm sure that look was all over my face. What does one say to a person who will never walk again? Such a great athlete, a leader, my captain, and my friend. I didn't know what to say. Joe greeted me from his bedside. I gave him a paperback book and strolled over to the window looking out onto the East Side River. I gazed out to the river as if in a trance. "Well, at least you've got a nice view", I muttered. From his bed, Joe rifled the book upside my head and scolded, "Hey Weasel, I'm not dead". He broke the ice. I explained to him as to my inability to cope with the thought of him not walking ever again. I couldn't comprehend such a new life for him in this manner, at the age of twenty-one. Joe lit me up with his explanation of how he intended to handle this "inconvenience" as he called it. In listening to him describing how this was just a new challenge and how his life would be full. He fired me up just like that halftime against the Saints. I couldn't believe how much better I felt after I left him. Typical Joe Reich. After that accident, though, the season was irrelevant.

I remember in speaking with Jerry about that night he had told me "I forget where I was, but I know I was in shock and it was very disappointing. I knew it was bad for the team because he was the heart and soul of the team. You take him out of the lineup and the fire is gone. Jackie was a great leader but Joe was different, Joe was a different type of leader. He was more vocal. He'd get in your face and push you. Yeah. We knew that the accident was bad and we knew that was bad for him. I just couldn't believe how a car can go into a curve and then flip over. And he was on his way to the party. If he was going home from the party after some drinking maybe it would have made some sense but he was completely sober."

About a year ago, as I was writing this book, I did hold a conversation about his mindset as the accident was unfolding. What he told me was alarming but not surprising in that it reflects his strength of mind and character that he has always maintained. It is best heard in his words.

152

"When the car spun out everything went in slow motion. They say your adrenaline gets so high things seem to go in slow motion. The car did a counter-clockwise spin three times and that's when I oversteered the car to compensate. On the second spin I said, 'holy shit, I screwed up this time'. That's all I could think, I had no control of the car anymore. It hit a pothole, it was a Volkswagen Beetle. After it went over, it sliced off the right side of the car so if anyone would have been riding with me on the passenger side, they would have died. The right side of the roof peeled back. The funny thing was I didn't think it was over, I knew I was in trouble, my father is going to yell at me. I felt like garbage thinking I screwed up this time. Once I lost control, I thought to myself 'hang on'. The most impressive part to me was that I had an eight-track player, I had a beautiful sound system going on and I was listening to Alice Cooper. I was unconscious for a little while then I came to and everything was upside down. I knew I had trouble breathing because I had busted my sternum. I said 'okay, control your breathing, I'm okay, I'm awake'. I was listening to No More Mr. Nice Guy. I'm thinking, damn I did a great job putting that eight-track into my Volkswagen. It still plays. I was so proud, that thing was still running. I didn't go into shock. It was a survival thing. The mechanism was to breathe slowly, calm down, calm my breathing until someone comes. This happened right across from Misericordia Hospital so that's where they took me. The only time that I thought I got bad news was when I was in Misericordia because as I was passing in and out, they're wheeling me down the hall and the priest was giving me last rites. I said 'holy shit, this is serious'. What really pissed me off is when I first saw my x-rays. I saw that the spine was disconnected I said 'I'm not going to be able to play this Sunday'. I thought there was a chance there that I could play like if I sprained something because I felt no pain, there was no pain being felt and I didn't realize that because I couldn't move my feet or anything. I had this thought 'no pain, okay. I'm okay except for the pain in my chest and we can fix that with some Ben Gay or whatever' but when I saw the x-rays, the first x-rays I said 'holy shit…that's not good'. I was taken to Rusk Institute-NYU. At that time that was one of the world-renowned specialty facilities. My brother-in-law, from Parkchester, was there first. He was actually there when they were reading me my last rites, he was walking the gurney down and I said, 'look, just tell my dad that I love him'. That's when I thought I was going to die. My mother and father found out about the accident a little bit later. My dad had a tough time with it. He would never show me that but I understood from other people that he had a really difficult time. My mother used to come down (to the hospital). My mom and my aunts were raised very

Christian. They got water from Our Lady of Lourdes. At one o'clock in the morning, while I'm sleeping, all of a sudden, I'm feeling water on me. She was throwing holy water on me to get me to walk again. I eventually got the hand-control car. It wasn't a brand- new car. It was a used car but with very little mileage. I brought it to City Island where they put hand controls on it. In City Island, they had this place, Kropke's. They invented this process. They cut the hand bars to fit just about any kind of car. They would actually weld them on. They were well renowned. I got the car in the springtime of '74. I recall that because of my memory of my dad driving me down to City Island with the car. We both went down there. One of the guys that worked there was a paraplegic and I was amazed by him. He had one of those little sports chairs that would rise up and down. He was getting underneath the cars, welding and doing this and that. He was probably into his fifties at that time. He was doing all that stuff and I said to myself, 'oh, wow, that's pretty impressive'. And that car got me through college. I was able to go back to college and get my degree in psychology. My first job, right after I graduated, was with the Office of Mental Retardation and Developmental Disabilities. Yeah, it worked out well. I was working for a Developmental Center as a social worker with paraplegic children. Then I worked for the State for thirty years. My major function with the New York State Advocate's office was for persons with disabilities. I became building code certified and they transferred me to New York State on accessibility issues, working with architects, and building inspectors. I got a chance to rewrite the building code. Well, only the accessibility portion. Myself and the United Spinal Institute for Paralyzed Veterans were a big player in rewriting the building codes for accessibility provisions."

I would be remiss not to mention the greatest game we ever played as a team in the seven years that we were together. It is known as the Joe Reich Benefit Game, played December 1973. This was not a league game but an exhibition put together by both Jerry Demers and Ed Stack. The purpose was to create a benefit fund that would aid in the purchase of that specialty-engineered car for Joe. We faced off against Eddie's Archer Street Rams. A team that Jimmy Oliveto once referred to as our arch-rivals. I always thought of them as our sister team as they were the mirror image of us in both coaches and right down to the style of play and sportsmanship. Jay and Eddie were not only long-time friends but identical in their persona. They were first rate, the two of them. They not only taught us how to play the game right but they mentored us beyond the game. They taught us to win with class and to lose with class. The game was held at German Stadium, on a Thursday night. There were seventeen hundred tickets sold. Joe was in attendance. What made this game legendary was not only for its cause but the intensity in which it was played. It was old-fashioned football with lots of hard, clean hitting. This game was so well played that at halftime, spectators in the stands were calling their friends to come out and watch this. We triumphed over the Rams 24-16. We opened the scoring with Jackie hitting Joe Golio, the fastest split end since Bob Hayes, which set up a three-yard dive by Cutty. Our second touchdown came on, but of course, a hook and lateral play executed, as always, to perfection by Tommy McGurl who lateraled to Vic Fernandez. Jackie threw another touchdown with minutes left to secure the win. He was awarded game MVP[47]. Please note, the extra-point, was worth two points, thank you.

***

In 1974 we moved over to a new league, the Metropolitan League in Queens as we had aged-out of the BUA. This league had two divisions. In our opener, we had snapped the St. Albans Chargers twenty-game win streak with a 22-0 victory. Once again, our defense had a stellar hold on the Chargers on four goal-line stands. In the second quarter, Jackie hit Vic Hernandez, our split end, on a sixty-yard pass play followed by a twelve-yard run by Cutty in the final quarter followed by a three-yard plunge again by Cutty[48]. We followed that game by beating the Islip Crusaders 22-0 with Cutty scoring three touchdowns. [49]We went on to beat Bayside, clinched the divisional title against the College Point Chiefs, destroyed the Patriots in a 44-0 match and there was a rematch against the St. Albans team which we won 24-0. We were for the season, undefeated, a familiar position for us. Beating a team twice in a year is hard. Beating them three times, as we found out, is was impossible. In the playoffs, we went against the Chargers for the third time that season. They finally got us. They would go on to face the Titans, who were undefeated in their division, and the Chargers lost to the Titans who took the League Championship.

By 1975 we moved up in age limit and joined the Pop Warner League. The year started off poorly. We had a good team but it was an older league. Some of the teams in Brooklyn and Queens that we played were teams that had excellent squads. This did not go well, at least for

---

[47] Bronx Press Review, December 1973
[48] Bronx Press Review, October 3, 1974
[49] Bronx Press Review, October 10, 1974

me. As Joe Regina so eloquently stated, "we were over-matched". Yes, we were. We lost a defensive stalwart with a season-ending injury and our defense wasn't the same without him. That was very disappointing for not only him but also for us as a team because he was a great player. That led to a lot of more points scored by the other teams. Jackie was no longer quarterbacking as was always his desire, he played wide receiver. This, I thought, changed the leadership of the offense. Going against older teams such as the Ramblers, the Islip Crusaders, the Staten Island Robbins, to name a few, we weren't winning. It was after a devastating loss in our second game out by the Belt Parkway, that I decided to pack it in. The team was in good hands, or should I say feet, with Mike Cedrone. The fun was gone for me and it wasn't just the losing. I was now living in Brooklyn, married, going to college full time and working for Blue Cross full time. It was too much of a strain for me. It was time. 1975 would be the last year that we would play as Warriors. A lot of our players went on to play with other teams such as the Crusaders and the Ramblers and some of them won championships. I'm sure they were a big part of the reason why that those teams won championships.

At this point, Jerry was coaching at Our Lady of Assumption, a Catholic, elementary school. He had taken on the operation of the O.L.A. Blue Devils, who had put an article in the church bulletin saying they needed a coach for their team. It was a small team. They were eleven, twelve years old and they were in a Bronx league. Jerry was running two teams at the same time. O.L.A. played on Saturdays and the Warrior-Rams played on Sundays. The equipment supplied by the church at that time was in a small little space and whatever the players received, they had to fit into so that some players were mismatched in the size of the equipment that they were handed, something you couldn't possibly do today but somehow everybody got equipment. Jerry went so far to tell me that he didn't know if they all had jocks but they all had helmets and shoulder pads and jerseys. They played for a year as the Blue Devils with blue jerseys with white shoulders, but after a year they were renamed the Warriors. From that point, this would be the start of what developed into the current program of intramural football. The younger team continued and played in the Bronx Midget Football League of the Pop Warner Football League. Most of the games were played at Van Courtlandt Park, because that is where they had a scale. The league had weight restrictions. Players would have to weigh in before each game. If you didn't weigh the correct amount you couldn't play, of course the coaches from each team were there to assure that the weight was correct. Two former players from our tackle-team, Joe Regina and Vic Anderson, assisted Jerry with coaching that team. Joe did reveal a little of his experience of working with these young players.

"Bobby, I was the line coach working with Ricky [Jerry's son] trying to impart football lessons the way they were taught to me. I would get very frustrated because nothing was sinking in. When we finally went to the season, you would see certain techniques being done, being carried out correctly, certain plays being run correctly. When we won the last game of the season, we were the champions of the league. Just being in the locker room and watching the kids celebrate was very satisfying. Everything came to fruition, you know. It was very gratifying. Something I got from Jay was you learn how to adapt to a situation such as working with younger aged kids, and how to get the same point across as you would to older players. He had to bring me back down to what we were dealing with, not so much as to who we were dealing with."

Basically, it was a Catholic grammar school league. Most of the teams had originated out of a church, quite like a C.Y.O. basketball program. Jay had told me, "The games were quite competitive. There was a powerhouse team in the league called the Road Runners but our young Warriors did break their eighteen-game consecutive winning streak. This was an excellent league. Essentially, the Road Runners would give four handoffs in a row, run around the outside, and one of them would usually break it. They were tough but we had a really good team. In the late seventies the Bronx Midget Football league started to disintegrate because of a team, the Morris Park Lions, who came into the league with a chip on their shoulder. They felt that all the other teams were against them and it was them against the world which caused quite a bit of problems for Sal Russo who was running the league at that time. Case in point, the Warrior had beaten the Lions in the finals 6-0. The Lions, coaches and players were upset enough that they refused to shake hands after the game. A fist fight broke out, the father of a Lion's player punched out the father who had been pulled his kid off the scrum. 'That was a bad scene'. It became difficult to run the league."

The league then turned into a combination league between the Bronx and the Hudson River group (Ossining, Dobbs Ferry, Hastings, Tarrytown, and Yonkers) in Westchester County. The Warriors combined with them to play in this league for a couple of years. Jerry would develop two travel teams while playing in Westchester because there were no leagues in the

Bronx. Jerry had a Junior and a Pee-Wee team. The Pee-Wee team ranged in ages of eight through ten and the Juniors ran from eleven years old to thirteen. Jay had conveyed to me that "it was nice to travel to Westchester, I will say that. The kids, as well as the coaches, loved going up there. We used to meet at P.S. 71 we didn't take a bus, the parents drove, everybody would pile into a car and drive up there and of course their fields were much better than our fields at that time. Pelham Bay Park, Rice Stadium were beginning to not only lose its grass but were not well maintained. Before each game we'd have to make a run with bags to pick up the stones on those Bronx fields. But Westchester was beautiful. You'd go up to beautiful green grass and play a game in a nice atmosphere. It was good competition, good clean competition. We enjoyed playing in Westchester quite a bit.". But the era of football was deteriorating and Jerry could see it coming in the early '80's. Teams had started to disappear because the coaches who had organized the teams had moved out of the Bronx and nobody would step up and continue the team. The early '80's was the last heyday of Bronx football.

***

I had wondered, after my kicking days, as a lot of us had, how much out-of-pocket and time Jerry had invested without anyone knowing. Kim Demers, his youngest daughter, gives a little insight from what she recollects as a young girl.

"I think that the time commitment that he had to give to the program in order to keep it running and successful, was time consuming. He was doing it voluntarily and he had very little help. I mean, nobody sees the background, behind the scenes. You know, you just don't show up and put these teams together and show up and play games. There is so much work that goes into this. And, you know, when he wasn't at the field, and he wasn't at work, he was home working on it. He was going around to get sponsors from all the local communities. It's a lot of work. He would go door to door up and down Jarvis Avenue, Middleton Road, Westchester Avenue, Crosby Avenue and all the business from all over the Bronx asking them for money for the program and to support teams. He had no shame doing that for the program. That is where all the connections that he's made over the years came from. How many people love him and rave about him? He would never ask anyone for something for himself. Going around to recruit, putting ads in every school, and talking to the students at the schools, and finding coaches. Working on proposals for money, for funding. It was more than just, I'm done organizing.

Making sure he had enough coaches and assistant coaches for the number of kids he had. Dividing and coming up with all the new teams. You know, doing the draft night with all his coaches. The certifications that you have to have. And funny as this may seem but I have this memory of the house phone, it was constantly ringing."

I interrupted Kim to validate the phone issue. "As a young guy I can remember, I could never get through to your father's phone line. I didn't live far from him, so I would just drive to your house and your mother would greet me with a big smile, 'Yeah, he's in the living room, he's in the dining room, and he's on the phone'."

Kim continued, "He never had, and this is one thing I did resent, in all of my life he never got a second phone line. He never got a separate line for the Warrior program so our home was plastered with phone numbers, schools, school boards, pizzerias, everywhere. And those six-hundred kids that were involved for any given season, let there be a sign of rain the night before, and that phone does not stop. And that's another thing that was funny about my house. My door was always an open door. It was a revolving door. No matter how bad the neighborhood started to get, we never….it was never locked, and people would come in and out, to see him. I never knew who I was going to run into in my own house because there was a constant revolving door of people coming to visit. And 'fuhgeddaboudit' if I tried to go for a walk around the corner or to lunch on Jarvis Avenue with either of them [Jerry and Geri]. You'd want to go to lunch with them but you would be out for hours because everyone would stop and talk to them along Jarvis Avenue. You know that was the running joke, that if we had to go around the corner, we didn't want to go with them because we'd never get back home. But those are all good things. Those are all the good things that I saw growing up. Knowing that my parents were loved."

I recounted a chat I had with her dad. "Your father did say to me, a couple of months ago, when we were in the Crosstown Diner. 'I regret that maybe I should have given more time to my daughters and my family'. But then he said, 'But this is my love, Bobby'."

Kim responded, "I understand it and I think everyone in my family may not have like it at times, but we understood and accepted it. [In regards to my mother] I think they were definitely meant to be, even though his first love was not her, it was the program. She, and maybe she didn't love that idea, but she embraced it because she respected it. She understood. You can't spend that much time doing that much for these many years. You can't be everything to everybody. And I think that and that's what I was trying to say to you, I think that we all understood. I mean, sure we all had our moments where we might have resented the program and resented the fact where we wished he was at our events instead of on the field. And it just didn't stop during football season. It would only be a couple of weeks that he would be available to us. The vacations we had were based on the football season. I'm sure it doesn't help the marriage and the relationship when he's gone six days out of the week, nights, and you know how long he's been doing it. Let's just put it this way, I think this is the honest and the best way to put it, the Warrior program is my father's first love. that's his first priority. I think that's a lot for a woman who's married to a man with four kids to accept in raising those four kids when he's working two jobs, umpiring, and on the field. You know, there was a point in time where the program got so big, he had over six-hundred kids playing and he had to be at practices. I don't know if he had to, but you know my Dad, he insisted on being at the field for every night of practice. Like he had to run practice every night of the week basically because there were so many kids playing, and then there were the games are on the weekends, and he's there for all the games the whole day. So, you know, my mom figured she couldn't beat 'em so she'd join 'em. If my mother didn't do the cheerleading when was she going to see him? She only did it because she had to spend most of her life on the field anyway, and he wasn't home, so she started something to be there with him. And she loved it too. She loved the excitement, of being on the field, being around the kids, and being around the parents. It was something they had in common and that now they could work together, her and my dad. And that's just who he is was. That was his first love and I understood that as I got older. As a kid I loved it, being on the field, growing up at Pelham Bay Park on the football field. You couldn't get better. It was just a great experience. Everybody knew him and my mom. Everybody loved my parents and you felt a great sense of pride and community. And I think that we all appreciated that the program was his love, and even though we weren't happy with it once in a while, that he wasn't always with us, we respected what he was doing, because he is like a second father to so many people. And people have told us that, my whole life I've been hearing it. My whole life. And like I said, we'd go to Jarvis Avenue and you know people would just stop us on a daily basis, talking to him, talking to my mother. Couldn't even get around the corner. So, I grew up seeing that. Seeing the love everyone had for him and my mother, and the appreciation. I also grew up seeing him helping all of these kids. Loving them like they were his own, and giving them what their parents weren't giving them and being there for them. It wasn't abnormal for me to come home to find strangers just hanging out watching TV in my living room. I remember sometimes coming home and kids being at my house because their parents hadn't bothered to pick them up after practice or a game. My dad took them home, and he would feed them. You know, at our house there was never an excess of money, there was no money for the extras. My parents didn't have the money to send me to college, but we always had enough. There was six of us and there were six pork chops bought, maybe even four, and we split them, we made the most of it. But he never had a problem bringing kids home that needed a meal, or needed some guidance, or needed somebody to show them that somebody cared. And I think that was a little unusual. I would come home from somewhere after being out with my friends, and there would be a football player in my room who lived in Manhattan, and their parents didn't come to pick them up. Didn't call. Didn't even look for their own kids. Or at the field with the kids that didn't have money. If there were kids around him with no lunch or money, he would buy them lunch on the football field. If they didn't have food, he would get it for them. And there were kids that would come to practice and not be able to get back home but he would drive them or make sure another coach would. I don't know. I mean, I don't know of many coaches that would go that extra mile, but he really went above and beyond. There were so many instances like these and that's just how I was raised. That was the norm for me. Especially when I was born in '77. I grew up as the program became full blown. It was at its maximum with the kids. We were already at the point where former players now had their sons playing. It was a great experience. I wouldn't trade my parents for anything. To be honest, I don't really think I ever felt neglected. I grew up on the field when I was about three, four years old. That's where I was, right by my mother's and my father's side, on the field. So, to me, that was just normal. The Warrior program, because it took up so much of his time, and it was our whole lives too. That's how we were raised, out on the field with all of these people. That is our family life, that is our home. What I'm saying is that growing up in our home, in that environment taught me the bigger picture. That there is a bigger picture, bigger than just yourself or us, the immediate family. It's the community. You don't just take care of your family. You take care of anyone who needs it. You help others and you do for everyone else and you do what you can. You put other people first. The lessons that they taught me are great valuable lessons. I'm lucky to have had such two strong, goodhearted parents."

I interrupted Kim with a passing thought that she brought forward in her dialog. "We never thought about losing. We never thought about failure. We worked on a process and we succeed. That's what your dad taught all of us. When we're losing, we never thought about 'Oh God, we're gonna lose this game.' No! How do we figure out a way to win? How do we figure out a way to succeed? And that transcends into business. I hate the negative because your dad taught me not to think that way."

Kim moved on in thought. "I always am a positive person. And you know, also was my mother too. Never quit. Never give up. They both shared a lot of the same great qualities."

"To me, it is apropos that they are both named Jerry and Geri. To me, they were one and the same only one's a woman and one's a man," I added.

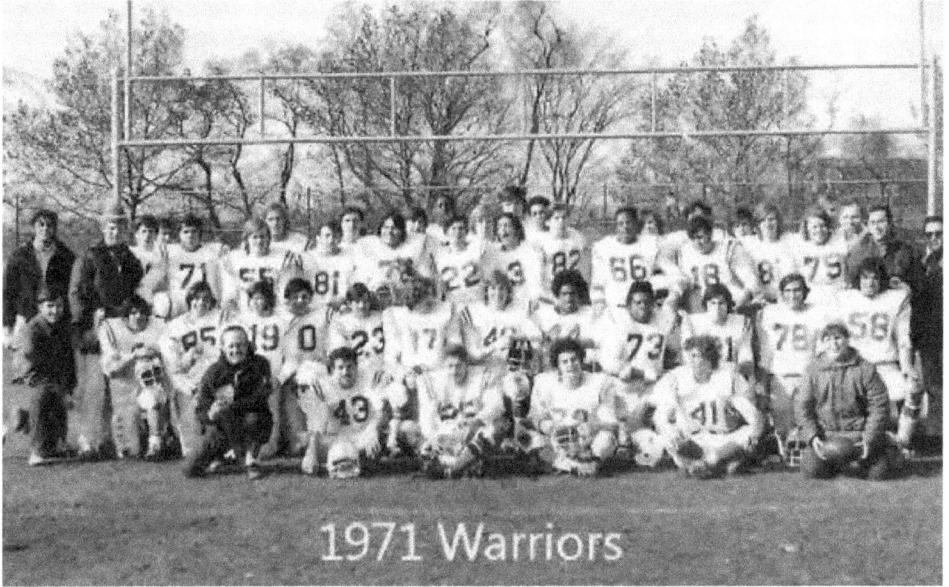
1971 Warriors

Warriors 1971 – B.U.A Divisional & League Championship Team (Undefeated)

WARRIORS

1970 Warriors Awards Dinner

Gary "Gary K" Kouzoujian - Interception

Tony Vastola (red jacket) addressing the offense 1973

Tommy Pryor (#16) following Dougie Williams (#75)

Chapter 8

Youth Football

Warrior Youth Football Organization – Photo Shoot 1999

Warriors Football officially began in 1952 as a club team playing out of East Harlem. Our Founder and current Executive VP Jay "The Chief" Demers was a player on that team. When he moved to the Bronx, the Warriors came with him. He eventually started and coached the Warriors Football Club in various Touch and Tackle leagues very successfully. In 1985, due to growing interest in the program, the Warriors Football Club grew into its own intramural league along with a cheerleader program, totaled over six-hundred participants. Many former player and cheerleaders still come back to support the program in various ways. In 2015, the league officially became the Warriors Football League, Inc and currently has approximately 225 youth and volunteer adult coaches in the program[50].

***

Old coaches don't die and they don't fade away…they keep coaching. In 1985 Jerry would reinvent the Warriors. He would create his grandest venture to date. I'm not sure if he had this in mind back in 1948. Teams were dropping out of leagues in the Bronx. The Bronx was

---

[50] Bronx Warriors Website

down to nobody, so he had to start his own league, an intramural league as he called it. He started that first year with four teams. The next year the turnout was even better as the league doubled in size. He added a new division, a Junior and Pee-Wee division. He had eight teams with four in each division. Gradually it grew to six teams in each division, during the early nineties. There was an older team, you might call them Seniors. Whoever was on the Junior team would eventually move up to the Senior team so there was no draft except for new players. And that system continued for years. All teams were named after former teams from the Bronx (Javelins, Rams, Saints, Navajos, etc.) but they were all Warriors.

I came to visit, maybe in 2001, and went to Lehman High School to catch up with the coach. There were at least a hundred kids practicing on the field. It was the youth football league, the Warrior Organization. I can see all these kids running around.

I asked Jay, "what's going on?"

He tells me, "Well Bobby, this is the Warrior football league".

I said, "Yeah, but they're all wearing different uniforms. That's the Rams, and that's the Javelins, and that's the Saints. And you said the league is the Warriors.", I was so confused. I asked, "Where's my Warrior team".

He replied, "There is no individual Warrior team. The whole thing is the Warriors, Bob! I told them that they are all Warriors. We put Warriors across the front of their jerseys, no matter what team they are on be it the Rams or the Saints, the Navajo's, the Javelins."

I caught on. "Like you honored the whole history of Bronx sandlot football, the original groups. Okay, but I'm not supposed to like the Saints, they were our rivals but now they're Warriors. You can't do this Jerry. It's like I have to root for the Russian hockey players on the Rangers that as a kid I was taught to hate in the '50s and the '60s. Not cool."

After practice, I went with Jerry to his place and listened intently as he ran through the beginnings of the intramural program.

"Bobby, all of our games are played at Rice Stadium which is much more convenient than traveling for half of your games especially if you were going to Brooklyn or Queens. There were even games that we went out to Staten Island for so it was good to be able to play in the community. We called it the Community Football league. We brought back some of the heads of

166

the programs like Eddie Stack of the Rams, Sal Catalano of the Saints, and Eddie Esposito of the Javelins. Mike Crescenzo, God bless him, he was really the one that helped us the most. He introduced me to Senator John Calandra who gave us our first gift of five-thousand dollars to get equipment for the teams. After that, once we were on the list of appropriations and we stayed on that list so that we got funding each year to continue the intramural program. The biggest help that I got in running the intramural program came from a gentleman in The Bronx who had three boys who all played in the program. His name is Ritchie Farino and he was my right-hand man for many years until he decided to run the hockey program, a roller hockey program at Waterbury playground which I had also started. We would play football up until December and as soon as the football season was over, we'd go and start a roller hockey season. Shoveling the snow and at that time there was no fencing around it, it was just a plain asphalt area. But at that time, I was high enough in the park system to get the commissioner of parks and recreation to have the whole area resurfaced so that helped quite a bit. But as the football program grew and grew to maybe three hundred kids and with roller hockey program also getting more kids, Ritchie decided that he would leave the football program and run the hockey program starting in October rather than in December. The help that Ritchie gave me was great and he had a station wagon (chuckles). He used to pick me up and we'd put all the equipment into his vehicle. At that time, we did not have a shed by the field to store our equipment. Your car was your storage area so whatever you needed, tackling dummies, blocking shields and first down markers, cones, or yard markers, had to go in the car. Ritchie was great, we did the whole program together. The program was a lot of fun, less competitive but I don't think the kids knew the difference since they haven't played travel ball before. Occasionally we would have a travel team and one year we had a travel team that won the City. But the trouble with travel teams in the intramural program is that it took away your best coaches, took away your best players so that they were hardly noticeable as part of the organization until the end of the season when they attended the awards program. We established a good relationship with Villa Barone (catering hall) for thirty years or so. We would hold our awards party at the Villa Barone each year. They became a sponsor of the league along with key sponsors that were with us since 1985 such as Giordano's Funeral Home, McNulty's Funeral Home whose son and grandson played on the Warriors, and they still sponsor us to this day. O'Connor Carpets which is a carpet place on Tremont Avenue in The Bronx whose owner's son played with us and he now runs the business and still sponsors us.

Schuyler Hill Funeral Home on Tremont Avenue under Jim McQuade and Ralph Balsamo whose son again played with us. They sponsored the football program also up until just recently. Starting the intramural program and continuing it up to this time was always kind of a little bit like work. What I love to do is coach because the relationship between a player and his coach or the player and his fellow players, well there is nothing like it in the world except the combat troops who rely on each other for their very lives. Football is very much like a combat situation and you get to feel the same way about the people you command and the people you work with and the people you play with. So, coaching was the one thing I loved the most and every now and then in the intramural program I was able to step down and coach a team. One year we had a thirteen to fifteen-year-old team that's how well we were doing with players at that time and I coached one of those teams. The rest of the time we were playing intramural ball with eight teams. Sooner or later we added another division, a mite division so we had three divisions and began playing games at Lehman High School. At the time Lehman High School was not so well secured as it is now and we were free to go in there for the last thirty-five years or so. In the beginning, the head of Lehman football team gave us just about whatever we needed. There were no permits required, we used the gyms when we needed them and they were glad to have somebody organized using their facility from the community rather than some group that might cause some damage to the place so Lehman was a big, big part of our Warrior organization. In 1989 we started another phase of the program called flag football. It came about because of a parent, that was a friend of a friend, who came to us and wanted to know what we could do to get his son, who was only six years old, involved in sports so we started flag football, We did it in coordination with the Parks Department which I was still Chief of Recreation in the Bronx and the PAL and the Warriors, it was a triumvirate relationship. This is where we first met Jimmy Pellicone, whose son played in the flag program and he coached. Jimmy later went on to be an administrator with us for twenty-six years now. Shortly thereafter in the tackle program, we met another gentleman that became an administrator, Dennis Kandell whose been my right-hand man. I have a lot of right hands. He has served twenty-six years. They're both still out there helping the current Warrior program in 2015. The flag program was very successful. A lot of kids didn't quite know what they were doing and we kept it that way just so that they could go out and have fun. I think they enjoyed picking grass and flowers just about as much as playing football. But they were cute, the parents loved it, they had good rapport amongst the group.

Some of them went on, after their flag career which was only for six and seven-year old's, at the time, but then it went up to eight-year old's. Most of the kids who turned eight wanted to play tackle football so it eventually it came back down to what it is now, five, six, and seven-year old. The program continued to grow through the eighties and nineties but I think that after about the year 2000, the numbers started to diminish. We went from four teams in the mite division, six teams in junior peewee and six teams in pewee to now four teams in the peewee and four teams in junior peewee so it has decreased and is continuing to do so. We'll see what happens in 2015. The kids today have many more things to do, as you know, like video games, electronics, it's all about fantasy sports right now and other sports that came into play primarily soccer, As the neighborhoods changed the desire for football decreased. Concussions are another issue. The threat of concussions as raised by some of the politicians also decreased the numbers. I'm sure that in the sixty-four years of the Warriors, have I ever (emphatic and proud) recall a concussion on any player under fourteen. I do recall a couple of older teams but not any of the younger kids. Our Assemblyman, Mike Benedetto has proposed a bill in the Senate and in the assembly to ban all football below the ages of fourteen in the whole state of New York. He has not been successful and it's unlikely that he'll be successful but you never know. Below is a copy of a letter Jerry sent to the editor of the Bronx Times Reporter back on November 24, 2005.

4

BRONX TIMES REPORTER   NOVEMBER 24, 2005

letters to the editor

Mayor's program reduces youth funding

Dear editor,

I read with amusement the story in the November 10 issue of the *Bronx Times Reporter* regarding the millions of dollars the mayor's Out of School Time program has set aside for after school activities.

Your correspondent probably didn't know that much of this money was secured by cutting off previously funded volunteer groups such as the Service Alliance for Youth, which has assisted local organizations such as the Warriors Flag and Tackle program, the Waterbury Roller Hockey League, the Pelham Bay Belles Softball League, Girl and Boy Scout units, the Warrior Cheerleaders, the Pelham Bay Little League, the Bronx Highlander Baseball Academy, Condors Baseball, the St. Theresa After School Center and the Warriors Football League Winter Program.

The Service Alliance for Youth was excluded from funding after 20 years (as were similar groups in the five boroughs) due to a rule change which required that all activities take place Monday through Friday from 3 to 6 p.m. and 8 a.m. to 6 p.m. during the summer. No weekends, no evenings when volunteers are available.

The millions of dollars now go to salaried groups such as the PAL, Pathways for Youth, Gloria Wise Center, etc.

Guess who will pay for this reduced funding to volunteer groups? Right! The participants.

We can only hope that our newly elected borough and community officials will come up with some innovative ways to help us regain our funding.

Jerry Demers, President
Service Alliance for Youth

I caught up with Rich Farino to get his history on the beginnings of what I have always referred to as the Warriors Youth Football League.

"Bob, I met Jay in August on 1985 on a field, when my oldest boy was ten and tried out for the team in what he called "The Community Youth Football League". They didn't call it the Warriors that first year. but we soon learned that it was the Warriors. I didn't know the man until apparently, he had gone to P.S. 71 and made his speech to try and get kids to join the league. My son told me about it. He wanted to try it so we went down to the field. I sat down in the old bleachers at Rice Stadium. Jay had all his assistants out on the field. You know a couple of guys he had from his travel team in the past years. This one guy, I think his name was Steve Fabrizzi and another ex-player were two mainstays in the program. They were out there putting the kids through their drills. My son had never participated in contact sports. Jay put him against one of his older kids. This kid was the biggest guy out there. My son immediately got knocked on his butt. Jay, as I was soon to learn that this would be his way, encouraged my boy to get up and try again. He got right back up as Jay encouraged him to keep going and you know, he did. My little chubby ten-year-old liked it. In short, that was Jay, encouraging the children to try their best, always. I came home and found Jay's street address and went over to his place to pay him. I sat down with him for a couple of minutes and he takes out this glossy envelope with an eight by ten piece of paper in it. He pulls it out and writes my son's name on there and writes the amount of money I give him and he somehow finds a pair of pants to give my son, we try on a helmet and we go home. This was the league. We wound up with seventy-five kids and four teams. That was the very first year. That first year of the league I started out as a sideline parent, but when Jay learned I had three boys and their ages he did a quick calculation and decreed that I would spend at least twelve years with him. As the year went on, because of my personality, I would just walk out on the field and ask the coach questions and if I could help them. You know, at first everyone was just putting me off but after a while, one of the coaches, Steve Fabrizzi could see that I was a little flakey and said, 'Okay, just hold the shields and let the kids hit you'. And then you know, I weaseled my way on to the field. By the end of the year, I was helping them coach one of the teams. My son played on a team coached by one of Jay's ex-players, Steve Fabrizzi, who was a former standout wide receiver for Jay's travel team and became a coach as he graduated from playing. Talking to Steve was like talking to Jay as Jay's philosophy of the game was handed down to this young man. During that first year, I was always on the field listening to Steve and

Jay so that I could get a feel for what they expected of everyone. That first year there were four teams, all had Warriors written across their jerseys, but with the four different colors the teams were named after old Bronx teams of the fifties, sixties, and the seventies: The Javelins, the Rams, the Saints coached by Ricky Demers and the Navajos. Jay lived three blocks from me in Pelham Bay and as the year progressed, I was a frequent visitor at his house, where I met his wife Geri and his children. The league was also a family affair for Jay as his wife coached a cheerleader squad and his son, Ricky, coached in the new-found league. It was at Jays' house where I started to take an interest in the way he was handling the paperwork for the league. Actually, he pulled out that same eight by eleven piece of paper with seventy-five names on it in a glassine envelope written in pencil with plenty of eraser marks on it. A league record at its best. I was more interested in the organization of the league than I was of the coaching aspect and I thought there should have been a better way. I told him that I would help him with the paperwork if he wanted. Oh, he took that hook, line, and sinker. I can't tell you how I went from somebody that got involved to see my kid play to someone who never saw their kid because I was so involved. It was then with Jay's permission that I had to reinvent the administration end of the game. We got along remarkably well right away. I listened to him and learned his way of thinking when it came to the group. He used to say to me all the time, 'As a leader of a group if all your teams come back feeling like they're number one, then you're successful. It's been a great year'. So, what he's talking about is fairness. He also told me "You treat these kids with fairness because they're not stupid and they are going to understand it when they get older. You know when you treat a kid fair, they understand, and they keep coming back. Our kids came back every year you know, and I think in the football league we had like a thirty percent turnover. I think it was mostly because kids would age out. And treat the coaches like men. Don't degrade anybody'. He used that first season to hone a set of rules for the players and coaches to abide by. The second year, we had a better registration and the league expanded from four teams in one division to two divisions with four teams in each. We had eight to ten-year old's in one division and twelve and thirteen-year old's in the other. What Jay decided to do was take a head coach and give him two teams, one in each division. He was thinking of the future. This way the kids would grow up with the same coach and would be able to understand something by the time he became eleven or twelve. The younger division was meant to be feeder-system for his thirteen and older teams. So that was the second year. As I said, I started

171

getting involved and I started doing the paperwork. I asked if I could look at that glossy envelope that Jay had so I could get an idea of what he wanted to know in his records and he couldn't find it. He lost it, so I had to make up a whole administrative process and as far as I know, they are still using some of it today. I wound up getting index cards and putting the kid's names on it and putting it in a box in alphabetical order. I had at that time a Commodore 64, an eight-bit home computer with a dot-matrix printer. A friend of mine gave me a database program. It was interesting. You could put all this information in but to get the information out, it took forever. It didn't show up on the screen. You'd press the button and your dot-matrix printer would go dot, dot, dot, dot, dot, it took forever. I told Jay that I was gonna print out a listing of one hundred twenty kids, but I said to him, 'Let's go for coffee because by the time we come back it might be done'. It was a great deal though because I was able to tell how many kids came from a particular zip code, how many kids were eleven, twelve, thirteen, what teams they were on and he was pretty appreciative of the work that I put into it."

"Jay set guidelines regarding age and weight to keep as much as possible an even keel with the team members. He insisted that the players should be almost equal in weight so that no one would get hurt by running into or getting hit by heavier kids. Safety was a way of life for us all. He also instituted a fairness rule which stated that all players must play either offense or defense for the first half of the game. We had many team names but collectively maintained that every player was a Warrior. He always addressed the group at large as Warriors. He made everyone, from the players to the coaches and parents feel as though they were part of the Warrior Family. During those early years, Jay tried to be with the group at least three times a week. Practice at the field in Pelham Bay Park was from six to dusk. At first, he would have everyone practice fundamentals in age groups, then by Labor Day, he would have a draft with the coaches to fill the teams. The children would come back to the same team, age permitting, and then another draft complete the rosters and fill the void of those who became too old for their teams. Those drafts alone were always a bonding rite for the coaches who also were called Warrior coaches as opposed to their team names. When daylight savings time ended and it got dark early, we moved into a gym at Lehman High School two nights a week for each division. We utilized two full gyms, separated into two gyms each, for the teams to have a private practice. He always insisted that fairness was number one priority. To that end, he would never allow a team to practice on its own. We kept an eye out for overzealous coaches and kept them in

172

check. He allowed me to not only administrate the league but to also coach. Jay handpicked all his coaches. His idea was if a father could be on the sideline for a year and not cause trouble, he might be worthy of being associated with the Warriors. Tackle was his love, but in 1989, with a small grant from the Police Athletic League, he started a flag football program for six to eight-year old's. At that point, we were over four hundred children in the program and still expanding. The reason was, and Jay will lovingly admit, was because I took all the pressure off of him by doing all the paperwork so that he could be free to recruit new players by making trips to the schools and talking to groups of children. He did it well. By the summer of '91, we had six hundred children involved in tackle, flag, and cheerleading. So well in fact that I had to recruit three administrators to do my work, of course, the cheerleaders were separate, run by his wife, Geri, and a slew of coaches. In '89, budget cuts by the Parks Department almost ended the roller hockey league, but with Jay's permission I stepped in and administrated that program. Just as I was taught in the Warrior program, fairness to the children will create a strong playing league. Being a disciple of Jay, the way I treated the children rolled over from the football to the hockey program. I am proud to say that I took the hockey from sixty players the first year to, by the time the Rangers won the cup in '94, to three hundred and sixty kids on roller skates with no rink, just a playground and two schoolyards with painted lines, all having a blast. Of course, the added work on my time caused me to bow out of the football program."

"Being a head of an organization and not just a team, as I soon learned, was something not new to Jerry. Lucky for us his position in the parks department afforded him the time to concentrate on organizing the group. As time went on and the league got bigger, we had to kind of come to some decisions. The one thing he wanted to do was get some sponsors for the teams. I had a bench in my basement and one of those picnic tables that we took in for the winter and me, Jay, and Robert Griffin. Robert was a salesman in his life. He's the guy that, when we were trying to figure out, how are we going put the sponsor's name on the back of the jersey. How much do we want to charge them? Jay and I thought, 'A hundred bucks, or two hundred'. Bobby was told us, 'No let's go for a thousand'. Yeah, so we asked for twenty-five hundred dollars and don't you know we got it. We would meet once a week and we would sit down there for hours and argue about who's going to pay for what and who's going to do it and how much money we're going to charge people, this and that. Jerry, in his excitement, yells out 'I don't have to charge the kids any money because I have money to pay for the uniforms'. That is how I learned that he had received a five-thousand-dollar grant from then State Senator John Calandra, in our first year, which community activist Mike Crescenzo, who was Jays' biggest supporter in those early days, had arranged. 'but', as he continued, 'if I hand out free jerseys then they will just take the jersey and go home and not have any reason to come back, but if I charge the parents money, the parents will make them come back'. So that's what we did. We came up with a figure. I think it was fifty dollars that first year. We gave the kid a jersey and we lent them the helmet and the pants. If they couldn't afford shoulder pads, we would try to help find some for them. Basically, they had to buy shoulder pads, a cup, and the mouth guard. Everything else we tried to give them. Between the grant and sponsorship money we were getting in the beginning, it all worked out. That second year Jay came up with an idea to raise money. He got an advertisement poster. He told us to go out and get sponsors to advertise on the posters and if you bring me back a thousand dollars' worth of sponsors' money, I'll give you this gear, shirts, pants, whatever, or a paid-in-full ski weekend. Only two of us took advantage of it. My wife and I and another person got ski weekends out of it."

"Those ski weekends were fun. We would pull out from Jay's house. Two busses going on a ski weekend with whoever else would drive up. I'll tell you, the first one, I can't remember the name of the place we went to, but they had a bar and they had a swing at the end of the bar with a female manikin and you can't imagine what went on with those guys with the drinks in them. I went up there probably February of eighty-seven. I have my three boys. My youngest was four at that time, maybe going on five. I was a poker player at that time, so we had a group that would sit down a play poker. You know we would have quarters on the table and one of the fathers at the table thought my kid was cute, so every time my kid would come by the table, he would give my kid a quarter, so of course, my kid kept coming by the table. I remember the time some father got drunk and started abusing his wife. It got bad enough that the daughter got nervous and ran out of the room to get one of the coaches. We were all at the bar. One of the coaches ran in first, tried to stop this guy and received a punch in the head in return. By now we're all coming in but it was Eddie Esposito who grabs this guy, looks him square in the eye and states, 'Now you die'. Eddie punched him in the head only to be tossed out of the room by Big Alfred. Big Alfred was one of the coaches. They call him Big Alfred for good reason. Al slams the door shut and all we hear is the sound of someone being thrown around into furniture and walls followed by a thud and then silence. Big Alfred came out of the room unscathed. At some time during the night, the guy disappeared. He walked over five miles, in the snow to get to the village, got on the next horse and got the heck out of dodge. We never saw this guy again. 'Now you die' became one of the weekend's slogans. We put it on t-shirts. One of the places we went to, we were asked to not come back, and it was a nice place. Apparently, we went up there and they also had a group of Girl Scouts and that didn't mix too well. Especially with the food fight in the cafeteria. You know these things happen."

"My relationship with Jay was such that I started doing all his paperwork. He didn't have to worry about who was on what team, who was registered, who paid, who had any equipment. All he had to do was think of ways to make things better. I don't think people realized it, Jay's name was on the league, but I ran a lot of it. I told the kids what to do, I told the coaches what to do, I made sure they had everything. I mean to the point that if the coaches needed whistles, I made sure they had them. If the coach needed bags, I made sure they had them, footballs, everybody had them. I drove a bucket truck for the phone company and I will tell you in the back of the bucket truck there where usually about fifteen boxes of jerseys. I drove a 1967 Plymouth Volare station wagon, we had it for years, and it was a workhorse. Believe me, we put so much stuff in it. My garage was full of old trophies, old posters, equipment, you name it, it was there. I gave up over time at my job to be with this group. I spent untold hours at night on the computer when we finally got the regular PS1 computers, everything became different. I used to call Mike Pisaniello up all the time and ask him questions. I would send him a copy of the league and he would send it back and we would talk about that all the time. Mike was my sanity guy. He helped me stay straight. We would come to the same conclusion, but I was rash, and I would jump to it and Mike was calm. He would think about it and then come to his conclusion. That's how he is. He's thoughtful and calm. Jay paid me the ultimate compliment. One day when we were sitting down a couple of years ago and we were talking. He said the worst thing he ever did was start the roller hockey league because it took me away from football. You know, that was just great. I was his left hand."

"He would sit in his office because he worked for the Parks Department at the time and he would get us all the permits. He would figure out where to get all the equipment from and stuff like that. Speaking of equipment, we didn't have the room for it in the park like they do now. We wound up using my house and my station wagon to go to the field with fifteen, twenty, sometimes thirty-five helmets crammed into the station wagon. Then sit there and try to fit kids and keep up with the paperwork and it was always a mob scene. Jerry used to laugh at me, but it worked out for the best. Everybody got taken care of. If the kid's helmet didn't fit, they could come back and try another one. At that point, we were probably up to about one-hundred-fifty to one-hundred-sixty kids. As one, we would practice three times a week before the season started at the Rice Stadium. At first, what he would do was have them go by age group and then we would have what we called the friendly draft. I'd have all the kid's names all separated into age and divisions. Then we would sit down, and I would give all the coaches a piece of paper and a pencil. Jay would have all the names written on the board and we would actually have a football draft where you would pick first, second, third and fourth. For example, if you had the fourth pick in the first round, then in the second round you went third and you moved up each round. It was our time to have fun as the coaching staff. Of course, sometimes we would disparage some of the children. Sometimes the children disparaged us. Of course, there were the young guys at the beginning of the draft where we didn't know the players, their abilities or what they could do. Outside of the fact that I had written down information such as their forty-yard dash, what the coaches thought of them on the field with a rating of one to three. You know if they were tough or weak. You know it was just fun. One of the coaches always drafted a boy if his name ended in a vowel. After the draft, we would go into daylight savings time and what we would do is practice twice a week in the gym at Leman Highschool and then we would have the games on a Saturday. While we were sitting in the gym watching the kids run back and forth, Jay and I would point at a kid and say, "What's his name?" If we didn't know, we would ask him. Eventually, we would learn all of the kid's names. The only reason I would know the kid's names was because I would write them down on an index card and then type them into the computer and write them down again. There were a lot of things that Jay wanted to sell, particularly clothing with the Warriors name on it. I didn't want to kill the kids with money so we would sell it just a little bit above cost so that we could recover our cost and give them a sense of identity. All the kids want to belong to something and he knew this so what we would do is if we sold t-shirts and they cost three-dollars and fifty-cents, we would sell them for five dollars. If the sweat pants cost us seven-dollar and fifty-cents, maybe we would get a ten-dollar bill out of it. Not only did we sell the stuff but I insisted that we give the coaches stuff. Just to make them feel like a part of the organization. I used to give out the jerseys and Jay used to collect all the fees. In other words, he collected the deposit to join and the rest of the fees as we gave the jerseys out. In the beginning, a coach might come up ten dollars short because he wasn't paying attention and wasn't doing the math right, so he would have to reach into his pocket. The next year, I took that all away from them. I told them, 'You know you guys don't have to do anything. I'll take care of the money. I don't want you to feel obligated if you are shorted.' Jay agreed with me and we did that. We went from two-hundred to two-hundred-fifty kids in 1987. When we had the travel team, my son became thirteen years old in 1988. He was on the travel team, so what we would do is, we would go up to these places like Yonkers and play these games. After the games I let them all come back to my house. My poor wife, God rest her soul, would make the macaroni. She would make five pounds of pasta and all the meat and stuff and we would all gather around the house and eat. We had more people eating than I coached. That was the last time we did that in a season. I couldn't afford it. Now we went from two-hundred-fifty kits kids to where we are pushing three-hundred. 1989 comes along and Jay says that we got a little money from the PAL, so we are going to start a flag football league. I looked at Jay and I said, "You know what Jay? I'm already doing paperwork for three-hundred kids. I don't think I want to do the paperwork for seventy more kids. He said, 'Okay, I'll do it myself.' That was interesting. He split the kids up himself and put them all on to teams and you know, it worked out good for a year. Now the following year we're up to four-hundred kids playing tackle, flag, and cheerleaders and I just can't do all the paperwork anymore myself. It was just getting ridiculous because not only am I doing the paperwork, I'm selling t-shirts and taking orders for jackets and stuff like that. I grabbed Mike Pisaniello and Dennis Kandell and Jimmy Pellicone and said, 'How would you guys like to be administrators?' and that was fine for about three weeks. They were stepping on each other's foot all the time and they said, 'Richie we can't do this.' And I said, 'I'll tell you what, Dennis you do the flag football, Mike you do the Pewee and Jimmy you do the Juniors.' And everybody was happy to have their own divisions and I was happy because I was starting to get away from that. I was starting to do a roller hockey program. I had my kids playing in that too. The roller hockey started with the Parks Department. Jay started that as a Parks Department thing and then when the Parks Department went into a fiscal crisis, they had to pull all of their people away from that, so I had to step in and take over. I wound up doing the Waterbury hockey league while they were still doing the football. I did that until probably '92 and I helped Jay by not letting him worry about the little things. By just letting him do the big things like recruiting and things like that. We had actually gotten the organization up to six-hundred kids or something like that. Standing at Rice Stadium field on a Saturday in August was somewhat ridiculous but it was really something to see, all those kids coming out and running around. After every warm up, we would pull some kids out and mess around with them or ask them stupid questions, we had fun."

"As a leader of the roller hockey, if the kids had a scheduling conflict and it was with football, I made sure the kids went to their football games first because the season was short. You know they only had ten games. I mean let them do that. I wish I had the respect like that from the little leagues because my kids would have to miss a game for practice with another sport or team and they wouldn't be able to play. Basically, through the nineties, I gave up the football to concentrate on the hockey and then in 2000 I gave up the hockey because it was wearing me out. I was fifty-two years old at that time. I actually I went back to the football and helped with it, but my head wasn't in it, so I left."

"A couple years later he asked me to do a little something but less than what I used to do. By 2014 I was just standing around the field, trying to get the parents to cooperate. They would pitch a fit about a penalty flag or something like that and that was it. I was done after that. I was doing baseball in the summer. In fall I was doing football and then during winter, I was doing roller hockey. There were two years I didn't see my wife for a single Saturday. One day she looks at me and says, 'That's enough'. Baseball was the first to go, and then football had to go because I was just too involved with the hockey. I wondered what I was doing at one point. It was just too much. You know it kept me away from the wife and it kept me away from the kids. But it was fun. I'll tell you, we wouldn't have done it unless we enjoyed it."

"What I found out and I told Jay, and you would understand this, the coaching staff and the players was not like what he had at P.S. 106. 106 was very personal to him with his twenty, thirty kids or whatever it was. Now he's the leader so he didn't have the interaction with the kids that he used to have, but he was still a father figure to some kids. He had a quarterback's club and he would take all the quarterbacks and hang out with them afterward and teach them about the game. Even some of the coaches. We had a lot of single parents. Usually, the mothers bringing their kids to the field and hoping we would discipline them and basically, we did. You know it's a team sport. It's not baseball where you have nine individuals. It's different and I always said that. I did baseball, I did hockey and the most enjoyment I got was going into a huddle with eleven nine-year old's and telling them what to do, breaking that huddle and watching them actually do it. It's the most satisfying thing in the world to me. It's an amazing sport. As a matter of fact, when Dennis Kandell's wife brought their kid in, he was only fifty-five pounds so we sent him home. We didn't want him to get hurt. She gave me and Jerry hell, wanting her son to play. So, she sends her brother over and we said the same thing. We said, 'Look we don't want the kid to get hurt'. Then Dennis showed up and used his charms on Jay and Jay relented because I think that Jay got tired of arguing with the family."

"What's happened today with the advent of the computer, the games and all the nonsense with the mothers hearing about concussion issues has changed everything in youth football. But when I first met Jay back in 1985 and he told me that I would be with him for twelve years he was right, and I did. He taught me, as a leader of a group, how to act. If you ask around about the roller hockey program about how successful it was, you would know he taught me well. I had no problems with coaches. I had no problems with kids. Like him, I hand-picked everybody. If you wanted to be a coach, you had to come through me first. You couldn't just walk on to the field. We would be running drills and you would see a guy come walking up to Jay saying, 'Yeah, I used to play football' with a beer in his hand, in a group full of kids. Jay would say, 'Okay, yeah. We'll let you know'. Just to get rid of him. Maybe you should talk to Dennis Kandell and get his perspective."

Pelham Bay Park is the largest municipal park in New York City with over almost twenty-eight-hundred acres is more than three times the size of Central Park. The park was created in 1888[51]. In the early 1920s. Rice Stadium, situated with Pelham Bay Park, was built with the aid of a $1M grant from Julia Rice, the widow of musician, lawyer, publisher, chess expert, and submarine pioneer, Isaac Leopold Rice[52]. In 1989 Rice Stadium succumbed to a major renovation. The statue of American Boy, installed in the Rice Stadium grandstand in 1932, was removed and found its new home in a dumpster, awaiting its new residence at a local dump site. Word got around to Mike Crescenzo who was a community activist, known as the "Mayor of Pelham Bay" and worked his political magic and rescued the "poor boy". *American Boy* was transported to its new location in between Pelham Bay Park's tennis courts and running track,

---

[51] www.nycgovparks.org/parks/pelham-bay-park/history
[52] forgotten-ny.com/2010/07/pelham-bay-bronx/

opposite from the bleachers. The colossal sculpture now sits atop a new pedestal surrounded by pipe rail fencing, shrubs, and grass-filled terracing. A commemorative bronze plaque explains how the sculpture was intended to reflect an ideal of youth and contains the original plaque's inscription. It was restored in 2002 and reinstalled in 2004 by the Parks Department[53].

I had taken the time, while I was in New York for a few days in September of 2015, to attended another Warrior afternoon at Rice Stadium. I sat in the bleachers, which were no longer concrete steps, but actually, an aluminum grandstand about fifteen rows. I was amazed at the activity going on all about me. About two-hundred players were involved in some form of football. On the field was a tackle game, the players were in the Junior division, complete with referees and coaches on the playing field. At the far end, the older boys were going through their drills in full equipment. Behind the stands were the Pee-Wees engaged in a flag football match. At the corner of the endzone, an EMT ambulance sat as a precaution. Many parents were in attendance encouraging their favorite player. A food truck held its ground in the parking lot. The park was vibrant. The tennis courts were being utilized. A group of eight athletes, led by a trainer were working on strength and conditioning at the new Adult Fitness Area. The outdoor fitness area's equipment included a sit-up bench, a parallel bar, a dip bench and mechanisms for chest presses, lateral pull-downs, vertical presses, upright cycles, chin-ups, leg extensions, and push-ups. Joggers and sprinters were running on the refurbished quarter-mile Mondo track, a synthetic surface. Far from the football field, near the playground, a soccer game was in full force. There was even a fenced off area for dog-lovers and their best friends. I was amazed at the cleanup this park had undergone.

I spotted Jerry and Dennis and went over to where they were stationed, sitting around a folding table. Jeff Ortiz was nearby assisting. I gave my hellos and hugs to all. I quickly whisked away Dennis, with the Coach's permission of course, so that we could talk without disruption. We sat in a big shed that housed equipment and paraphernalia.

"Dennis, you started telling me last night how you started with all this. You were talking about your kid."

---

[53] forgotten-ny.com/2010/07/pelham-bay-bronx/

Dennis went into full remembrance. "My son, Chris, and I started back in 1986 when he was eight-years-old. Today he is thirty-six. He was playing and I was on the sideline. I saw from the sidelines that the administrators were needing some assistance, so I jumped in and offered my services. This is now my twenty-seventh season. I saw what Jay was presenting, a sports package that worked for our community, for kids in our community. It just made me want to be more involved. When I first started with tackle, I want to believe there were six teams in each division and then we added on a seven and eight-year-old mite division tackle program. Don't quote me on that. You can get that from Jay. The reasoning behind my motivation to do this, it all stems from when I was growing up and my father was a community person where we lived, upstate for the summers. How he got involved with youth softball, swimming, barbeques for adults, and I think I took after his legacy. He passed away thirty-some-odd years ago. Jay, with his demeanor and the way he handled everything, it seemed like I gained another father. I was able to talk to him about things, not having a father at that young age of my life. I just came and Jay was that person that I looked up to and I was able to ask for guidance. He became my mentor and my best friend. I worked with children for many years for the New York City Housing Authority and I worked with seniors. Jay could always steer me in the right direction when needed. What especially made me take to Jay was his calm disposition. Watching him working with children, giving back something to them, guiding them and teaching them. Offering guidance through school. Always giving them the motivation to stay in school, do your best. As a leader, he is also teaching these kids to lead. We have our young players, kids who played for us for many years, coming back to us as they get a little older. Now they are part of our organization, either refereeing, and coaching. We have their kids playing, so it is not a short-term relationship that any one of these guys has with Jay. It's not some guy walking onto the field and telling us that he wants to coach. They have been there before. Their children are coming to play. All of what Jay does as such a positive role model to all these people, and there are thousands of kids that have been through this program."

"So, you've been through this program through thick and thin. You've seen it flourish. You've seen it dwindle. Am I correct in that?" I asked.

Without hesitation, Dennis shot back. "Yeah. One-hundred percent correct. I saw where we had over five-hundred kids participating in the program and we added the Warrior Cheerleaders. And I saw our ups and I saw our downs, and now I see it starting to build back up, and that's because the unit stays together. The people who have been here. And a new fellow, Joe DeSimone, who coached for us. His kids play for us. His daughter cheer for us. He took over this program now with the support and backing of the administrator (Jerry) that he has, and is bringing it to the next level, and rebuilding a program that will…I can't see it ever dying. Never see it dying as long as we are all here and alive. Passing it on. The baton gets passed on. In this case, the football gets passed on. And everybody here is a volunteer. They put in their time. There are no paychecks around here. This is all work from the heart. And we see if someone doesn't have that heart, we kindly tell them, 'Thank you, but no thank you'. My involvement, my time in this program is never-ending. I do it twelve months out of the year. I go from registration startup to practices on the field, to the program that we do in between registration when the season is starting. I prepare for the awards ceremony that we have in February. We do a winter program in January, a sports program for our kids and the community kids. We even do it in a high school, and that's two nights a week, an hour and a half for kids. It's two hours for the administrators that do it. So, all total, I'm a twenty-four/seven-person for The Warriors. It's a full-time job. If Jay calls, Joe calls, we're there! It's going, practicing, and I'm the administrator of the flag football program, I'm also the administrator for the whole entire program. It just doesn't stop when I finish flag and go home at seven o'clock. It doesn't work that way. It could be ten o'clock at night. It could be ten-thirty. It's a love that if you haven't ever experienced love, you don't know what I'm talking about, but for me, this is family. Just like my own family, you have to always give. And that's what I do for Jay. When Jay leaves this program, I'm still there, but I am not getting any younger. I hope to pass the baton on to someone who has the self-motivation to keep something that is very good for a community, to continue it. We want them to have fun, yet educate and teach them sportsmanship because that's what it's about. We're playing within ourselves. We're a league within ourselves. Once in a while, we will play an outside team for what we call the 'Friendship Bowl', to take our kids to make friends with another group of kids. But we are all Warriors. They get the same trophies. They share in the same parties. And out of the group of kids that I've seen, there are groups that remain friends forever. Like your group with Joe Regina, Jackie Cawley, John Macchiaroli, Tommy McGurl, Joe Reich and you. I couldn't believe what Joe Regina put together with your monthly huddle meetings. You could see the quality of the guys that sit and come to that dinner. I was there one time for Jay's birthday. They had a cake. I came down and I saw all these guys from your group and the P.S. 106 group."

"We here now, we have a variety of people from different communities coming to us now. It's not just a Throggs Neck-Pelham Bay organization. This is an entire city organization because we never turn a kid away that comes from Queens. We won't turn a kid away that comes from Yonkers. And that's a good part of it because besides the kids playing together, they're seeing different cultures, different upbringings. That helps every child out. It helps the inner-city kids and it helps the kids that come from middle class. And no matter if you have it or you don't, we build character into a person. We build responsibility. Everything that our kids experience in the Warrior organization is mostly a positive example for these kids and hopefully, they will take it with them to where ever they go in life. That is the important factor. When people hear 'you played for the Warriors' they know your education was perfect. The education that we give here is perfect, and they come out with some respect. We don't get all of the kids. You always have those few that go astray, but we try our damnedest to get it done. We try to keep those kids altogether. I always give back in life. God gave me a chance. I had three heart attacks in my sixty-three years and I've got diabetes. Jay has had the same, heart attacks and diabetes. I was with him when he had his heart attack after dinner. Our other administrator, Jimmy, heart attack and diabetes, so I guess that's just something you have to have to be an administrator of this organization. You need to have a heart attack or diabetes to be a part of this organization."

We shared the dark humor with a laugh.

Dennis went on. "We have to keep going in life and this is what keeps me going. My family understands it. My whole family were Warriors. My son, Chris, my daughter, Dawn was a cheerleader, my granddaughter, Destiny was a cheerleader, my wife, Phyllis was a cheerleading coach along with Jay's wife, Geri. My daughter was six-years-old. My kids are thirteen months apart. My daughter came in, I'm gonna say, she was probably around six or seven. Geri, almost twenty-five years later, terminated the program, and then she passed away. She didn't want anyone carrying on her legacy of the program, even though there were people offering, and you have to respect her for that. She did good for the community, good for the organization, and good for Jay. She was his backbone. It's the organization, that makes people want to do whatever they can do to support. I have guys holding chains out here. They could be really sitting in the bleachers or on the sidelines watching their kid, but they are doing a service for us. And the referees are all here religiously every week, and also during the offseason, they come down. We meet. It's a nonstop devotion to Warrior football. We have sponsors and this is very important, that have been with us for over thirty years sponsoring us with money. We go into schools. We talk to kids in schools. We give the principal paperwork. We want them to be part of what we're doing. And if you go to the schools, 'Oh, I'm here from the Warriors', no problem. That's how inviting they are to us because we are a good organization with a good reputation. The overall objective is to show people that things happen positively in communities. In recreation, in sports, and in just everyday life, you want to give back something. That there are people that do this. People want to do this! Hopefully, this program will last forever. It's a joy. It satisfies people's lives, and for one it satisfies my life. And you know, no matter where you go. I've met people when I was on vacation, and I might have had a Warrior T-shirt on, and I'm walking around and someone would come up to me and ask, 'Is that in the Bronx? Is Jay still…' And you say to yourself, 'Oh my God, this guy [Jerry] knows everybody! People know of Jay Demers, and you can't ask for any better than that. You really, really can't. He's the ultimate. And like I say, Jay is family to me and Phyliss. When he had his heart attack we were out to dinner with Jay and Geri. They go home, he had the heart attack, and Geri called me, Jay is in the hospital. 'I'll be right there' I told her and I stayed the whole night until I had to leave. And recently when he was in the hospital, the same nurse I had at Einstein, that did my stents, took care of Jay in that same room. So, when she said, 'Dennis what are you doing here?' I said to the nurse, 'this is my friend, my mentor, a father to me. Make sure you gave him the same care you gave me and more. Make sure you give him one-hundred percent'. And she did. So…What to say about Jay? The proof is in the pudding and that says it all."

At this point, a younger man, perhaps in his forties, entered the shed. He began to rummage through boxes, obviously looking for something. He broke Dennis' train of thought. Dennis knowing the inventory and where everything was stored asked him, more of a command, as to what he was searching for. The young man replied that a particular coach needed something but without telling Dennis what that something was. Dennis has been around the program for so long, and knows each and every one and what they usually need, reached into a plastic tub and found what was being sought, a plastic water bottle. It was as if Dennis was a telepathic savant.

Dennis turned to me apologetic for the interruption. I smiled and with a chuckle told this was not a problem. For me, this was like my team driving coaches crazy only ten-fold. Dennis introduced me to our intrusion.

"Bobby, this is Anthony Panissidi. Anthony, tell this gentleman, this ex-Warrior how you started with us."

Anthony had no choice but to obey Dennis' administrative order. "I played when I was eight, nine and ten years old. Probably sometime in the eighties. I remember because Dennis' daughter was a cheerleader and his son and I were actually on my team. I remember we played on the Ramblers. It was like a Pop Warner league thing. There weren't many teams at that time. There were only two divisions. You had the Juniors and then the Pee-wee league. There was no flag team yet. Eight, nine-year old's and then light [in weight and size] ten-year old's and because I was a peanut, I got to stay back a year. Then after that, you graduated out when you were fourteen. The Juniors were like you know, the heavy tens year old's and older. When I left, when I stopped playing, I came back and coached for about five or six years. That's when Morris Park folded, and a lot of the kids came over. We had a lot. We had flag football. We had Pee-wee. We had the Mites and the Juniors. We went from ages five, six, seven-year old's all the way up to fourteen-years old. It was ten times bigger than when I played but even so, it was a great experience for me. You know every kid at that age wants to be a professional football player."

Curious, I probed Anthony regarding his relationship with Jerry.

He was quick to answer, now with a gleam in his eyes. "Of course, I had a great relationship with him, I mean, how could you not. He had his hands into everything, not in a bad way. He was the general pretty much. The Chief, so to say, he is just such a great guy. Between the time I played and coached, there was a big gap, but he remembered who I was. He remembered what team I played for. I mean it's one of those things and it's kind of astounding because so many kids went through that program for so many years. The fact that he remembered who I was, I only played for three years. I got in there and graduated through the program, so it was an experience. It was fun, and it was more fun coaching than it was playing. At that time, it was a league. We had the kids all the way from flag football and as they went through the program, they just graduated into the big brother program. We coached those kids from the age of seven until they were fourteen or so. Most of the kids I still see in the old neighborhood. Kids that I'm friends with today are guys that I coached. But getting back to Jerry. He kind of instilled a lot of values in us, especially at a young age. You know, how organized everything was. We were on a team but you felt like you were part of something bigger. The coach treated all the kids the same way but when you coached, that's when you felt it most because he kind of gave you free reign with the kids. As far as an impact, I don't want to say it was like it the military, it's hard to explain, trying to put it into words but all in all, he's just one of the greatest guys I've ever met in my life. As far as being in touch with so many kids and so many families and remembering all of them. As I said, there had to be a good ten, fifteen years between my playing and coaching and he remembered who I was. He welcomes you right in and gives you responsibility. Any advice you needed, he was there. Sometimes I'd be running a practice and he'd walk by and call me over, 'Try this, do this. Maybe do this a little different. He's standing a little wrong'. I mean that's what he was. He was the guy in charge but he was always visible. He was at every practice. He was at every meeting. He was everywhere and always there, and he was always the first one there. I think for him it was more of the brand, a family than it was for any kind of individual praise. You know it wasn't about personal achievements. It was about growing that Warriors brand and that's what it really was. Even the ski weekends. When we got to go away as coaches. You know, the comradery and the brotherhood. To this day you see those guys and you have that mutual respect for each other. It's hard to put into words exactly. I'm sure you understand where I'm coming from."

I assured Anthony that I did know where he was coming from. I knew he was talking about the discipline and an organized way to have these young footballers learn the game and have fun at the same time. I inquired as to if at any point in time if he got the sense that maybe Jerry was teaching more than just football.

"Yes exactly. That's what I mean. It wasn't about individual accomplishments like we won this game, we won that game. It was more about values. I remember him instructing us coaches that we couldn't run the score up if you were up by more than two touchdowns. It was stuff like that to let the kids enjoy themselves but give them a sense of competitiveness. Jerry always made time to stop by each team and talk to them and to certain kids. He would ask them 'What position would you like to play?' I never have seen him play favorites. Even when he coached because there was a couple of years that he actually had his own team and he coached them even though he was the head administrator. I wish I had stayed longer but with work schedules and then moving away, it was just too hard. You get these kids when they are little peanuts and then boom, here they are, at age fourteen. They're like little adults. I think that's when I decided to stop because at that point, it was a whole new group of kids and you had just spent five, six years with these other kids. It was kind of sad to see them go. I didn't want to do that all over again. You know you get attached. It was one of those types of things. But, as far as Jerry goes, I feel like if I ran into him today in the supermarket, that he would for a fact know who I am and that we would have a conversation like it was yesterday."

"My thing is, if you lose, you've got to be gracious, in losing just like winning. It's things like that that he taught us. You know the score doesn't matter. You went out and you played hard. I haven't coached in probably over ten years and just to run into so many kids that were nine and ten years old and they shout out to me, 'Hey coach. How are you doing?' That's what I mean. They're grownups, they have families and kids now and the fact that they still call me coach means a lot to me. I would still call Eddie Esposito coach and I worked with the guy for four years. The same thing with Jay. You know, 'Hey coach'. It's a sign of respect. It's definitely, definitely not just about football."

Anthony was joined by a younger man, John Alba. The shed was becoming a cavalcade of Warriors, past, present, and future. Dennis was like the school teacher instructing his kids to say hello to the visiting parent.

"Hey John, say hello to Bob Nieder, he played in the early '70s. John shot me a look like I was a relic but greeted me politely with a handshake. Dennis informed John that it was me who was writing, or as I say, trying to write the Warrior story. This raised interest in John. Dennis, telling me that we were done, got up from his chair and told John to have a seat and tell me his story.

I initiated our conversation. "Tell me and I always start with this John. Tell me the year and/or how old were you when you got to the Warriors."

"I started in 2006. That was my first year playing. I think I was twelve years old. I started in the Junior Division."

I could see that John wasn't a big talker so I probed him with a follow-up question. "Okay, how did you learn of this Warrior league? I got a feeling that you're gonna tell me that you got a flyer at school or one of your friends played in the Warrior league."

"I loved football for a long time. My mother was always afraid for me to play tackle. But one year, I think I was in seventh grade, my friend's mother found an ad in the paper. I think it was the Bronx Times or something. It was some kind of flyer she saw, and she told us all about it. We all went down, checked it out and we ended up signing up for it."

"How long did you play?"

"I played...I was a player in the Warriors from '06 to '09."

"What was the experience like?"

John was now opening up. "I remember my first day like it was yesterday. I can tell you that on my first day I wound up playing quarterback for the Warriors. Actually, when I started my first year, I was a wide receiver but quickly after that, I became a quarterback. I was a quarterback all through high school and the semi-pro teams that I played for. I kind of stayed with that. Jay put me into the position of quarterback. I was on the field and I was just throwing and catching a football with somebody and Jay was sitting in the bleachers. He saw me, and he walked over to the field. He introduced himself to me and told me who he was. He told me that I had a really good arm and he wound up putting me on his team, the Chiefs. He wasn't coaching but the Chiefs were his team the year prior. He had just given it up to someone else, but he wanted me on that team. That team wound up being the best team in the whole division. I think we went eight and one that year. Yeah, it was a good team. I think he wanted me to learn behind some of those players because it was my first year, which I did. Then the following year we had a Pop Warner travel team. I became the starting quarterback on that team and it just went on from there."

"Did you do any coaching?"

"Yeah, I coached. Me, I quickly built a relationship with Jay. My first year of coaching, me and Jay, we coached together. When I went to the travel team, Jay was the head coach of that team. That year, that's when we became really good friends. Jay used to be a quarterback as you know."

I feigned surprise at this enlightenment. What would a sixty-three-year-old know about anything in the world of a twenty-two-year-old?

John continued. "He has such an offensive mind. Me, I also have a very offensive mind and we just used to communicate with plays and in certain situations, we would just communicate with each other and we always ended up on the same page, always on the same wavelength. The best thing we had on the field was that we had the same mindset. I would call a play or Jay would call a play and that's what we both were thinking about doing. So, we had a great player-coach relationship. Quarterback coach relationship actually. You know you could even say it was actually a lot of fun to do that. We both knew what we were doing. He already knew what was going to happen. I knew what he was gonna call. It made it made it pretty fun."

I couldn't contain myself hearing this. "John, I've got to tell you. This is exactly the same story as it was for one of the greatest Warriors, a quarterback and a captain, Jackie Cawley. He started back in 1968 and played through 1975. Like you, he didn't want to be a quarterback. He was an excellent wide receiver. Like you, he has told me about having that same mindset with Jay that you just talked about. It's eerie, both of you guys are telling the same story forty years apart. Now Jerry is a quarterback man. He can pick out a quarterback in the middle of the night in pure darkness and as you have learned, he's brilliant offensively."

The excitement grew in John's eyes. "Yeah, I know Jackie. I was coached by younger brother, Willie Cawley. Willie was my coach at Cardinal Spellman High School. He was a good coach. Yeah, so, me and Jerry developed that relationship really quick when he coached me, but he was more of my friend. He taught all of us and I'm still close to some of the guys I played with. The relationships I developed from being in the Warriors you know, being around Jay, it was more than football. It was more about learning how to be a teammate and how to work well together. I took lessons from the Warriors that I still implement to this day. Just learning how to build relationships and getting along with others. That was one of the best lessons that I was able to grasp from being in the Warriors. I know this one thing about Jay too. Jerry would not let us run up the score if we were winning. Jay wasn't the type to demoralize people. When we were up by just enough to make sure that we held onto that game, we would stop scoring because he wasn't like that. He didn't want to run the score up and as I said, he didn't want to demoralize any other kid. It was all about the fun of the game and even about the opponent. There was no need

189

to embarrass anyone. Let's not humiliate these guys. Let's walk out of here with the win. If we don't get the win, it's okay. It wasn't about winning with Jay. You didn't hear Jay yell very much. Not at all. But you knew, if you got a certain look from him, you knew you screwed up. I threw a few balls in the past where I got that look from Jay. It's not good," he laughed.

"Are you coaching now?"

"I would love to coach but the problem for me is I just don't have the time to do it. This past year is actually the first year that I'm not coaching. From time to time we try to get together for lunch or dinner. He just called me a few months back. We don't keep in touch as much as I would like but we still speak. What I'm saying is that is what it's all about. Just the fact that all these years later, guys are still talking and getting together because of Jay. Jay is that type of guy. If he ever asked me for a favor then I would do it. My brother played for the Warriors too. When Jay was in the hospital a few years ago we would always go to the hospital. If Jay asked for a favor, we just did it. He never asked because that's just how he is but if he ever did there would be no hesitation. And there's one more thing I have to say regarding him teaching me football as a quarterback. To this day, from when I was young, Jay taught me this rule. I can't remember when it was, where it was or who we were playing. I was on the goal line and I wanted to throw the ball. Just to throw the defense off however whenever we got down there, we would be running it. I asked Jay this one question and he said, 'Never throw the ball on the goal line.' And to this day it has stuck with me. You know you have four downs, just pound it in. Just get it in there somehow. Never throw the ball at the goal line. Bad things happen."

I laughed out loud recalling a conversation I had with Jay the day after the Patriots beat the Seahawks for the Super Bowl. "John do you know why he's telling you that? I know exactly why he's telling you that."

"Why?"

"Somewhere in the fifties. When he played on the original team. I think it was maybe 1956, he was in that same situation as Russell Wilson. He threw a pass over the middle, into the end zone and the guy intercepts it and runs it all the way back for the winning touchdown."

"Oh my God," John responded in astonishment.

"I didn't know that until that Superbowl where Seattle had Marshawn Lynch running all over the place and at the end of the game Wilson threw that ball from what, the two-yard line, over the middle only to have Malcolm Butler pick it off. So, the next day, in talking with Jerry I said, 'You know Jerry, that wasn't a bad play, but that guy made a great break on that ball'. Man did he light up. He was yelling at me, 'No Bobby. You never do that. You never do that'. And then he told me the story. There's one thing I've learned, if Jay says something regarding offense, then that's gospel. If Jay says that this is the way it is, then that is the way it is. I don't question it. Besides, I'm a kicker. What do I know?"

I made my exit from the shed. I was about to take a seat in the bleachers and watch all of these Warriors running around, when I was accosted by Dennis who grabbed me by the arm.

"Come with me", he commanded not giving me much of a choice. "I want you to meet someone. Hey Jim, come here, I want you to talk to this guy."

A tall man with gray hair was shuffling papers at the folding table and dealing with three parents. "Not right now Dennis, I'm in the middle of something", he called out. He had that no-nonsense look about him. I wasn't sure if I wanted to talk with this man. Dennis wouldn't lose this little battle.

"Jim, talk to Bobby, he's writing a book about the Warriors. I'll take over what you're doing.

Jim walked toward me. I found Jim to be very engaging and pleasant. We shook hands and I explained exactly what this book was all about. I gave him a little of my past Warrior history and as I do with everyone I meet. I asked him what year did he come and what brought him to the organization.

"I came to the Warriors in 1990. My wife took my son, Jimmy, who was five-years-old at that time to Pelham Bay Park and as she told me, there was quite a crowd there, primarily kids running around playing football. So that day, she signed up Jimmy for flag football. Understand that I am a football fanatic so you can imagine my disappointment that I didn't get to see my son in his first football game. Needless to say, I went with him the next weekend. I was a parent on the sideline, yelling and screaming, cheering him on. I would walk up and down the sidelines yelling 'defense, defense'. Jerry saw my enthusiasm. The following year they needed some help so he asked me to coach. I think Jerry figured out that it was better to get me off the parents' sidelines and put me on the other sideline to coach. The first and second year, Pete Kilgallen was the coach of the team and I helped him out. The third year it was Donald Van Bomel and I took over the team. Pete went ahead and did other things for us. That's how I started with Jay. I stayed there with my son and coached in flag football which was fine, I had no problem doing that. But when he moved up to tackle, I was one of the assistant coaches. Jay put me with one of the teams. I realized it myself that I wasn't really cut out to…I mean I know football like the back of my hand, I know everything about it, but I know that but I couldn't teach it to kids. I just wasn't good at that and I guess Jay realized that also because that's when he came to me knowing that I was very big into computers. I was doing work for my company with computers creating and putting together spreadsheets, formulas, designs, and all that other stuff. Remember this is in an era where computers were in the beginning stages of existence, especially in the home, so he asked me to help him out on that end. I told him I would be more than happy to do it and that's how it started. I became the paper guru as you might say. I was doing basic info, things like that, rosters, information on the players, and make spreadsheets up. Jay wanted to do weekly articles about the organization in our local paper, the Bronx Times and he asked me if I could help out with that and I said yeah, sure. It started out where I would have to wait for the coaches to feed me information and that was coming very sparsely. One coach did nothing and another coach did this so that's when I decided to make up some forms. I stood on the sidelines every single game and I actually wrote down what was going on. So, at the end of the day, I was able to sit down and write articles about every game. So that's when I started publishing articles every week in the newspaper and they've been doing it ever since. Jeff Ortiz took over for me after I told Jay and Joe DeSimone, 'listen, I can't do this anymore, I just don't have the time and my head's not in it' so Jeff took over. It became a pain the butt. It was easier to do it on the field, actually doing it myself but to depend on the coaches to supply you the information, that's a pain in the butt and Jeff knew that also. He would start doing a lot of ad-libbing of his own. A lot of it wasn't right but nobody cared, nobody knew. It was fun but that's what we're up to right now. Jeff really did a great job for us, considering what he had to work with. Yesterday when Joe DeSimone came over, he brought me stuff that eventually Jay and I have to go over. I realized how much involved it was to do all that stuff but I'll get it all into the computer to make life easier. And I'll tell you where we are currently as an organization. When Joe DeSimone decided to take over, he incorporated us. We were never incorporated before. We used to work under the Service Alliance for Youth banner but when that stopped, we were out there with no protection so Joe incorporated us. Now we have to have titles so I was made the secretary. Jay asked me if I wanted to become president. I thought about it and I thought about it and I said 'Jay, if you want to give me the title that's fine but we've got to make it so that people understand, when the parents are complaining, they're not coming to me because that's not my job, they've got to go to you'. And he says, 'Yeah, that works out'. I talked to my son about it. He loves Jay, he's one of these kids that grew up with Jay. That man could do no wrong in my son's eyes, so he was more than willing to help us out. He said 'why don't you do something like this', and he knows this stuff because the company he works for, he does their IT work. He tells me 'why don't you make Jay founder/president and you can be executive vice-president/treasurer so this way all the big decisions with the parents he handles and you handle all the other stuff'. I thought about it some more and I realized that's the way it worked with the Little League. I was the executive vice-president and a guy named Mike was the president. He did all that presidential stuff with the parents and personnel within the league and I took care of scheduling, the coaches, the paperwork. I helped expand the girls' softball league in Pelham Bay. I didn't like the way that program was going so I took it out of Little League and I put it into the Babe Ruth league. They used to play in all the Babe Ruth tournaments. We used to make it to the regional games in Jersey and Pennsylvania. Finally, I was asked to become Commissioner of Metro New York which consists of the five boroughs, Nassau, Suffolk, and Westchester so I was the State Metro New York Commissioner. But getting back to the Warriors, we're chartered now as a corporation, under the auspices of the State. We're chartered as a non-profit; we have tax-exemption status. We don't get any funds from the State but it protects us, the individuals from being sued. When you're not incorporated, a kid gets hurts and the parents can sue the individuals but as a corporation, you can't sue the individuals, but you can sue the corporation. At one time we decided to go with a travel team for the older kids so we joined Pop Warner down in Brooklyn and eventually I became a member of the executive board of New York City Pop Warner. At that time, I also belonged to the National Sports Coaches Association, they're located in Florida by the way. I was certified to teach their training course. I'm still in that and I do that for our coaches, not the actual football part but how to deal with kids. I was into a lot.

The only thing I didn't do with the Warriors were the ski weekends, everybody tells me about it, how much fun they had but I wasn't into that."

"That's impressive, all of this coming out of 1990."

"Right, it all started there, you're one-hundred percent right. I wasn't from this area. I grew up in the northeast section of the Bronx on Laconia Avenue near 233rd Street. When I married my wife, I moved here into the Pelham Bay area and I didn't know anybody. Because of my involvement with the Warrior Organization and the way it expanded, all because of the opportunity, it opened up a whole new world for me, the people I met and the friendships that were developed. I liked what I saw when I was first standing on the sideline and as time went on, I liked what I was working with, working with kids, all kids. I decided that this is right for me. And I'll tell you about Jay being Jay. I consider him a great friend, a mentor, and an older brother because we're close in age. Mentor more than anything else. I learned an awful lot about handling kids from him. He taught me patience and to be a little calmer, relaxed. I'm still working at it [laughs]. I want to be here. I would love to be able to see my grandson play for the Warriors. It would be great for me if I could see that. He's not even a year old yet so I've got a long way to go."

"Not really, Jim. He'll be playing flag in almost four years."

[Jim laughs] "Yeah. But I'll tell you, it would be a loss to the youth of the Bronx if we lost the Warrior program, if it didn't exist.

"We're known, Jim. There's a history of class and distinction with the Warriors. We have a guy now living in Jacksonville, Florida, Lew Lubarsky. He played on that famed 1967 touch-tackle team out of P.S. 106 that won the city championship. Today, he's a season pass holder for the Jaguars. A local radio station down there asked the fans for their 'questions to the coach' for a segment they were doing. This was held on a football field, about sixty people were in attendance. You had to be selected to be there. Anyhow, this radio personality calls out asking if a Lew Lubarsky is in attendance and of course Lew responds. The question he asked Jacksonville's Head Coach Doug Marrone was, 'knowing that you're from the Bronx, have you ever heard of the Warriors'. Coach Marrone answered without hesitation, 'Of course I've heard of the Bronx Warriors'."

"That's what we've always been, Bob. In fact, leagues now are coming after us wanting us to join their league because they know of our reputation. But as long as we have the number of kids, where we don't have to go to one team per age bracket, that's a last resort to join another league or go interleague. I don't want to see that. Our intramural program is what makes us unique from everybody else. We play everything against each other. Yeah, each team has a different name but we're all Warriors. The front of the jersey says, Warriors. We're all together. And the coaches we have all know this. They teach their kids to win but they all tell each other the same thing in the end, remember, we're all Warriors. We've got Warrior shirts, sweatshirts, jackets. And here's something about Jay, you were a family, Jay is like the father of the family and Geri is the mother. He does all these things for everybody. We go places together, we go on trips together, he has parties at his house for us, the people that are part of his organization. He more or less started a family. And between the two of us, they made it so that we are a family. We feel like a family, we feel like we belonged."

The next afternoon, I paid a visit to Ricky Demers, Jay's son. Not seeing Ricky since he was a young boy, about fifteen-years-old back then, I was stunned to be greeted by a forty-four-year-old adult. It seems that we hold people, in our mind's eye, as to who they were and what they looked like when they were young forgetting that thirty years have passed and that people age. No handshake was necessary after the strong hug we shared. I entered his place and was greeted by his buddy, Momo, a large Boxer. We sat on the couch and chatted as there was a lot of catching up to do. My mind shot back in time to when I first met Ricky. He was ten-years-old, a small guy, sitting on a sofa in Jerry's house on Hobart Avenue. I figured he was someone who played on a young Warrior team, waiting for his parents to pick him up. I guess they never showed up as over the next several weeks, Ricky would be there every time I would go to Jay's. I didn't know what to make of this young boy. Jay did introduce him to me simply giving me his name. Nothing more, nothing less. Ricky, we would all come to learn, is his adoptive son.

I initiated the dialogue with "grown-up" Ricky. "How old were you when you meet your dad?"

"I was about ten years old. It was 1981. The summer of 1981. He adopted me through the Little Flower Agencies."

"You know, he told me that he fell in love with you as soon as he saw you. So, you go home with this man. Do you remember that day?"

"I do. I remember when he walked in the door at the agency. He had a cowboy hat on, he had a beard and long raincoat. I just thought that he was another social worker that I was going off with because that's the way it was, you know, the foster home system. Meeting this social worker, meeting that social worker. The previous day I was before the judge with my biological mom, in the family court system in Queens. I had no idea that this was part of an adoption process. So, when he shows up, I just went with this guy. I didn't know who he was. I didn't question it. We came here to the Bronx, but I didn't know he was taking me home with him. Actually, at that age, I didn't even care cause, because my life was just so upside-down anyways. I had a nicotine addiction, at ten-years-old. I had a stealing problem. I smoked dust at the age of ten, in Queens. I was on the streets. I was molested by two men, strange men. This was my life prior to here, before being with dad. I mean, unbeknown to my father. I was still smoking behind his back. I had a pack of Marlboros inside my thigh pad and I would go out and play. We're playing at Van Cortlandt Park and at halftime, I'm running behind the stadium to have a smoke by myself. I had a lot of bad habits coming into his home. I did stop stealing when I came into my new home. So, getting back to meeting dad and thinking he was another caseworker, I just went where ever the system took me and it didn't bother me. Nobody was home when we first got there. That's when I met his dog, a big German Sheppard, named King. So, it was just me, my father and King at the time. I'm thinking, when we first walk into this house, that I'll be here for a few days, maybe. Eventually, I'll be going back home to Queens. That night I met Karen and then I met Kerry, then my mother came home from work and then we went to pick up Kim from nursery school. It was one of those situations. I was like, 'Alright, well it's better than being back in Queens'."

I stopped Rickey, "Do you know what your sister Kim said about first meeting you? She told me that 'My parents came to my nursery school and he was hiding in the backseat of the Volkswagen, and then he popped out at me'. I had asked her if she was excited by this and her reply was, 'I loved it. Loved it, loved it, loved it. It was great. He completed our family'."

Ricky chuckled at the recollection. "Right away I had an attachment to my father because he was the male figure, which I never had. It was always, my past, either my biological mother or my grandmother or my aunts and cousins. They were all females. At dad's house, there were guys that were coming to the house more often at that time, Steve Fabrizzi, George Nardone to name a few. They were like regulars in the household and they treated me well. My dad remembers talking to my cousin Serina, a few years later and she said, 'Wow. You know what? He turned out so good. You did a good job with him'. And my father replies, 'What does that mean?' My biological family thought I was so bad. I had no supervision with them. I was out smoking cigarettes, smoking marijuana, stealing, but it was that when I was with dad's family, I was a different person."

I shifted our talk to his playing days.

"He brought football to me. I thought I liked baseball, but I wasn't really into it. I didn't play little league baseball. I didn't play any sports. My first sport was football. I liked playing in an actual organized league. I went right to football, not really knowing the game, not knowing the rules but, it came along because I was living in a football house. When I first started to play, 1981, I was a defensive back. I wasn't really good during my first year. I played on the second string so it wasn't favoritism. It was just a learning period but during the offseason, we would go to Stevenson High School and we would play. They had the winter program and he's still doing the winter program to this day. So, I was involved. I was involved in playing hockey in the gym. You know, dodge ball. My second year, 1982 was my first season as a starter. I was playing defensive end and I was playing center (laughing) on the offense. So, I was playing both ways the second year and third year. My first team was called, of course, the Warriors. Yeah, and there were only three teams. There was the Peewee's, the Junior Midgets and the Midgets. I played two years in the Junior Division. My last year in 1985 was with the thirteen-year-old in the Senior Division. I even played a year at Cardinal Spellman as a matter of fact. My dad coached every team. Then I turned to coaching for two years after that. At this point in time, dad was more in an administrative role but throughout the years, he would coach a team. In 2010 after all these years that I've been out of the system, I came back and coached a team with him. We coached the Rams and we were undefeated that year." Ricky was laughing recalling the thought.

"What was that like, working with your dad?"

"Oh, my father? My dad took over the offense. I was the defense. And it was a lot of fun. (laughing) There was a lot of bickering back and forth with him and me. The bickering was when he didn't like when I placed the defensive backs too deep. He felt that they should be up closer. But because these guys were small, I had to give them ten yards, you know. These kids were eleven, twelve, and thirteen. I would run my defense and he would try to give me input, but I wanted to do my own thing and there were times that he would get mad at me on the field. There was one game where dad is walking over to the end zone to meet the guy who he thought was about to score a touchdown but my defense stopped him. I'm telling him, 'Okay Dad, you can come back now'. My wife says I'm exactly like him, even though we're not blood. We're both passive."

I stopped Ricky. "But your dad has a very strong way of getting what he wants".

"Absolutely, He's passive but he has character and he won't break that character. After all these years, I would never move away from him. I always have thoughts of moving out of state, moving further away. I would not move while he was still alive so that I could be near him."

I asked Ricky of how his mother, Geri, fit into all of this.

"She was always very supportive of me. I'm sure she had issues with my dad. You know, in my perception, in that household in regard to football, I think it came down to her mindset. This is why I think she thought, "If I can't beat em, join em.""

"That's exactly what your father said. My god, you're identical in thought."

"That was my perception because I remember hearing a lot of things that she would be upset about. I would hear 'It's always football. It's always football. We don't have time for this and that but there's football'. I'm sure that drove my mother crazy because everything was about sports but I don't think that was the cause of their separation. Even though they separated, she still coached the cheerleaders."

"Ricky, I've got to tell you that when your mom and dad separated, all of us, the guys that played from 1968 to 1975 assumed we were the reason for this. I did hold a conversation with your dad and he very firmly told me that wasn't the case. To tell you the truth, a lot of us, me for one, didn't have a clue of the separation because they continued on as if they were married, best of friends."

The next day, before I boarded a late-night flight back home, I met up with Joe DeSimone at Jimmy Ryan's. Joe, an alumnus of P.S. 119, and a long-time friend going back almost fifty years greeted me in his usual manner. I may be The Weasel but to Joe, I'm "Ugly". That is how he has always called me for those almost fifty years, With one exception. It was the early '80's. I was in management employed by Blue Cross/Blue Shield. One of my accounts was Con Edison and their Mutual Aid Society [an organization formed to provide mutual aid, benefit, and/or insurance among its members43]. On a Thursday evening, I was to wine and dine executives of the Mutual Aid Society at a high-end restaurant, Mr. Leo's Southern Cuisine. God bless the corporate account. We were all dressed appropriately in suits and ties. As we walked briskly on a bustling 27th Street we came upon one of their generator trucks, complete with full lighting sitting over an open manhole. It was about six o'clock. The sound of its diesel engine filled the neighborhood letting everyone know that these guys don't punch a clock. "Dig we must", an executive named Ray commented. I heard the call of the wild above the noise. "Hey, Weasel." My head snapped to the right only to see Joe DeSimone, climbing out of the manhole. He wore what looked like a miner's hard hat, grimy but with that ever-present smile. I yelled out in excitement, "Joe." The executives loved the moment.

Joe "D" as we would call him, retired after thirty-nine years as Manager at Con Edison Development. We sat at a booth over pints to catch up on family, old memories, and all things Warrior as he now holds the position of head administrator of the organization. A server approached our table. Joe, being a part-time bartender at Ryan's, introduced me to Teresa.

Joe: "Teresa, this is my good friend, Ugly."

Me" I'm Bob. I know I'm not a good-looking man but am I that ugly?

Joe: "Yeah."

Terresa: "No."

Joe: "Just say yes."

Terresa: "Why? I don't think he is."

Bob: (laughing) "He's called me ugly all my life."

Joe: "Ah he's ugly. He's very ugly. Look he's gotten better. He's gotten more ugly. It's true."

Some things just never change. I decided it was time for my inquisition.

"Joe, when did you start with the Warriors?"

"When my daughter Alexis was five. She's thirty-three now so eighteen, (laughing) twenty-eight years ago. She was trying out for cheerleading, yes. Then my sons came of age and I gradually got pulled into coaching there. You know, a flag team. Me and Jack Cawley coached together when we first started, so I started coaching twenty-five years ago."

"When I heard that you were the new administrator, I had to call Jay and squeeze 'em a little. I asked him, "'ay what are you doing, what are you doing with the Warriors'? and he says, 'Well you know, I'm getting a little older and I can use a younger person to run the program, so I picked this guy, Joe DeSimone'. I proceed to read him the riot act. 'No, Jay? Do you know this friggin' guy? Joe DeSimone? He's your new guy. I can't believe you picked this guy. He's the worst'. I could hear the silence. After his continued hesitation, I brought him back to reality. 'Jay I've known Joe since high school age from 119. You couldn't have picked a better person to run this organization. He's good with people. I've never seen him lose control. When he gets mad, he's going to give you that grin, roll his eyes, laugh and walk away."

"What is it that the administrator of the organization does? What do you do?"

"For the Warriors now. I'm kind of the final say on any decisions but administratively, Jay was very hands-on, so I obviously had to pick up the hands-on process. First of all, we reach out to sponsors to try to get some funding for the league because we're non-profit, but we're not under non-profit status yet because of the switching over from the Service Alliance for Youth. We just separated. We are now the Warrior Football League Incorporated. We incorporated ourselves under my watch here and we're in the process of going for tax-exempt status. Right now, I'm dealing with photographers. I get a photographer to take photos once a year and that's our only fundraiser. Then I make sure all the equipment is, you know, the jerseys are all ordered. Coaches' shirts, whistles, all those kind of minutia things. I got lucky in that we still have Jay's two right-hand men stayed on, Dennis Kandell and Jimmy Pellicone. With being there kind of helps the transition and Jay, of course, is a consultant advisor but I still defer to him. I know his wisdom and his years of experience. It's a tough thing but you know I'm trying to put my little mark on things as well. Some things I just want to modernize a little bit. You know Jay is still sending out snail mail (laughing). He doesn't have a computer or a cell phone, but I got away from that and I do most of my stuff on email. I think we are reaching out to more people. We're in the process of joining with these web partners. They put your information up for free if you're a new client. They're going to post our league stats and how to reach us. And as you now know we're unique in the fact that we're a league and not a team. Like Coop City or Mount Vernon, they'll have one team in two or three divisions. They don't play intramurals. We're pretty much a little league structure. Intramural, everything played at one spot. We're centrally located at Pelham Bay Park where you can get to by a lot of transportation. The uniqueness of it I think gives a lot of parents' comfort. I believe that there are only two in the city that are actual leagues and we are one of them. Jim Pellicone would know for sure. Kid's aren't getting on buses, going to strange places. The parents, we all know each other. It's a great experience. I love that part of it. I enjoy being around football again in this capacity. I just fall in love with the interactions with the kids. I love to see them happy. I love what the Warriors do especially with providing a very safe environment that is unique. You know all those kids. Seeing them excel, seeing them change, get better. You know my little saying to them is, you know, everyone says you have to be the best so best is a priority. There's nothing beyond best but not everyone can't be the best, but everyone can get better. Hearing our message, it's not about winning. I mean everyone is competitive, everyone that is there as far as administrator or coach have played sports at some level so there's that competitiveness that nobody wants to lose. [Joe played offensive tackle at Cardinal Hayes High School and went on to become head coach at Cardinal Spellman High School, along with Willie Cawley, leading them to three championships, one of which was against his alma mater.] So yeah, we want to win but we understand that losing is part of the game and we try to instill that to the players. At the end of the day what I tell everybody, my little mantra is, "We've got nine different teams in tackle. We've got five in flag. You're gonna all play each other. You're all gonna try to win the championship but at the end of the day whether you're a Navaho or a Spartan, at the end of the day, you're a Warrior. When you walk off the field, congratulate your friend. They're one of your brothers. They can compete because if there weren't leagues like ours, a lot of these kids wouldn't play any tackle football. They would then be put through tryouts and even if they were put on the team, they weren't going to play. Here you're guaranteed to play at least a half of a football game."

"Yeah, I like that. It's what I always say to my wife. You know young kids should be taught to play the game and have fun. When they're older. Maybe high school then they can learn the killer instinct. You know, if they have that talent."

Joe moved on. "Yeah, I'm with that. You know we do give individual trophies for participation. Again, I'm all for rewarding the best but when you see the kids. Especially the flag players coming up with a smile on their face and it's probably the first time they've ever got a trophy. That makes it all worthwhile. But right now, it's this administrator stuff. And Jay is just sitting there laughing and he's happier than anybody because if anybody goes to him with an issue he just says, 'Tell Joe'. And then he laughs at my reaction because I tell him, 'Really, is this that big a problem'? I love being around football, I love being able to improve things, but I don't make any moves without consulting with Jay. With him, Jimmy, and Dennis, and I added a couple of more guys because Jim and Dennis were doing so much. I added a treasurer, I added a director of safety, a safety officer. I added an EMT this year that we didn't have. Through our website and our talks, we are making people be safety conscious. I'm sure most administrators and coaches are thinking the same but I kind of stress it. You know concussions in youth sports, that's a deterrent to what we are trying to do now. Parents are pulling their kids out of sports because so many politicians are talking about it. Rightly they should talk about it, but they are scaring people out of the sport so I kind of try to build a report with having an EMT there. By making them aware, it's a very real possibility. It's a contact sport. It's something we are working toward and I talk to the parents all the time about it. I'm big on safety. That's part of the clinic I ran. I had invited all of the Warrior coaches to come down. I try to show them the techniques they should use like proper blocking and tackling. We watched videos on it. We're trying to teach the game. My style of coaching has always been that if the players understand what it is that they're doing then it makes it easier to do. It sticks in their head because not only do they know how to do it, but they know why they're doing it. We are pushing our coaches to go in that direction and it's happening that way and they are receptive to it. I told our officials when I met with them regarding the certification this year, throw the flag on anything that is around the head. Use your discretion but when you see helmet to helmet or head tackling things like that I said, 'I want to see you throwing a flag'. We don't care how it affects the game. We care about how it affects the kids.

"Joe, I want to thank you for what you're doing. I've got to tell you that we tackle guys and the guys before us at the 106, we look at the organization almost like we're alumni of a major college you know. That's fifty years past and we want to know who's running our program? Who's taking care of our kids? Do you feel any of that or is it…?"

"I think I've been feeling it since I've been talking to you. I don't think I felt it because I don't talk to that many ex-Warriors. I don't you know…Jack [Cawley] is happy when I see him. I've heard that, but I haven't heard, if you know what I mean. Well, there's some of that but I wish we had more contact with them with the ex-Warriors. I would like that. I don't know if they would be interested but I would like to do have an alumni touch game and a picnic after. Maybe that's something to delve into with Jeff since he has all the contacts. Yeah, I'll investigate that and maybe before the end of the season we'll see if we can do a little alumni game at the park."

"You know that Jerry would be the quarterback and he cheats, his daughter told me that."

"Yes, I know but Bobby I've got to tell you, he's enjoying himself right now. He's thrilled right now. He's back in his environment. He's working with quarterbacks. He wants to coach. Yeah so, he's very much into that. You can just see, he's revived once I came on. From walking with two canes to him running around the field. It's pretty amazing. Now thanks to the internet and online training, we have all of our coaches go through an online certification through the National Association for Youth Sports and they have to get that certification before they can come on board and coach. But that doesn't guarantee that their character is going to be good. We have to get a feel for them."

"Joe, how much time do you put in on the administration level? Can you define it on a weekly basis?"

"Now that we're about to start my workload will probably start to lighten up. Prior to this, what I did, I kind of thought that I had to put my own little signature on it, so what I did is…I convinced them that we should start a free training clinic. I called it the Warrior Training Clinic. We started at the end of March. My pitch to Jay was, 'Look it's not going to cost us anything. I'm going to try to get a sponsor and we can get some tee shirts. We have balls, we have dummies and I'll get stuff from Spellman like cones and whatever we need so let's put our name on something free and see how many kids that show up'. So, we did that. I went around to the schools in the area. Put posters up in bars and restaurants, stores, all over the neighborhood.

We put it in the Penny Pincher and the Bronx Times. It was appealing to kids seven years old, thirteen years old. Free training. By the time that we were done, we had probably one-hundred-fifty kids registered. Hours? When I started, I was putting in an hour a day on the computer, just ordering things that we could purchase for the league. Now, it's about six or eight hours. I'm an all- in kind of guy or as Jim Pellicone told me, 'a hands-on guy'. I'm always looking for ways that we can get grants. Right now, we're shut out of any donations from the government agencies because as I told you, we don't have our tax-exempt status yet, but we'll get there. We got twenty grand last year. This year we don't get anything. So, we're trying to promote as much as we can. We rely on our sponsors."

I had to ask Joe one more question. "Now that you're around Jay a lot, what's your impression of the man."

"You know Bobby, I first met Jay when he would referee and umpire my games. He was always the head official. He always carried himself with the best demeanor and a lot of knowledge. From that standpoint, I looked up to him. A guy with a little authority who was to be taken seriously. He was still an active coach with your team. He's a high-character guy. For him, it much more than your football knowledge. Football knowledge is a plus, but your character is much more important to be a coach with us. Organizationally, he knows the way, way more than me. You know, he'll come to me with these index cards that he scribbles on, literally scribbles on. (laughing) I can't read them but once a week he'll hand me a card. 'You should do this. You might want to think about doing this'. And he has calendars with dates. On this date we're doing this and, on this date, we're doing that, and I say 'Alright'. His authority always comes through, very decisive like a natural leader. He says that I'm very optimistic. I wonder if at some point the bottom is going to fall out for me because of the enormity of it all. I don't know how he's done it all these years. He has this air of authority, but it never overwhelms him. He's just Jay. You know, he said something very poignant the other night when we had our draft a couple of weeks ago toward the end. Besides being a great guy, he also has a great sense of humor too. He knows how to throw the underhanded, the backhanded insult, with a little sarcasm. It's a great ice breaker. Anyways so we both do that to each other. At one point he turned to me and he shakes my hand and he says, 'I want to thank you'. This league wouldn't have survived if you hadn't taken over'. He says, 'It wasn't gonna last. We would have had a couple travel teams and that would be it'. So, I'm laughing you know (laughing) and I say, 'You're breaking my balls, right'?

and he says, 'No, no. I'm serious'. But I couldn't take him seriously because it was always that with us. We were always giving each other shots. When I realized he wasn't kidding I said, 'You know Jay, that means a lot to me'. More than anybody has said to me in a long time'. I hold that as dear to me as one of my kids telling me they couldn't love someone as they do me. It was a very…I walked out of that room and I had to soak it in a little. That blew me away. I mentioned it to a couple of other people. I said, 'You know, Jay just paid to me the greatest compliment that he never had to pay me'. And I just said, 'For a guy like that to say that to me…knowing my role in something so important'. I thought that was one of the greatest compliments. That was a very important moment for me."

***

Meeting Richie, Dennis, and Jimmy, and knowing Jerry, I could see why this era of Warrior football has been so successful. Even though the personalities are different, Jerry being who he always has been and is to this day, organized, keen of vision, a leader and a teacher to all, kids, teenagers, and adults. Richie, a driven dedicated man willing to do whatever for the people in his sphere but with a wicked sense of humor, and Dennis, a person who oozes the 'milk of human kindness', a guy who cares about all those around him and gives his all for the good of the whole. And Jimmy, an "M & M", hard on the outside but soft on the inside, also working diligently for the organization. This foursome, together for over twenty-five years, mesh well to not only get the job done but to provide young boys and teenager enjoyment and an alternative to going down the wrong road in life. Not one of these men ever think about themselves, what they do is simply give to everybody for a greater good. Dedicated men with great families, working selflessly for the community. They have now placed the future of the organization into the qualified, and caring hands of Joe DeSimone.

Youth Organization League, Rice Stadium, Pelham Bay Park, Bronx, NY - 1999

Coach Ricky Demers 2000

Warrior Youth Football Game at Rice Stadium – 2009

Photo Shoot at Rice Stadium - 2017

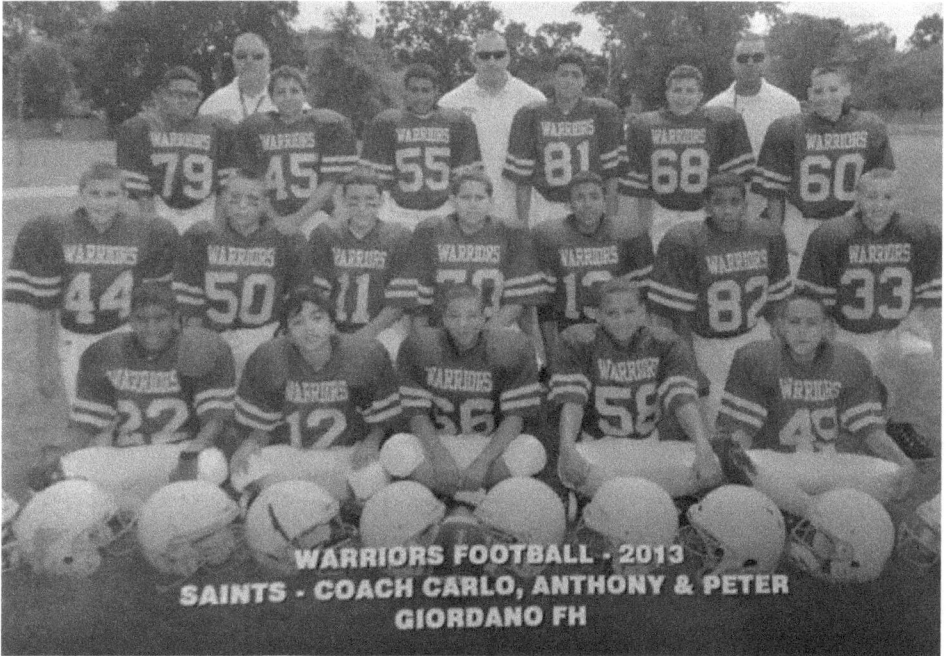

WARRIORS FOOTBALL - 2013
SAINTS - COACH CARLO, ANTHONY & PETER
GIORDANO FH

Warriors visit Good Morning America Studio, Times Square, NY – 2015
Dennis Kandell (far right, red jacket) & Joe DeSimone (behind Dennis)

Chapter 9

Goodbye to Geri

Geri and Kim Demers – Awards Diner at Villa Barone, Bronx NY – 2011

"Good morning everyone. On behalf of the family, I would like to thank everyone for coming. Even though it may have been too short, Geri lived a blessed life. It was a life of faith and virtue and was a fine example to us all."

"They say you don't know how strong you are until you have to be. I believe that it's true for most people that walk this earth, but Geri had strength beyond compare. She's the strongest person I know, filled with boundless energy, so full of life. These are all the things I've been hearing the past few days and they are so true. If we could bottle her spirit and hand it out, the world would be a happier place. She always had a smile ear to ear for you and never took one second for granted, hosting every party and barbeque she could. She enjoyed every song, singing them out loud, dancing every chance she got. When a new line dance at a cheer competition would come out, she made sure the girls would teach it to her. She was always on the move, and with her Hurricanes, she took the world by storm!

Geri was not only physically strong, proving it by cartwheeling circles around us and in all the parades, but she was everyone's rock as well. She would welcome friends into her home, be it for a night, or a week, or even months if some misfortune was bestowed upon them. She held her daughters' hands during the births of their children and nursed everyone back to health when necessary. She adored her grandchildren and spoke about them with pride to all who would listen. Jade and Amber were lucky enough to have cheered for her and will forever be grandma's MVPs. Callie was her shopping buddy and if there were a new pair of shoes to be had, Callie and grandma had them. Justice was her little man and the apple of her eye. And Fallon, there aren't enough words, but simply put, she was her girl. She loved being a grandma. Nurturing was just her way."

"I remember one of my first impressions of Geri. I was very young and Kim and I were the babies on a team of older cheerleaders. Kim was upset about something and dared to walk away saying, "I'm telling daddy," and as she whipped around to walk away, Geri grabbed her ponytail to pull her back. My first and only thought was, "Oh no, she's just like my mom." And that she was. A mom not only to her four children but to thousands of kids everywhere. She taught much more than cheerleading. She taught us self-confidence, grace, and self-respect and molded many little girls into dignified young women. She was respected, loved, and admired by so many. The extent to how she touched lives is unimaginable and a mere thank you seems insufficient. I know she's watching us all from above, still taking care of us from there. And when we join her on that ski trip in heaven, we'll be sure to greet her with a "Hi, hello, we're really glad to see you!"

"Hello, my name is Jennifer Volpe. That is the eulogy I read at Our Lady of Assumption, on Sunday, January 13, 2013. It was very emotional for me."

"I first met Geri in 1985 when I first joined the Warrior Cheerleaders, I was ten-years-old. Over the years, Geri is like my other mom, she was definitely my second mom. She was very strong-willed and strict, but with a lot of love. She would get her point across, but she also instilled a lot of good responsibility in all of us. She loved dancing. She loved going out. But she always made sure that everyone understood that we have a job to do and you get up the next day and you do it. She would tell us, 'Don't call me on Sunday morning and tell me you can't make it to the field because you were out the night before'. She was very influential. She taught us a good work ethic and responsibility. If Geri said something, that was it. There would be girls that sometimes worried about an issue and they would go to the other coaches or tell their moms because they were afraid. Not afraid of Geri, but afraid of disappointing her ever. You did not want to disappoint her. Even my kids. There was no way they wanted to disappoint her. Like my daughters. We would go to a separate tumbling class and the minute they would get the routine down, the first thing they said was, 'I can't wait to show Geri'. They always wanted to get her approval because there was nothing like it if you made Geri proud. Her face, the way she would look at you and light up. The way she would grab these girls and swing them around in a great big bear hug. There was nothing like it. She would make you feel like you were the most important thing in the world. And I would like everyone to be very clear on this point. She didn't stop cheerleading because she was sick. What had happened was, the year before, she had decided this was going to be her last year. She was ready to enjoy her grandkids and enjoy life and she was ready to let go of the program. She had no idea at this point in time that she was sick. Then over the summer, she found out that she was sick. She was actually watching Kim's kids and I don't know. Something ended up happening and something didn't feel right, so she ended up going to the doctor. That's when they discovered what was going on, but this wasn't until August of that year. Unfortunately, it came on like vengeance. It was a shock to all of us. She was everyone's mom, and everyone knew it. She was respected and loved in that way."

***

One Greatest Moment I Had – Keri Demers

A long night of practice both the football and cheerleading at Pelham Bay Park. The air was humid with a light breeze. All of the children were gone. The park was almost empty and getting dark. It was dusk, the sun going down. I was in the parking lot but very close to the field. I can see my dad walking from the left side of the field and my mom walking toward him from the right side. The sun was setting and as I watched there was a silhouette of them meeting and a quick kiss on the lips. Both exhausted. There was silence. I stood there quietly watching this moment, I know they didn't even realize I was there. But that perfect memory plays very loud in my mind. I will never forget that moment.

Chapter 10

The Cheerleaders

Bronx Warriors Cheerleaders – 2008 (Geri Demers-front row, center)

The Bronx Warriors Football Program moved into the modern era with the advent of the girls. Not to play but to cheer them on. The Bronx Warriors Cheerleading program was officially established in 1986. I had a chat with several cheerleaders, some of whom would go on to coach in the organization. My first stop on this tour would be with Kerry Demers, Jay and Geri's middle daughter, now a mother herself at age fifty. We embraced upon meeting. I had seen Kerry over the years, periodically. My memory of her is as a five-year-old, a little thing sitting on the couch in her parent's home on Hobart Avenue. Kerry promptly jumped into her "way-back" machine.

"From as far back as I can remember, the word "Warrior" was as common as the word "hello'. The Warriors were not just some seasonal league but a program that the community put their sons in. Years ago, children just played on the block or in the neighborhood. There were not many clubs out there at that time and if there were, families in our community couldn't afford it. My father stood on that field at Pelham Bay Park and offered the community a place for sons to go and play at very little money. He found a few others who were interested in this plan and started a team. My father and his coaches were volunteers. These were people outside of their full-time jobs, raising their own families, who committed to this journey of building a community. Every staff member made sacrifices in order to commit to this. Time away from their family, time away from their recreational activity and again, volunteers. From the time my dad started with a team of thirty, it had grown to over two hundred. You can imagine where my father spent all of his time. So, when families were on that field you knew these guys were all heart and passionate about what they were doing. They were spending all their spare time with strangers' kids for free. They believed in the cause. The Warriors were far from any league or common club. When you joined the Warriors, you were now part of this select family. Each child, parent, and relative mattered. What this meant was each child was looked after even if they needed a ride home to parent not at home yet. They would come back to our house have dinner, watch television until a family member was reached. Then my dad started expanding this club and started booking waterpark trips, movies and eventually a ski weekend every year. It was always on the holidays, Christmas, New Year's Eve, when all Warriors would come to the house before heading to their destinations. This was a tradition. The Warrior name was like an epidemic. We were known throughout the entire Bronx. No matter where you went you would see that red coat with the Warrior logo. I remember always feeling so proud. I believe it was 1980, I was twelve-years-old, I rounded up some neighborhood girls and we practiced cheers. Our uniforms were simple white skirts, red shirts and Chinese slippers and we cheered a few games. Then around 1984, 1985 when I was older, I wanted to get a team and seriously coach them. I had a group of girls from City Island and my little sister, Kim. The Warrior cheerleaders had made their own name. In 1986, that's when my mom started. As the saying goes, 'If you can't beat them, join them'. That was the beginning of the Warriors cheerleaders."

I chuckled at what was becoming a family reference to Geri's involvement.

"Mom had taken cheerleading to an entire new level. The ages started at five through fifteen. All were welcome. No child was excluded. At that time there were many schools that picked only a certain "few" to join. My mom said 'Bullshit' everyone has a place on this team. There were our baby sisters just trying to cheer on the sidelines waiting until they were old enough to be a cheerleader. Sure enough, next season there they were. So that's how the cycle began just like football. The children would start at age five, six, age out and become coaches. They would get married and have their kids play, and so on and son. We matched the age groups to cheer for the football age equivalent groups. Just like football, the cheerleading took off with every season. The team kept getting larger and larger. Again, coaches were volunteers. We started practicing at Lehman High School gym just like the Warriors football teams. They had one gym and we had the other. We started practicing stunts more seriously. Eventually we hired professional cheer stunt choreographers from Florida for serious training camps. We discovered how talented and dedicated these kids, parents and coaches were. My mom started enrolling the girls in competitions. It was amazing. Most of the time we came home with first, second, or third place trophies. Probably one of my favorites was Jennifer Esposito, now Jennifer Volpe. She was, my little shy ten-year-old who became the backbone of the Warrior cheerleaders. I can see her now, as I did back then, when she first walked over with her dad, hair in two pigtails, very timid. From that day forward, she never stopped. She was a star, a gift, and steadfast. She was talented, organized and ran this league to stardom. I know for a fact that my mom could not have had the success she did without Jen. She was dedicated, reliable, and responsible. She knew the rules of what we could and could not do as a competitive group. This girl, married, having four children, three girls in cheer and a son in football, never quit. Cheerleading was now more serious. We had skirts and Warrior jerseys, and we cheered every game. Great experience! This is where Jennifer Volpe became the head of the Warrior cheerleaders. You should talk to Kim and Jen."

Kerry drew a breath, as she stepped out of her time machine. It was obvious to me that the memory of her mother was still emotional for her. A peck on her cheek, a tight hug, complete with warm wishes and I was off to see her sister. Kim Demers, the youngest of the Demers, who was more than happy to reminisce.

"When we first started it out during 1985 it was my sister Kerry who was in charge of the cheerleaders. I was eight-years-old. My sister did that first year and then my mother took it over and did it the following year. My Mom figured if she couldn't beat 'em so she'd join 'em."

I laughed at the repetition of this phrase amongst the Demers family. "You know, you're the fourth Demers to say that! Your father said that to me. Last Thursday, Ricky said the same exact thing, Kerry, and now you just said the same thing!"

"Well, because it's the truth, and everybody in my family knows it! She only did it because she had to spend most of her life on the field anyway, and he wasn't home, so she started something to be there with him. And she loved it. She loved the excitement on the field. Being around the kids. Being around the parents. And it was something they now had in common, that they could work together, her and my dad. That's why I think they were the perfect couple. We used to go to the games and be on the field every weekend before there was cheerleading. That's why I think cheerleading became such a natural next step for mom. Once she started doing it, she realized that it was a good idea. It just took off. That first year, it was just five or six of us girls when we started, when my sister coached, but then when my mom got involved that's when it really became a cheer program. She made it into a program like the Warrior football program. She made it a big program and then kept taking it every year to the next level, where we had squads and teams. It just kept growing and growing. She was just like my father with the letters, sending them out, and working with the parents. That's who she was and that's why I think that she was perfect for my father. Like him, she welcomed everyone. She was always working to help and work long and hard. My mother's biggest worry I think was only that she spent more money than either one of them could make. We evolved to where we entered competitions and then it became more of a real cheer program instead of just cheering for the football team. It became its own entity where the cheerleaders just were too high and mighty that they had no time to cheer for the boys." She laughed at her sarcastic humor. "I have friends, obviously, growing up through the program. A lot of my relationships that are still maintained today started when we met as kids on the field, and through the program. You know, it's funny, talking to the football players, they all are afraid of my dad. They would tell me, 'I can't do this to coach' or, 'I wouldn't mess around with coach!' And I would be surprised hearing from other guys that played for my dad how they were scared of him. Because he wasn't, to me, my mother was the disciplinarian in our family. She was the one that really disciplined us. But there were moments

216

that when my father blew, you knew to run. Run for the hills! But he didn't really have that on a daily basis, which was rare. That was not his personality or manner at home. I'm not sure why I brought that up…I guess it just memories. As I said, the people that I have met through the program are an extended family to us, and that's how I was brought up. This is my family. And all of the people that came back after playing and/or coaching would come to the bus trips and the ski trips and the murder mysteries skits he would throw in our house. We just had such a great time. And that's one thing I will also say, it's surprising to me how many people my father has reached and has helped and how many people my father knows. But growing up, I found that he would never ask anyone for anything. He wouldn't impose or use his connections or his relationships to benefit himself. My mom, she was a secretary. She worked in the superintendent's office at Lehman High School for a number of years. She worked at Westchester Square Hospital as a secretary in the social worker's department. She always worked, as a secretary. My Mother knew everyone because everyone loved her. If she wanted a job, she just went around the corner, bump into a few people, and the next week she'd have a new job as a secretary somewhere. Her energy was endless.

I stopped Kim for the moment. "My God, I have a picture of your mother from that night at Westchester Square Manor and it's Kerry hugging her from behind. Your mother looked as beautiful as I ever remember from when I was a little boy. She was gorgeous. And in that picture, to their right is Karen (oldest daughter). Behind Karen are Ricky and his daughter. Your dad is to the left. I love that picture. But you young ladies carry your Mother's lessons with you. That's what I told your sister, Kerry. I found your mom to be an incredibly strong-willed and good-hearted person."

Kim cut me off at the pass. "And that's exactly who she is. It's amazing that you could pick up on that because that is exactly what my Mother was. Those words you just used to describe her, I couldn't have said it better at church…those are the words to describe her."

Today, Kim is approaching her mid-forties, mother of six, a son and daughter of her own and four step-children. It's like the movie, "With Six You Get Eggroll". Kim is a graduate of Penn State and started her law career as a public defender but is now a partner, alongside her future husband in her firm practicing family law, matrimonial law, and criminal law.

My next visit was with Jennifer Volpe, a forty-four-year-old and mother of four, ages sixteen to twenty-two who teaches at P.S. 105 in the Morris Park section of the Bronx. Her degree is in elementary education with a masters in special education. She works in an Integrated Co-Teaching (ICT) classroom which is where students with disabilities are educated with age-appropriate peers in a general education classroom setting and receive a general education curriculum on an individual need basis[54]. Jen jumped right into the conversation of being a cheerleader.

"I remember I was there in 1985. I actually went because my brother was playing for the football team. My brother is two years older than me. I was ten and he was twelve. I had actually gone to a game and there were cheerleaders. When I was growing up if you didn't play softball as a girl there was nothing else for us to do. It was nice to go and be a part of something and be around other neighborhood kids. And at one point in time, Geri had over two hundred girls. But that very first day when I had shown up, there were about seven of them. There was Kim, Geri's daughter, and then six older girls. Kim was eight at that time. I just remember going there and my dad talking to somebody. He asked me if I wanted to join but I don't remember exactly what happened. I just know that I was there the following week. I was in a skirt. (laughing) And Kim and I just bonded because we were the babies. The other six girls were about thirteen years old. They came from City Island. That was the first team with Kerry coaching us, she was our original coach. Geri took over the next year. Kerry was still with us as a coach. That second year there was still Kim, Angela, and me but that's when we started getting girls from different areas such as Pelham Bay and the north Bronx. They made two or three teams. I cheered all through middle school with Geri and coached all through high school with her. Then I went to college in Albany for two years and I actually cheered for a Continental Basketball Association team, the Pontiacs, and their dance team. I transferred to New Paltz for my junior year and I was a cheerleader there. I was living in New Paltz, but I was commuting back and forth so I could coach cheerleading with her again but I loved it. Cheerleading was my life. I remember, I think it was 1994, when stunting really got incorporated in cheerleading. Geri actually gave me a team where the girls were doing more tumbling. and they were a little more athletic so they were able to do the stunting that I was taught in college. We had a team, almost twenty girls ranging

---

[54] www.uft.org/teaching/integrated-co-teaching-ict

between the ages of seven and thirteen, that wound up going to competition. They were the best girls from the Warriors that were put on to this team. Because they were able to tumble and do stunting. They had the sharpest movements. Geri put them on this team and it was our first experience at a competition. At that exhibition, it was at Monsignor Scanlon High School and I'll never forget this, our girls came out and did a couple of cheers. We then put the music on that I chose to dance to and they did a falling extension during the routine. The crowd went silent because they had never seen anything like it before (laughing). That was actually really cool. A falling extension is where two girls are holding one girl by her feet and she's up in the air in a half extension. The other two girls get behind her and as she falls back, and they pop her back up. Now you see that all the time. You see the girls falling. You see the girls flipping but at that time, nobody really did anything like that, so it was really cool. From that point on, we managed to enter them in more competitions starting the following year. It evolved from having that one team that went to competition to where we started having tryouts. Geri never really cut anybody because she didn't have the heart to do that (laughing) which was fine. It was all inclusive. She wanted everyone to be able to say that they were a cheerleader at one point in time. That was her catchphrase. Then it evolved into having three competition teams. That's when it all started to get more serious. We had the three teams. We had the little babies. They were seven, eight and nine. Then we had the next group that was ten or eleven and then we had the junior high school team. At one point we did have a high school team but only for a couple of years. The girls competed in New Jersey at Great Adventure and the local schools around here. We, as a group got big. There were so many teams because like I said before, Geri didn't turn anyone away. I want to say that it was mid-nineties when that happened. Then the numbers started to trickle down as other programs such as Saint Teresa's started to build their programs. We started to lose girls to their high school teams. Geri was always great about that too. She was always supportive that you have to be a part of your school. You have to be part of your environment. She was always good with the other coaches and stuff. You know we would go to their competitions and she always had a good rapport with most of them. We would watch the programs and we saw that they were stealing…or I should say they borrowed our material, routine. But that's okay. I am proud to say that we were one of the first with everything. In the Bronx, we were one of the first organizations that did cheerleading. Then we were the first group that did stunting and tumbling. When we started doing new routines, people were really impressed by it. It was pretty cool. I remember the year my daughter was on a team. She was in fifth grade. They were entered into a sixth grade and under competition and they won and they were crowned the grand champion. They actually received the highest score out of every team that competed that day. This includes the middle schools (seventh and eighth-grade girls). That was huge. They would go on to do really well. They always managed to place and like I said as it kept getting more competitive, we just got better. I had connections with choreographers in Florida. We used to have them come up and run cheerleading camps right before the season started. This was toward the last six years of cheerleading. It's really funny for me, it was really weird to make that transition from being a cheerleader when I was younger to where we go into competition.   At first, the Warriors were a traveling team, we were a travel team. I remember, as a cheerleader going to Dobbs Ferry and Tarrytown and the boys would play against other teams so we would cheer for them. We, as cheerleaders, didn't compete. Suddenly the Warriors became its own league. It had so many kids that they were able to make their own league, so we didn't travel anymore. The boys wound up competing against…each other. The boys had their own thing, and it kind of upset us girls. We were wondering, 'Well, what are we doing? (laughing). We're not cheering against anybody, now we have to cheer for both teams. There's not like one team you want to win because they're all Warriors.' It got kind of hard. For me as a coach on our sideline, for the cheerleaders, on Sunday it was more of a practice. To try out something new. To try out a new half time routine, because we were just entertaining all of the Warrior parents. We used to practice indoors at Owen Dolen Park, right in the middle of Westchester Square, and at Lehman High School and then in August we were always in Pelham Bay. I've been there [Warrior organization] my whole life. The Warriors are their own family. We all grew up together. That's where I met my husband. I have to say… my husband and I are the only warrior couple."

"Yes Jen, I've been told that by Jay. Tell me your story."

"When we were like teenagers my husband played on a Warrior team when I first started. He was twelve. He played with my brother and they became good friends. They must have been in seventh grade. We, as cheerleaders knew who the boys were because we were cheering for them. Carlo [husband] and I knew each other. Jay and Geri always did the yearly trip to Great Adventure for us kids. Then they did the annual ski trip in January and because Angela and I were like best friends with Kim, we always wound up going on these ski trips every year. They didn't invite the cheerleaders until later on so Angela, Kim and I were the only girls there along

220

with the boys. (laughing). And Kerry was our chaperone which is why we got into a lot of trouble. On these ski trips, as teenagers, we would all just be hanging out all the time. At this point, I was fifteen. One of the nights on the ski trip, me and Carlo just started talking, differently than normal. We weren't really serious in high school, but we were friends and we would just hang out sometimes. It wasn't until a ski trip when we were both in college that we really started dating. And that was pretty much all she wrote. We got married and we have four children. All four of our kids have been with the Warriors. Carlo, my husband, has always been a big football guy."

"Oh my God, he looks like an NFL middle linebacker."

"Well, he played for Mount St. Michael High School and then he played for Saint John's University, so, he played through college. He's always played football."

"What position did he play?"

"Um, lineman. Is that right?"

"You're such a girl."

"He was one of the big guys that tackled everybody."

"Yeah, I can see that."

"When I got pregnant and as I said, I have four kids, first three are girls. So, every time I got pregnant for Geri and Jay… it was like reliving their youth. (laughing). But Jay was waiting for Carlo and me to have a son and I would tease him. What do you mean? It's another cheerleader. (laughing). Everyone was asking, 'When is the boy coming?' When my son was finally born, my oldest daughter was seven. She was already cheering for the Warriors, so we never really left the field. I was always coaching. Even through my pregnancies. Then Carlo started coaching football for my son. When my son, Carlo Jr., was finally born everyone was saying, 'He's going to play football Jen'. And I would tell them, 'No he's not'. Because I didn't want him to get hurt of course. They probably shouldn't have, but they let him play because he was always so big. At four years old, he was playing flag football with them. I think he was six maybe seven when he went off to tackle football. My third daughter, Samantha, and my son, they both started with the Warriors when they were four. They were both really athletic and Sam was already tumbling. Geri said to me, 'Just put her in a skirt'. (laughing). I protested telling Geri that

221

'She's too little'. Geri came back at me, 'I don't care. Just put her in a skirt. She can be the mascot'. Eventually, we moved out of the Bronx to Pelham, but I kept bringing them back so that they could stay with the Warriors. They didn't have youth football or youth cheerleading here in Pelham and I didn't want them to lose that Warrior connection because this is our home. Today my son is about to go to Pelham High School and be their quarterback. Jay's excited. And my daughter is a really good athlete too in basketball and volleyball, but when she got into high school, she told me, 'Mommy, I want to get back into cheerleading'. (laughing) So, she's cheering for the high school football team. And Geri was always so good to them. She was like their other grandma. She was always encouraging them with whatever they wanted to do. Not just my kids. All of the girls, all the time. We had one cheerleader who, not wanting to but had to, choose between her competitive dance and our cheerleading. Geri had a very long conversation with her and she chose dance. We were very excited for her. It's not like we wanted to keep them all for cheerleading. Whatever the girls wanted and whatever they excelled at is what we were encouraging, and Geri was very good at that. Oh, she was definitely a second mom." Jen pause in reflection of her past. A smile was ever present throughout.

I figured I would pull her back to when she was younger by asking if the Cheerleaders had ever performed at a parade. If was as if I snapped her out of a hypnotic trance.

"Oh yes. One of my favorite memories is that she loved to march the St. Patty's Day parade. We marched in it a lot. We marched in the Columbus Day parade and the Veteran's Day parade. All throughout the nineties. Up until 2012, we were marching. They [parade committee] knew there were so many girls and we would march in those parades. We would cartwheel up Fifth Avenue all the way to St. Patrick's Cathedral. Of course, I did those cartwheels. I had no choice because I was one of the few that tumbled from when I was little. There wasn't many of us that were tumblers but if you were, you were cartwheeling. Geri didn't care if I was thirty years old and just had my fourth kid. I had to be in the front with her and I had to tumble. (laughing). She was tumbling too. The year after, Geri passed on January 2013, that year we marched in her honor. We all marched in the Saint Patrick's Day parade. I had to lead the parade that day. I don't know how or who exactly made it happen, but the St. Patrick's Day Parade Committee made Geri an honorary Grand Marshall that year. All the girls came out. We had our banner for Geri. But that was the last year that we marched. We didn't march again the following year. When Geri decided to 'retire' from the cheerleaders, I had her and some other people talking to me because they wanted me to be the one to take over the program. She did not know of her impending illness at that time. She was so physical. I was thirty-seven at this point. We finished the season. We had the last Warrior dinner that she was at which was in February of 2012 at Villa Barone. That night that was for all the girls [cheerleaders] to get their trophies and awards. We had created a shadow box with one of our newest uniforms. We had a collage of pictures made for her. We had all this stuff for her because she was retiring. She was trying to talk me into running the cheerleader for the upcoming season. She said she wasn't going to hand the program over to just anyone to run it. She didn't want to give it to somebody that wouldn't deal with it the way she did her whole life. She wanted me to take it over. At that point in time, I had my kids that were all in sports. They were all ranging in ages from nine to sixteen. All four of them were in basketball and dance. We were all over the place. There was no way that I could. I look back now and I can't believe I even had the time to coach cheerleading at that time in my life with all my kids being young. She was the head honcho and we all knew it and we all followed suit. I definitely enjoyed my role and my place. You know, she was the one that called all of the shots and she was the one to deal with difficult parents. I didn't really have to deal with that. Which was good. And you know, I liked being able to follow in her footsteps, but I didn't want to take over the program. Not because I didn't think I could do it. I had been doing that the whole time with her. There was one season where she was sick, so she wasn't around one season. I basically had to end up doing the whole program, but I just didn't feel right doing it without her. She was okay with my decision. She knew my kids were getting older. She knew I was running all over. She didn't hold it against me, but she definitely did say that she didn't want to give it to anyone else. Which touched me of course, but I just couldn't. I didn't have what she had. She had made her decision and she was letting people know that this was the decision that she was coming to. I didn't want to take it all on because it was a lot more than just cheerleading. It's easy for me to show up and coach and give those kids my knowledge. It's another to deal with the waivers and the permission slips, the insurance policies and the business side. So, by the time we had the Warrior dinner in February, it was very much known to all of the girls and all of the parents that this was the last year. By the end of it, the program was closing. Geri was retiring so there would not be a place for these cheerleaders the following year. We knew of other schools and we were reaching out to other coaches, or within the parish and within the neighborhood so that our girls could go to other school teams. We didn't just leave the girls high and dry. It was sad though. She wasn't able to enjoy life the way she had planned. There are a lot of girls that are now coaching. They are in their twenties now and they're the coaches at their old high schools. I know that's something that she's smiling about. She just adored them all. She mothered all of the guys that came through her house, the football players, so she went ahead and took on all the girls. At the beginning of the season, she was always good about making sure the coaches always got together at her house. You know, have a barbeque so that we could go over what we were going to do. Geri definitely kept us closer than just a coaching staff and I enjoyed being her right-hand woman. And the one thing she taught me, and I have carried this into my teaching career, never deny a child anything. Geri would never deny any child. Just because you don't fit the mold of what a cheerleader should be, just because you don't tumble, or you don't get into that little skirt, you can still be a cheerleader. You should not be denied that opportunity. Everybody has their talents. You just have to tap into it. Geri would find a way with each child and that's why everyone was always able to fit in. Yeah, sometimes we had to move the formation around to make it look better or give someone a different position or make them hold a sign, but they were still cheerleading with us and that's all that mattered. They were out there, and they were giving it their all and they were happy. That's all that counted."

I forged on into the world of Warrior Cheerleading with a phone call to Phyliss Kandel, Dennis' wife. She was expecting my call.

"Hi, this is Phyliss Kandel."

"Hello Phyliss, this is Bob Nieder. You're on the air. It's a pleasure to talk to you. I never met you but I've got a feeling you're the better half."

"Awe, he's a good man."

"Yes, he is. Alright, tell me how you get involved with the Warrior cheerleaders."

"Well, I got involved once my son started playing football. I'm sure you've heard that story. Jay used to go to the schools and hand out flyers, so my son Christopher, he was six-years-old, came home with a flyer and so did my girlfriend Debbie's son. My son was very into sports. He played baseball and hockey, so he wanted to play football. I went down to register my son for football with my girlfriend Debbie and her son but Jay would not sign up my son. Jay signed Debbie's son, Foster, because he was a lot bigger than Christopher. My son was crying. Jay spoke to Christopher and then told me 'We can't take your son because he's too tiny, he's under-weight, he's too small'. He was just making up excuses. So, I proceed to read Jay the riot act. "'I'm sorry, I don't put limitations on my son. Why are you putting limitations on my son? How dare you'. I cursed him out. And I had the biggest fight with Jay. I made the biggest scene ever.'

We were laughing over the phone. "Did Dennis know Jay at this point?"

"No Dennis didn't know him at all."

Unbeknownst to me at the time of this phone call, Phyliss was in a car riding around with Dennis and Jerry. From the background, I heard Jay defend himself, "I just saw a little midget walking in. I didn't know he was a ballplayer."

I mockingly scolded Jerry. "Shame on you Jay because when I played, we had about seven guys that were undersized. Jeez, Jay, we had a whole team of munchkins. We had linebackers and a defensive end or two who were about five-feet-six at age eighteen, com'on now.

Jay was on the ropes. "Bobby, he was only six years old."

Phyliss shot back at Jay, "I don't care. A ballplayer is a ballplayer. And you know what? He's been with the Warriors for thirty years now, five as a player and twenty-five as a referee. And they still call him a midget. That's his nickname, Midge." Once our laughter subsided Phyliss continued with cheerleading. "Geri had about maybe fifteen cheerleaders and, my daughter, Dawn, was six when she started there, the mid-eighties. When my daughter became sixteen, she also became a coach because that's how it was. She never wanted to leave. (laughing). Today she is thirty-nine. Geri had a very strict program. She was very dedicated. So, I decided to help her out with whatever needed to be done. And the program grew. It got so big that we didn't have to advertise. At one point, we had over three hundred girls. It was getting so that we couldn't keep up with it, all those girls at one time. So, we started breaking them up into age groups and assigned the older girls to coach. At one point, I had a few girls with special needs because that was very important to Geri. Geri herself was a mentor to many of the girls, especially my daughter. I think Dawn liked Geri more than she did her own mom at that time. (laughing) You know when I hear her talk and I look at her, she reminds of Geri and I tell her, 'Oh my god. You're so much like Geri." And what ended up happening was that these cheerleaders became a family of friends that never let go. Up until this day, a lot of the cheerleaders are still friends. As a matter of fact, one of the cheerleaders that was with us when she was nine, she moved to North Carolina. She came to visit us here in South Carolina, just a few weeks ago. So, Geri's memory lives on and on, through many people's hearts. She was dedicated. She was also demanding because she wanted to teach these girls consistency. She wanted to teach them what it meant to be on a team, devotion, sportsmanship, responsibility. And as the years went on, we became bigger and bigger and we started entering competitions and nine out of ten times we would win. She had many first-place trophies. Then she divided our group into three. The units I think we had were the Peewees, the Juniors and the Seniors. We also went down to the football field and cheered for the football players. And that was done every Sunday and if the travel team went out, us girls would go out with the travel team. (long pause) It's still very hard for me because Jay was like a dad and Geri was a second mother to us all. And her loss affected so many people. I can't tell you how many people were at her wake. I can remember when my daughter got really sick. We didn't know what was wrong with her. She ended up having brain surgery. I would pick up that phone and Geri would be right on the phone telling me, 'You know Phyllis, everything is going to be alright. You've got to be strong. It's going to be alright'. And I couldn't have gotten through that without her. You know you don't find people like Geri and Jay. In this world, they've been my role model. I have to say that, and I very much miss Geri because we used to fight all the time (laughing) because she was just like my daughter. Everything had to be perfect. We used to have to do tryouts because there were so many girls. Well, I would do the tryouts and everyone made it. Geri and Jen would say, 'You can't do tryouts anymore because everyone is one the team anyhow'. So, I said okay. That's how we got the special kids because I said, 'Okay I'm taking them too. You guys take the others and I'll take the ones who don't know anything'." (laughing)

Me being a boy had to ask her. "Let me ask you something Phyllis because there is a lot obviously as a guy who grows up in an era where cheerleaders are for colleges only, what is involved in a cheerleader practice workout? What do you have them do? Let's say it's the first time a young lady wants to be part of the Warrior cheerleading group."

"Well, what we would do is, we would start with a warm-up. Stretch and whatever and then we would show them a short, maybe a thirty-six-dance count of eight. So, we would show them a cheer, a very small cheer and then they would come down for like a week and we would practice with them. Then we would have the different age groups come to do a tryout. In the beginning, cheerleading was more about cheerleading. As time went on it became more of a competition between cheerleading and dance."

"Like choreography?"

"Yes, we would come up our own choreography and make our own music. I mean we did that I think, I want to say, the last three to five years. Geri had a choreographer come in but before that me, Dawn, and Jennifer would come up with the choreography, the dance. Then it became even harder because now they have to learn backflips and these crazy stunts. We would go on the internet, look it up and have our girls do the same thing. We'd go home, and Geri would give us homework. 'Okay, you've got to come up with two cheers by next Wednesday'. We were like, 'How are we gonna come up with these cheers' but we did. Geri actually got scholarships for a few girls going into private high schools. She had one cheer. And I'll tell you this, this is how powerful her cheerleading squad was. Every other cheerleading squad, Saint Teresa, Our Lady of Assumption used our cheers. And we know they used our cheers because we made them up. They may have used different moves, but the basic moves were ours. Her signature cheer was called the Hello Cheer and that stands out in my mind."

Hi, hello, we're really glad to see you!
We cheer for the Warriors and we're here to greet you
With a hi there and a hello
From us to you we say (team cartwheels)
HELLO!

"Every parade we went to, that woman would cartwheel down the avenue. You would not believe it. She would have the big girls like Jen, Dawn and herself, they would be in the front and they would cartwheel down the parade. Her favorite parade was the Saint Patrick's Day parade. I'm telling you, parades were amazing, amazing. Yeah, we were the Warriors. And that never ended until she was gone. I mean we would as coaches, we became so close, we would all go to her house and hand washed uniforms and pompoms. And she never thought of anybody but the girls. Her girls were her girls. I did it with her for twenty-five years. I heard you tell my husband 'Once you're a Warrior, you're a Warrior for life'. That's true and you want to know something? That is one of the things that was said at her wake. That we would always be Warriors. I mean for us as a cheerleading family, if one of us is going through something, we put it on Facebook and you'll get a ton of cheerleaders responding, 'Come on let's put out a Warrior prayer'. It's a family you know? And then there were our ski weekends and the cheerleaders were now part of it. We all went up buses and buses of us. They were all so different and great. I loved the entertainment, our entertainment. Jay had his skits and they were hilarious. We would all have to come up with skits, even the kids. There was that one game we would play. It was called the shit game, it was a bullshit game. Everybody had a name. For example, I was shy shit because I was very quiet. Dennis was clean shit because he was in the cleaning business. I can't remember the resorts we went to but I do remember that there was a couple of them that we got thrown out of. There was one where we had a cake fight. This was upstate New York and it was Geri and Jay's anniversary. We had a big cake and one thing led to another and we had a big cake fight. All the cheerleaders would make sure they all got feety pajamas and they would all come out in their feety pajamas. You know, to this day we're still moms to a lot of those girls. Maybe you should talk to my daughter about all this."

"I would love to. When is she available?"

"She's available right now. She's sitting right next to me."

A different voice came on the phone and we exchanged greetings. Having heard from Phyliss on how and when Dawn had become a Warrior, my obvious question to her was what was the experience like for her. Her response was as immediate as a New York minute.

"I loved it. I loved it because I was a part of it. I loved cheerleading, but I loved being a part of a team. I remember, being close to my brother Chris, we would do everything together. When he would have a practice, we all would go. Then I started cheerleading and that was it. I was hooked. I can also remember the first time I met Geri. I think my dad might have taken me over to meet her and I spoke to everybody. Geri just took me in. I was put on the team and I started. They had older girls there, twelve and thirteen years old and they were nice to me. But that just gave me more encouragement to want to be like the older girls. Geri and I always had a tight bond. Even when I was little. For me at that age, I had a lot of insecurities, so I think being with the Warriors helped me overcome some of my insecurity. And, Geri never made any of your insecurities come out. Everybody was equal no matter what. She didn't favor anybody for what they looked like or for what they could do. Everyone was equal, and she pushed you to be who you wanted to be. I wound up cheerleading into high school, then I stopped for maybe three or four years but I came back and I started coaching."

"Tell me more about your relationship with Geri. Who was this woman to you, what was she to you? What is her influence on your life?"

"Oh God. You're going to make me cry. To me, she was my other mother. She was the person that kept me strong. She was the person that taught me to be strong and to never give up. And now that I'm am an adult, I apply all those lessons because my life is not the easiest life, so I sit there, and I say, 'What would Geri do?' To me, she was also my friend. When I got married and I had to make some tough decisions in my life, she was the person I would go to. She was my go-to person. You know like my mom was there, but sometimes you just need that other person and she was that person for me. She kept me grounded and was the one that would keep me on the right path like, 'I'm going to take you with me and this is the road we are going down.' And she kept me ready for the day when I had a daughter, Destiny. I think that really changed our relationship because I have a daughter with special needs. Geri took her and treated her like I don't think anybody else would, other than my parents. I think that because Geri had Karen, she knew how to deal with Destiny and she basically helped us through it." [Karen is the oldest of Jay and Geri's children. Karen is a special needs individual. Today she is fifty-two years old living with Jay.] "I got to see how Geri interacted with her but until it's, you know, your own child… it's a lot to deal with. It's a lot different when it's yours. When I saw how Geri was with Karen that is how I would treat Destiny. I go to her level. I talk to her. I show her what she needs to be doing or we do it until she feels confident. I slowly put her into situations and we talk about them. Geri always told me, 'Never sugar coat anything. Always talk to her like she is an adult. Always make her understand what she needs to know'. Destiny is really shy. How can you be shy and be a cheerleader? But she loved cheerleading. I mean that's all we did in the house because that's what mommy loved to do. Geri would not let her shy away from doing it because she was scared or had anxiety being close to other people. Geri would take her to the side and teach her by herself to do the cheers so that she knew what she was doing. Geri would slowly walk her over to the group and ask Destiny, 'Okay, is this close enough?' and Destiny would quietly tell Geri, 'Yeah' and eventually she got into the group. She wasn't one of the most outstanding cheerleaders, but she wouldn't have been able to do that if Geri didn't push her and help her and get her through it. She would do a lot of confidence building. You know, 'You can do it. I'm here for you. Never give up.' Destiny can tell you to this day if something gets hard, she will say to me, 'Mommy, Geri wouldn't want me to give up, would she?' and I tell her, Nope'. My daughter doesn't like to try new things so if she doesn't know what something is then she will have anxiety. But Geri would tell her, 'No, you can get through it. You can do anything you want to do' and she helped her. Some of the parents didn't like it. They would say that Geri was 'favoring her'. Geri didn't care what they had to say. Geri would tell the others, 'Don't question me on why I'm doing what I'm doing. There are reasons why I do what I do'. That's why Destiny was able to succeed so much in her career of cheerleading and dance. It was because of Geri. At that point, if I had problems with my daughter, I would call Geri. I would plead, 'Geri, I don't know what to do. Can you try to talk to her'? Geri would get on the phone and talk to Destiny and she would be calm by the time she got off the phone. She played a big role in our lives. Geri would always tell me her favorite saying, 'God gives you the strength and you always get through it'. And that's what I still say to this day, over and over again. 'God give me the strength'. At times, Destiny might be down emotional but then all the sudden she has a burst of energy and I look at her and think 'I guess he gave you the strength'."

"My God, Dawn, you've touched my heart. I am so glad we had this conversation. I had no idea that your daughter is a special needs child."

"Bob, it was a pleasure talking to you. And if you ever want to have a conversation with my daughter, give me a call this weekend. I'm sure she won't talk long but her point of view of Geri is pretty amazing."

That following Saturday, I did place a call to Dawn. I mentioned to her that it might be easier and more comfortable for Destiny, now age fifteen, to hold a conversation with her mother rather than with a stranger. This is what we've got.

"So, Destiny, how old were you when you started cheerleading?"

"Like five."

"And what was it like for you when you first went out on the field and met Geri?"

"It was nerve-wracking but exciting at the same time."

"And how did Geri help you on your first day?"

"We created a special bond so like she was more I guess, not focused on me but she understood me since me, you and grand-mom were also cheerleaders and coaches. So somehow, we had a special bond even though it was the first day."

"Okay. And as you became more involved in cheerleading in which ways was Geri there to help you?"

"When I felt like I couldn't do stuff properly she would get in my head and help me think 'don't say can't, you can do this'. She motivated me to do things that I thought I couldn't do."

"And how do you feel that being a Warrior cheerleader and meeting Geri and being part of a team affected your life today?"

"Like, like…repeat the question."

Dawn repeated the question.

"Like, teaching me teamwork, saying to me and all my friends that if we were going out and we can't decide on something we all compromise…like we're on a team still. And like, if I'm doing something that I enjoy, and I feel that I can't perfect it, I think about what Geri would have said to me and I would know that I can do it. It would motivate me to do it right or get it the way I wanted to."

"That's good. Now that you're older and you had a lot of years as being a cheerleader what lessons have you learned from being a cheerleader?"

"To never say never, don't say can't. Basically, if you said you can't or something, you're into doing a lot of push-ups."

"That's very true."

"So, that's the lesson that I learned. Always be cheerful, never be so down with something that you make other people down. Like if you go to competition and you're cheering and you're cheerful then the rest of the crowd is not sad, they're always cheering and cheerful."

"So, you think if you're happy other people are going to be happy?"

"Hopefully yes."

"That's good. And your relationship you said was a bond from the beginning with Geri. How do you think that you could explain your bond with Geri?"

"Geri was like another grandma to me. She was not just my coach, she was my grandma basically. She was always talking to me whether it was a cheerleader matter or a life matter, she always told me to push myself to do more than I can do. She was always there for me no matter what. We had that special bond. Not like coach and cheerleader, it was like grandmother and granddaughter."

"That's beautiful. She loved you just the same. Now, when you get older and you'll have your kids, one day, do you recommend putting them in a recreational sport that you were in like that? Do you think they would benefit from that?"

"Honestly, if it's a coach like Geri, then definitely. If not, then they probably would not benefit. They would not get the same life skills that I got from Geri than from a different coach that is not like Geri."

"So, you believe that Geri was the reason you succeeded.

"Yes."

"It's amazing…beautiful. I think you said a lot. I think you did a good job. I'm proud of you."

Geri Demers (top left), Dennis Kandell (top center), Jerry Demers (top right)

Geri Demers & Jennifer Volpe

Geri & Jay Demers – Appreciation Day at Rice Stadium, Pelham Bay Park, Bronx, N.Y.

Cheerleader Uniform - 2000

Gerri Demers (top row), Kerry Demers (front, center), & Jennifer Volpe (first row, right)

Fairleigh Dickinson University, N.J. – 2009 Geri Demers (front row, center), Jade Demers (Geri's granddaughter to her left), Jennifer Volpe (second row, left)

Destiny Martinez & Geri Demers - 2009

Fordham University Competition, Bronx, N.Y. - 2009

Warrior Cheerleaders 1985 – (bottom row) Michelle Howard, Kristi Mincieli, Danielle Mazzella (middle row) Jennifer Volpe (#77), Joanne Hubener, Anne Marie Thompsen, Kim Demers (#52) (top row) Kim Vincent

Chapter 11

Epilogue

67th Anniversary - Awards Dinner, Scavello's on the Island – City Island, Bronx, NY – February 2019

On Thursday, February 21, 2019, I attended the Sixty-seventh Annual Awards Ceremony of the Warrior Football League. It was held at Scavello's on the Island. Scavello's is a family owned business that specializes in catering in City Island. They provided an elegant dining experience in an inviting lavish setting along with great food and friendly, professional service in a comfortable atmosphere. The Warriors have held many an event there and as always it was a great evening. Roughly one-hundred-fifty, players, coaches, parents, and guests were in attendance. I was honored to be a part of the affair. A wonderful night it was. I was seated at a table alongside Jeff Ortiz' dear and charming wife, Rosemarie, along with her daughter Jessica and her husband Billy Lawston, Roe's son Andrew with his fiancé Lena and of course Jeff's favorite, grandson Bobby. The affair was dedicated to Jeff as he had suddenly passed away on September 1, 2018. A massive heart attack during his sleep took him from us. A true Warrior, from P.S. 106 all the way through the Youth Football Organization assisting Jay up until his passing. Joe presented Roe with a plaque honoring Jeff. Jeff was with us all night, in spirit, as he adorned the cover of the program along with many pictures and tributes to him within it. The speeches were on point stressing the Warrior Way, fun and safety, and celebrating the players. Joe Desimone led the way as master of ceremonies. It was as if I was listening to Jay. Councilman Mark Gjonaj gave a particularly inspirational speech. Even yours truly gave a speech. Thankfully I kept it short and sweet. I am best left to my writing and not my rambling on, especially to ten to fifteen-year-olds who want their trophies. As I was handed the microphone, the circle had been completed for me. As I told the crowd, as I looked upon everyone, that in 1970 when I received my first Warrior trophy, I had wondered who the group of old guys was sitting at another table. A coach informed me that they were Warriors that played in the past. The old guys might have been all of fifty years old. I guess I am now one of the "old guys" at age sixty-six. I explained to the players of how proud I am to be a Warrior and I am proud of my young Warrior brothers who carry our tradition. They are surrounded by great coaches and parents guiding their futures, who only want for their success and what's best for them. For most, their Warriors experience will mean more as they age. It will be carried for life because being a Bronx Warrior is where we live, and this is who we are. Our heritage, our history. We have been around longer than many NFL teams. Certainly, a great evening. The highlight of this affair for me was meeting Julius Lopez, an ex-Warrior at age thirteen. Julius "Sarcoma Warrior" as he was announced was presented with a trophy. The nickname needs no explanation. I did speak with the young man later. The charm in his eyes and the magic of his smile stole my heart. He lit me up. In speaking with his father Tim, I was informed that Julius was diagnosed with sarcoma at age ten. His necrosis was at ninety-eight percent in his right femur right above the knee. He has surgery at Montefiore Hospital where he received a full knee replacement. They caught it in time. Only two percent of the tumor is still active but his prognosis is very good. He has been cancer free for two years. Julius' love is football but because of this he cannot play. He stays involved working with the coaches. The correlation between Julius and Joe Reich, in my mind, very similar in their spirit and fight. The Warrior Way is a positive. There may be a setback but we don't quit, we don't lose. Have I mentioned that it was a perfect event?

This would be Joe DeSimone's last moment as Head Administrator of the Warrior Football League as he is stepping away to coach Cardinal Spellman. The organization is losing a good man and he will be missed. Jerry will be back in play as Founder and Executive President with Jim Pellicone's able assistance as President.

I know that this organization and what Jerry has built and what he provides to the community will be in great hands.

***

It may have been the enjoyment of the awards dinner that triggered a flood of reminiscences as a Warrior or maybe it was sitting with Jeff Ortiz' family as they honored Jeff's passing and what he meant to the organization for the past fifty years, perhaps it was a combination of the two that nudged my memory. It was a conversation we had a little after the affair at Westchester Manor back in 2012. I had asked him what was involved in setting up the event and what brought it about. I think Jeff best explained how we think of the Coach.

"It began with the "boys" from P.S. 106 community, with fond memories of Jerry Demers that decided to organize a reunion to honor and thank Jay for his dedication and service to the youth of the community. I got a lot of assistance from Mike Pisanello and Joe Regina. Jerry not only coordinated football for the boys at P.S. 106, but also hockey, basketball, punch ball, soccer, whiffle ball, and even trivia games when it rained. He organized all types of sports back then. We had a softball team and hockey leagues. He always had us playing sports all of the time, keeping us out of trouble. We had a touch tackle team when I was about 15 years old and Jerry was the coach," Ortiz said. "He would take us to his house and show us films. It was almost like going to school, the way we studied [football] plays. That team went onto win the city championship, un-scored upon. Around 1971 was when people started to lose touch, with going away to college and moving to other states. Recently, a group of us decided to try to get in contact with everyone to bring everyone back together for a reunion. We have people coming from all over the country, so that will be a little surprise for Jerry. It would be a gathering of former players to show their love and affection to the man who influenced all of their lives as we honor him. In this joyous task of contacting all my old friends there is one common thing that I have discovered and that is, that most of us have been involved in coaching our kid's as well as other kid's in sports. I believe that is what Jay taught each and every one of us, the gift of giving back and caring for our youth."

Jerry has been awarded a proclamation from the President of the Borough of the Bronx, Adolfo Carrión, Jr. which reads as follows; Whereas the Warrior Football Club is celebrating fifty-seven years as a Bronx youth organization, devoted to giving young people a separate yet competitive environment to develop athletes and cheerleaders and whereas fifty-seven years of service to the youth of this great city. Whereas, I Adolfo Carrión, Jr., President of the Borough of the Bronx, due heartedly proclaim February 21st, 2008, Warrior Football Club recognition day. Jay has also received a similar proclamation presented to him by Senator Jeff Klein and Councilman Mark Gjonaj on February 22, 2018 and he was honored with a plaque by Bronx YMCA on September 6, 2018 for his years of selfless work in the community. What we would like to see, sooner than later, is for the County of the Bronx to rename our home field, Rice Stadium, to Jerry Demers Field at Rice Stadium. That would be a true testament to a great and influential man.

***

The world of a Warrior begins with the first steps into a world of brotherhood, compassion, and camaraderie. Looking back, I now realize that to win a football game was irrelevant, though we won most. Being a Warrior would become a life lesson under a coach, who became a father figure to most of us, and friendships that would last forever. Young boys don't listen to their fathers because we know more than them at that adolescent time of our lives. Of course, there are always others talking to us, telling us the very same message as do our dads. Those are the people we heed. From a soft voice heard, at age eighteen, to volumes said to me over the years, the lessons taught and the lessons learned, carried throughout my life. Life lessons that I absorbed as a teenager transcended into the rest of my life in marriage, in business, and in relationships. We were all taught this and we all carried it forward. Jerry, never on a soapbox or pounding the drum delivered subtle messages in isolated, quiet moments. In life, we come upon crossroads, the fork in the road and the road we choose to take that defines our future, our lives. Jerry led us down the right path, a good path. I've always said that there is a "Warrior Way". We knew it as players. We were taught "the Warrior Way". We all seem to fit a certain mold that emanated out of Jerry and if you didn't fit that mold, that Warrior Way, that particular way about all of us, you didn't stay for long. The Warrior Way is a mindset. A way passed on for decades and generations. A way of class and distinction. It is both a behavioral and a mental process, a positive wavelength. The frustration of losing or failure at the moment doesn't enter our equation because each failure becomes a stepping stone to success. With each failure, we get closer to success if we don't resign ourselves to it. And to trust the Warrior Way gives comfort because it never fails us.

Perhaps the homages for Jerry, Jay, the Coach, the Chief have been repetitious and endless. I could have provided many more. He was not comfortable with this but as I told him, "For most, tributes come after death, you happen to be receiving them now so enjoy it while you can." I teasing also said, "Jay, at your age you aren't close to your bright exit but at eighty years old you are running that deep fly pattern towards life's endzone, we all are. Enjoy the praise for your life's work, you earned this."

Jerry Demers is more than just a brilliant coach to me, he is a gentleman in the truest sense and respected by all. I have always considered him as my second father. I missed my dad dearly but I do have Jerry. When the football Giants win that big game, I can't share it with my father but I can and do with Jay. The conversations I would have with dad are now held with Jerry. He softens my loss to this day. Jay is who he is, at all times, when no one is watching. Small in stature, big of heart. I have asked everyone to define the man. Vic Anderson had the best response in one word, consistency. It's more than football for this man. It has always been about molding, shaping and influencing lives. Like Johnny Appleseed, he spread his football seeds, nurtured us and grew us well. The lessons he taught beyond the field to over ten-thousand kids and teenagers.

I can only speak for myself but everyone he touched could step up to this plate and explain his impact in their world. What he taught I brought into my career. His team concept gave me the ability to work seamlessly within the group. Being organized in my task. Learning to build relationships and getting along with others even through group strengths and weaknesses. Not accepting failure and in the face of it searching for success. That is the Warrior Way. A lot of who we are, what we've become, the way we think, how we handle adversity in our lives, the success we've achieved. A lot of us are the product of Jerome Demers, generations of us.

Writing our history and the legacy of one man has been a gift and quite a journey. This has been a blessing as Frank Botti told me and he's right. The stories that I heard from older men

242

who were in their adolescence in the late forties to men who were teenagers in the mid-sixties, to young adults from recalling their youth. I don't know that this story that I have written would interest anyone but I do hope that every young person and adult has hopefully had a Warrior-like experience in their life. I hope that our experience has touched you and that it brings you back to your youth, good days, and good memories. My experience with the Warriors and my coach, Jerry Demers, has provided this for me and I'm certain, for all my teammates as well. It is the reason that I feel privileged to be a Warrior and to share it with my teammates, my true friends, forty-five years later.

***

During an early evening, on a field in the Bronx, a football stadium they came from afar and near. Seemingly from everywhere they came, children, adults, and the elderly. From all points in the Bronx, upper Manhattan, and Westchester they came, one by one then in small groups then in droves. Not a footstep, not a voice was heard, there was quiet. Hordes of players of all ages descended onto mid-field. What were a few, grew to be hundreds. It grew into thousands and thousands. They all encircled a diminutive man. A special man, a unique man. Each one leaning forward, an arm on the back or shoulder of the player in front of them. En masse we waited in complete silence for the call. His soft voice echoed, carrying into the night far, for all to hear. "Our Lady of Victory". The response was thunderous as we shouted in unison, "Pray for us". The stadium came to rest with momentary silence. The voice let loose, "Kali". We all roared in return, "Kali", the ground trembled. Again, Kali was invoked from the man. We followed by an even louder response. A third and final Kali and again we called out, thousands of Kali's rang out into the night. Our invocation was heard by all of sandlot football, everywhere.

Post Script

All for A Number

Rice Stadium at Pelham Bay Park

I had to go up o New York to get a number. This I will explain at a later point. Getting off my flight at JFK airport, I boarded the Train to the Plane which took me to Sutphin Boulevard – Archer Avenue in Queens. May 11, 2021, was a perfect weather day. A clear blue sky brightened an old store-infested, bustling neighborhood. A creaky, shaking escalator took me down to the E train. I stood at the subway platform awaiting its arrival. The screeching squeal of the train's brakes against its steel wheels as it approached was all it took to flood my mind and jog its memories of almost fifty years of life in New York City. Good thoughts put a smile on my face. I got on and even though it was off hours, I was stunned to find the car devoid of passengers, six travelers in all. It was the sign of our pandemic times. More people working from home or out of work. After thirty years of riding belly-to-belly rush hour, I welcomed the space and a seat. My destination was Buhre Avenue in the Bronx where I would be picked up by the

Coach, Jay. Without much of a wait, he pulled up in his new Toyota sedan in front of George's Restaurant. As always, big hugs and smiles were exchanged. I would stay two nights with Jay and his eldest daughter, Karen, watching Yankee games.

It wasn't long before we took off to Rice Stadium for the Tuesday evening Warrior Youth Organization's clinic. We walked the entranceway, Middletown Road and Stadium Avenue. A strange feeling overcame me. In about three weeks, this walkway would become Joe DeSimone Way. I had known Joe for almost fifty-five years. One of the nicest, caring, giving a person one could know. He coached with the Warriors for more than 25 years and served as president from 2015 to 2018 when Jay stepped down from the position. Joe also coached Cardinal Spellman, both junior varsity and varsity football. He led the team to two Division City Championships in 2006 and 2008 and was inducted into Spellman High School Hall of Fame. If you were to ask his players what they took from him they would tell you that his mantra was "it's not just important to be successful on the field, but rather a good person off of it" Shades of Jay. I will miss him calling me by the name he forever tagged me with, "Ugly".

Stadium was teeming with activity. Joggers and walkers, both young and old around the track. A large group of very young boys and girls engaged in parent-organized soccer drills. A calisthenic group worked out off to the side of the field. We got to the shed where all the equipment was stored. It was good to see Jimmy Pellicone, still at the helm as Jay's right-hand man. It was odd that there was no Dennis Kandell. Dennis and Phyliss, along with their daughter Dawn and their granddaughter, Destiny, the greatest of all Warriors, had the nerve to retire to South Carolina living the life of luxury. Also, there was no Richie Farino. Sadly, Rich was taken from us by the ravage of COVID-19 on December 19, 2020. A Navy man, who was handy with a camera and video recorder, served in Viet Nam. He patrolled the waterways searching for the bad guys. He will be sorely missed for his directness and all that he gave to the kids.

Two foldout tables in front of the shed were swarming with young boys, some signing in and others with their parents registering to be in the program. This was a free two-hour clinic held Tuesday, Thursday, and Saturday. Its purpose was to get the kids interested so that they would sign up for the football program that would commence in

June. The excitement in these young boys was evident as they could not wait to hit the field. There was madness on the field, sixty-five boys in all, ages five to thirteen. They broke down into three groups, five to seven, eight to ten, and eleven to thirteen. Two coaches per group ran them through agility drills. The enthusiasm was through the roof. I could see the gleam in Jay's eyes, the broad smile on his face. I believe this is what keeps the Coach young at age eighty-three. At one point, he took to the field to assist with instruction to the older group.

The next morning, breakfast was served at the Crosstown Diner. To this day, I do not understand how two eggs, over medium, are so much bigger than two eggs in Florida. Perhaps it is the price. Over coffee, we got down to business. I needed my number.

"Jay let's start with what's going on today. You had a clinic, what is that all about? The purpose or the aim."

"Bobby, the clinic is merely meant to be an addition to giving the kids a good time teaching them a little football. The clinic is to recruit. We give a free clinic and then we hope that some of these kids will come out when we start practice in August for the flag football.

So again, the ages out there, the groupings.

Jerry: The ages are five to seven, eight to ten, and eleven to thirteen. We're hoping to make it five to seven, eight to ten, and eleven to thirteen. But last year, we had so few players that we had to make it five to nine and ten to fourteen. So, it was very difficult."

"The reason for low attendance?"

"The reason for low attendance is twofold. One is the Parks Department would not give out permits during the Covid for tackle football, so we had to play flag. The other was more devastating if they keep it up. The Board of Education sent out a memo to all the schools saying that no program that isn't free could pass out flyers. That really hurt."

"So, they are actually stealing kids from you by having free programs?"

"Well, they have their own programs, not free programs."

"I'm a little confused, I don't know how that impacted the Warrior Organization."

"Well, they refused… we used to go to each school, thirty schools, and give out packages of twenty-five flyers for how many classes they had. We covered everybody in thirty schools. Each got a personal flyer, but they cut that out."

"So, you can't recruit."

"Exactly, we can't spread the word like we used to."

"I've got to tell you, it's odd not to see Dennis out there."

"He's a great loss because Dennis talked to the parents. He would talk to anybody and he had no fear of asking them what they did for a living or anything else. Jimmy is not as social as Dennis."

"Yes, and he told me that himself. He's a great help but on a different level."

"Oh, yes, he does the paperwork fine but he's not a social being. And I'm getting too old to do it alone."

"So, who's your go-to guy? Do you have a coach out there that you think might step up to fill Dennis' void?"

"Well, Eric the coach with the older group, is the leader of the clinic. He is the next up-and-coming coach and Anthony Bruno which is, he been with us probably two years now, he's an up-and-coming coach too."

"How long has Eric been with the Organization?"

"Two years."

"We're going to go positives and negatives, but at this time of sixty-nine years of Warrior football, where do you see the downside, you know, we've got the Covid, we've got concussion concerns, we've got the funding or lack of it from the Board of Ed. Is there a fear that this will come to an end?"

"The downside of the football program is it used to have six hundred kids in the program and now we have eighty to ninety to a hundred. Sports is not the only thing in the world like it was when we were young. If you didn't play sports, you were out of it."

"There was something said last night about coaches. I heard you saying that you need more coaches. I would imagine that you would recruit parents or somebody?"

"Jimmy is working on putting out a message on our website that coaches are needed. I recommended it to him…see what comes out and pick the best of what comes out. He would rather talk individually to the persons and judge them by their response, by what they say."

"What's the upside in your mind? You're always positive Jay, that's a Warrior attribute."

"The upside is that it has gone seventy years (laughs). And the upside is that we have the inside track on the permits. A lot of people are playing soccer, they don't know anything about the permits (chuckles), which helps them in a way because nobody checks their use of the field. But the upside is that we'll have the permits Monday, Tuesday, Thursday, Friday, and during the season, on Saturday."

"I just wonder, when you go to bed at the end of your life, what do you take with you (I choked up with this question)."

"I take with me the knowledge that I have done something to improve the lives of so many kids, maybe ten-thousand, maybe more, I don't know because we used to do a Winter Program every year with five sports in it. So, I will be very happy.

"Jay, I always tell people, that you were more than a football coach, that you were more of a mentor. You were a second dad to a lot of us. An older brother to the older guys. And it was more about life lessons, doing things the right way. We won a lot of games, the 106 guys, won a city championship, but it was beyond that. Ollie said it, we had a conversation, he said, "a lot of things that I learned from Jay, I applied it to my life, my marriage, my job", and I told him that I did the same. In my marriage, in business, in the corporate world. These were lessons from Jay, and I said that I've been blessed. And when I talk about him in Florida, I always say that we all know someone like this. It could be a religious person, a teacher, a community leader, or a neighbor that do those great things for young people. And then I tell them his story. They go crazy when I tell them that "He's doing it, seventy years down the road".

"Well, I can't say that it was intentional. It was just my personality. My family life was very happy. We didn't even know that we were poor (big laugh). I didn't get a television set until I was fourteen years old. And I had my brother, my older brother Frank was eight years older than me. He was a saint…he is a saint."

"I miss him."

"Yeah, I miss him very much."

"You were on the field yesterday Jay, and I know that you still have a lot to offer to these young guys for the sport beyond everything else that you do. What are you getting…when you go out there what are you talking to them about? I saw them doing calisthenics, agility drills."

"I don't believe too much in agility and the working out. That's for the older boys. I talk to them about what skill they have and what they can do with it and let them practice what I say."

"So, you ask them what they like to do?"

"Bobby, I can tell, I can see what their strengths are. One of my best skills was recognizing talent and taking talent in and incorporating it into my program."

"Isn't that how you did Jackie Cawley? You saw that he was a quarterback."

"Yeah, he was a little reluctant."

"No, he didn't want to play quarterback. He wanted to play receiver. They all want to play receiver because it's away from the contact (chuckles)."

"I mean, when you saw Bernie Lyons, what goes through your head that you say I'm going to give up my position because he's better?"

"Well, we used to play in St. Catherine's Park on 68th Street, touch football. And I saw him down there. He was only one year younger than me, but I saw that he could catch, he could throw better than me, everything."

"And that's really where your coaching started, isn't it?"

"Yes, oh yeah. Coaching down at the playground level. I even played the line a little bit."

"You were how old when you started coaching?"

"Thirteen, I'd say fourteen, but that was the first year we really had a team. Eleven guys, nine helmets, seven shoulder guards, and different uniforms."

"When you transitioned from the original touch team that won the City, 1967. Bernie Kaufman's team, Lo Lubarsky, and Eric Wolfe's team, and we became the tackle team, and then again, the organization transforms again into the Youth Organizational League."

Jerry interrupted me. "It takes a lot to keep a team together. With a youth team, you have to collect the money and all the other stuff."

"What is the greatest pleasure that the Youth Organization gave you? I know about the tackle team and the older guys, the 106 years."

"Seeing the kids that I like. In a way, it is hard because most of them don't come back like they used to. You don't see them anymore. Our group, the Huddle is unusual in that you guys have kept together for over forty years. I enjoy the pleasure of creating that and watching it develop.

Jerry: Well, it kept building so I kind of took it for granted that it would go on for as long as I was around. I made a point of committing to the football team. That was my commitment, my life."

"Are you going to coach this year? I heard somebody say that you might be with the older group."

"I'd like to. I'd like to coach one more year in touch football and we may need more coaches if the attendance keeps up the same. But, last year, at the first meeting, there were a hundred and twenty kids and they gradually whittled themselves down and didn't play. So, this year, seventy-five is not a big number, really. Although we were surprised."

"It's not compared to what you're used to."

"What would stop you from not coaching this year because you said that you would like to coach. There's a little hesitancy in that statement."

"I think they think that I'm too old."

"Who? Bring them to me. (we shared a big laugh)"

"People…if you can't move like a player, they think you forgot everything you use to know as a coach. So, I think that's the main restriction. The younger coaches don't know that I can do what they're doing only better and with seventy years of knowledge."

"Are you going to talk to them about this?"

"Jimmy said he was going to talk to them. I told Jimmy that I thought it was him trying to protect me. Trying to protect me from getting sore legs. What we are seeing, Jimmy and I are that the numbers have been down for the last ten years. Every year, a little bit less. In our day, sports were everything. Back then, sports were like a religion. You didn't have to be great.

You might the last guy picked, but you're picked. To be out there with everyone else, it's a thrill. Especially if you're the last guy because then you're playing with the good guys. Well, I think from the sixth grade and on I was always the organizer, something like Jeff Ortiz. You need someone like Jeff or Frank Botti. You need someone who will make decisions for the good of the whole. Jeff learned from me going back to when he was a kid in the playground. And it's amazing how what you do has such an effect on other people."

Just two guys tawkin' sports. A perfect morning back home in the Bronx.

***

Head of table, clockwise, Art Langer, Jerry Demers, Joe Regina, Tom McGurl Vic Anderson, George Nardone (standing), Tom Piccininni (standing), Frank Botti, Jack Cawley, Ron Watson & yours truly

Wednesday night was our night at the Wicked Wolf, the Huddle. Jay was excited. He told me that he hadn't seen the guys in fourteen months, two Februarys ago when the virus broke out. We weren't sure how many of us would show up. I guess that there might be, at most, six of us based on a few verbal commitments, but that we would have a great time even if it was me and him. We got there early. Within moments after taking a seat at the bar, Joe Regina sauntered in. We moved to the restaurant side of the establishment, drinks in hand. By six o'clock, the guys wandered in. Ron Watson, Tommy Piccininni and Vic Anderson, Tommy McGurl, George Nardone, Frank Botti, Artie Langer, Jackie Cawley. We kept adding tables. Eleven of us in all, maybe twelve if you count Johnny Match who joined us via phone. The coach ate it up. A perfect evening amongst brothers, fifty years strong. We had become our fathers in that conversation ranged across the long table from reminiscing the "good old days of our teens" to catching up with today, our wives, our kids, our grandchildren. And yes, "Gorgeous" George's famous "puddle play" was once again invoked. I sat back soaking it all in between Artie and Ron and was humbled listening to their travels and efforts all over the globe. I watched Frank as he talked and showed pictures, with pride, of his new grandchild, Gianna. The excitable talk was all over and across the table. With a sly

252

smile, a moment of simpatico rolled through my mind. A few tears found their way down my cheek. I looked up at Joe Regina choked with emotion. "Joe, this is what's it's all about. It doesn't get better than this. You can't beat this." I put my head down, palm on my forehead to stop myself from bawling. I looked up at Joe and found that he was doing the same. I can't believe I broke down Joe. The evening ended a good hour after scheduled. Jay and I stayed up until midnight rehashing the great time we had. We did the same the next morning at the Crosstown Diner. The love, the camaraderie amongst all of us will never end.

Oh, I almost forgot to tell you, the number. The sole reason for my visit was to obtain a Library of Congress number. When this book was first published, I became my own publishing firm, No. 3 Publishing Company. What I did not know at that time was that you have to apply for this before the book is published which I did not do. I called the Library of Congress and they verified this. I might be dumb, but I'm not stupid. I asked that if I wrote a second edition could I get a number. They said yes. Due to new FCC cell phone recording regulations, I could not record Jay over my phone from Florida, so I hopped a plane. As a writer, I may not be John Steinbeck, Stephen King, heck, I'm not even Thomas Pryor, but it is a prideful thing for me to have our book in the Library of Congress. As Jay has proudly told me, "when we are all gone, the book will be there forever".

Fallen Warriors

May their souls rest in eternity. Good people who left us before theirtime, never to be forgotten.

1. Geraldine L. "Geri" (Wissler) Demers – Warrior YouthOrganization (cheerleader "chief")

2. Francis J. "Frank" Demers – First Warrior Team (original "chief)

3. Steve Caputo – First Warrior Team

4. George Melicharek – First Warrior Team

5. Thomas McQuade – First Warrior Team

6. Kenny Aronoff - P.S. 106 & 1967 City Championship SeniorWarrior Team

7. Alan Beberman - P.S. 106

8. Dennis Cronin – P.S. 106

9. Allen Johnson – P.S. 106 & Warrior Youth Organization (coach)

10. Johnny O'Donnel - P.S. 106

11. Jeff Ortiz –P.S. 106 & 1967 City Championship Senior Warrior Team, WarriorTackle Team & Warrior Youth Organization (administration)

12. William "Billy Beaver" Price – P.S. 106

13. Abe Raskin – P.S. 106

14. Tricia Simmons - P.S. 106

15. Frankie Starr- P.S. 106

16. Robert Stein - P.S. 106 & 1967 Runner Up City ChampionshipJunior Warrior Team

17. Lauren Zeltner - P.S. 106 – 1967 City Championship Senior Warrior Team

18. *Mike Cedrone – Warrior Tackle Team*

19. *Billy Coma – Warrior Tackle Team*

20. *Neil Balsamo – Warrior Tackle Team*

21. *Anthony Lombard – Warrior Tackle Team*

22. *Joe Menesik – Warrior Tackle Team*

23. *Larry Munoz – Warrior Tackle Team*

24. *Dougie Williams – Warrior Tackle Team*

25. *Bob Bonamassa – Friend of the Warrior Family*

26. *Joe DeSimone – Warrior Youth Organization (coach & President)*

27. *Rich Farino - Warrior Youth Organization (administration)*

28. *John "Omar" Burke, Sr. – Warrior Youth Organization (coach)*

29. *John Burke, Jr. - Warrior Youth Organization (player & coach)*

30. *Gerry DeFabia - Warrior Youth Organization (coach)*

31. *Lloyd Edmundson, Jr. - Warrior Youth Organization (player)*

32. *Eddie Esposito, Sr. – Javelin Coach & Warrior Youth Organization(coach)*

33. *Jason Farino - Warrior Youth Organization (player)*

34. *Robert Griffin - Warrior Youth Organization (coach)*

35. *Bob Howard – Warrior Youth Organization*

36. *John Kelly - Warrior Youth Organization (coach)*

37. *Patricia Lang - Warrior Youth Organization (volunteer EMT)*

38. *Mike Rocco - Warrior Youth Organization (player)*

39. *Skip Rose – Warrior Youth Organization (volunteer EMT)*

40. *Fran Solarzano - Warrior Youth Organization*

41. *Frank Volpe - Warrior Youth Organization (administration)*

Appendix

NOTICE TO PASSENGERS

Effective Sunday, July 11, 1948, the 167th STREET CROSSTOWN, 138th STREET CROSSTOWN, WESTCHESTER AVENUE and ST. ANN'S AVENUE will be MOTORIZED.

Effective same date, exchange of Free Transfers between the 167th St. Crosstown and the Broadway - Kingsbridge, Third and Amsterdam Avenue will be Discontinued.

A charge of two cents will continue to be made for Transfers from the Williamsbridge Road, Eastchester Road and Throggs Neck Buses to South Bound Westchester Avenue Buses and Vice - Versa.

ORIGINAL POSTER ANNOUNCING THE END OF TROLLEY CAR SERVICE

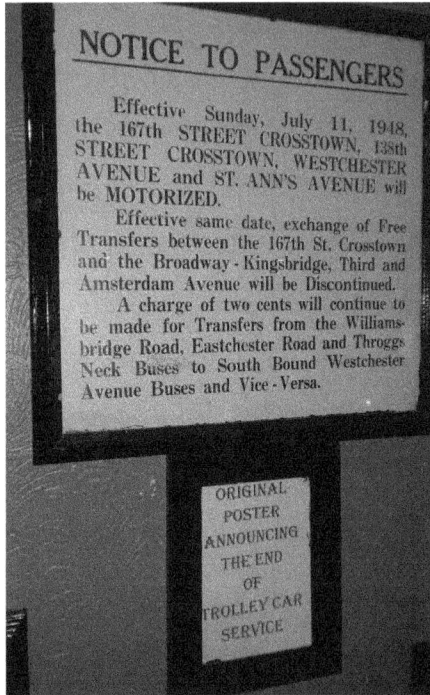

Jimmy Ryan's Bar & Grill, Bronx, NY

1952 – Central Park

1952 – Central Park

1952 – Central Park

1952 – Central Park

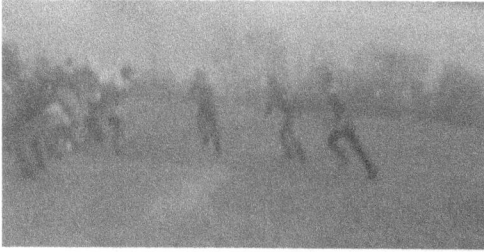
1952 – Central Park

1952 – Central Park

1952 – Central Park

1952 – Central Park

Jerry "Jay" Demers

Jerry "Jay" Demers

Jerry, Geri, Karen, Kim, Kerry

Jerry at P.S. 106

Eric Wulf – The "Wulfie" Riser

Pick-up Game at P.S.106

Joey Reich

Jack Kaufman

P.S. 106 (l to r) Joe Reich, Jerry Maringionne, Tony Bosco, Ken Synder, Mike Pisaniello

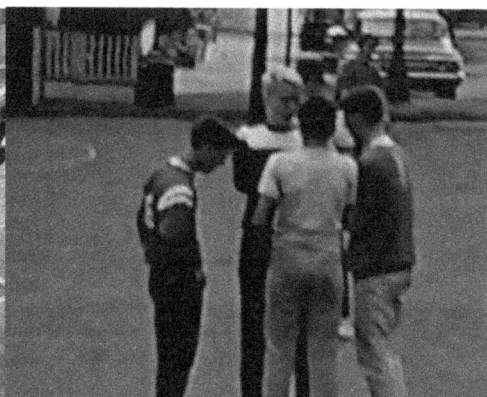
Game Planning at P.S. 106

P.S. 106 – circa 1967

Bowling at Fiesta Lanes August 1966

Jeff Ortiz

Artie Langer

Bronx Park East – circa 1967

Lew Lubarsky – The Famous Lubarsky Check Swing

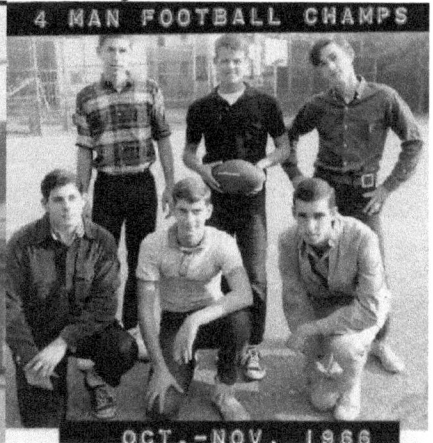

Pre-game Calisthenics – circa 1967

4 MAN FOOTBALL CHAMPS

OCT. - NOV. 1966

Front Row - Neil Shapiro, Bob Kurtz, Jeff Goldberg,
Rear Row – Lew Lubarsky, Eric Wulf, Tony LaMagna

Ron Watson

Neil Altabet & Ricky Slatin

Jim Oliveto (left) & Tony Vastola (driver)

Danny Miller

Meatball (Rich Ruggerio) and Jay

The City Champs

1967 N.Y.C. Touch Tackle Team – Front Row – Spencer Blank, Neil Rabinowitz, Ken Aronoff, Tony LaMagna, Loren Zeltner. Rear Row – Jack Kaufman, Lew Lubarsky, Neil Altabet, Eric Wulf, Jeff Oritz, Sam Sciciolone.

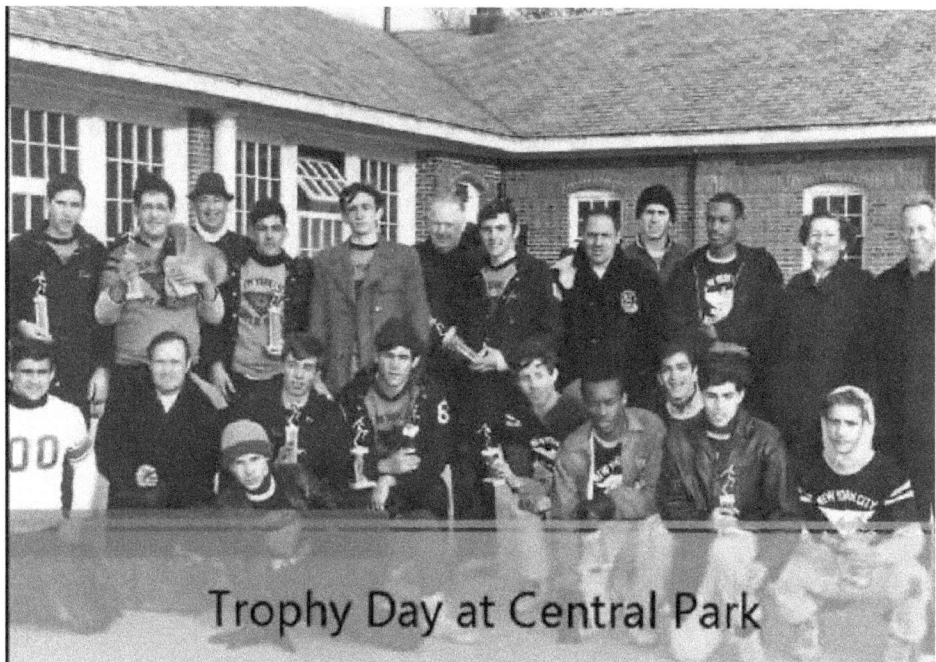

Trophy Day at Central Park

1967 N.Y.C. Champions – Senior Touch Tackle Team – Jerry Demers second from right bottom row. Individuals pictured are the same as those in previous photo.

263

Danny Miller & Jerry

Jerry's Famous Mustang - 1967

Jerry Demers passing over the middle – circa 1967

1973 Tackle Team

McGurl - Williams - ? - Ninivaggi - Hume - Sullivan

1968 Warrior Tackle Team

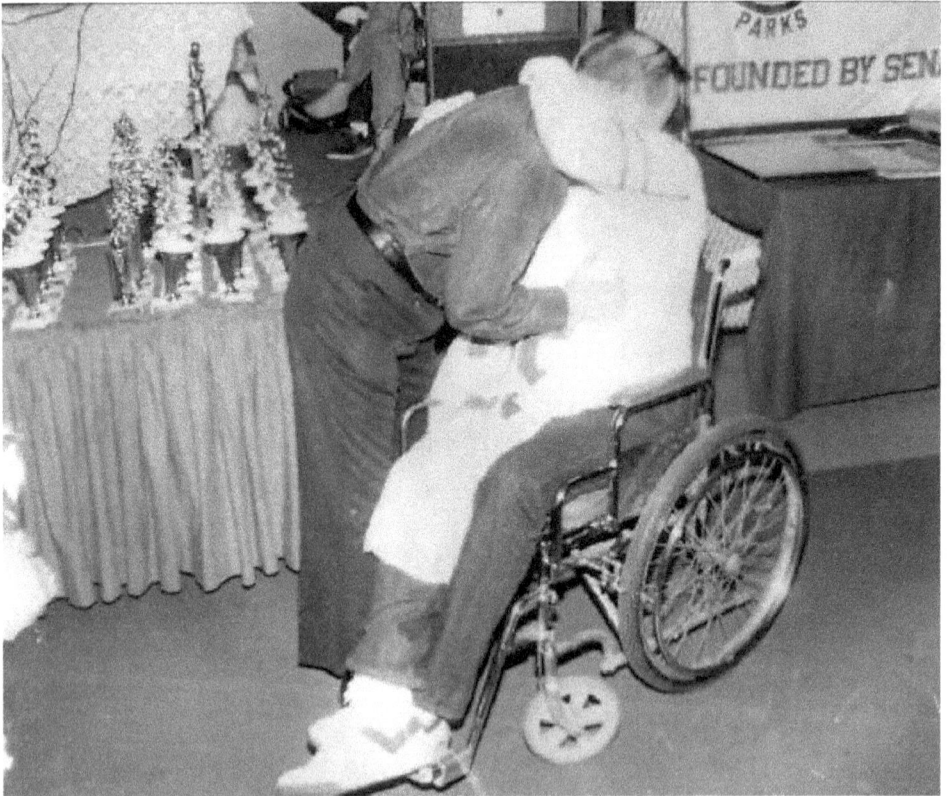

Jay & Joey - Warriors Retire Joey Reich's Number - #25

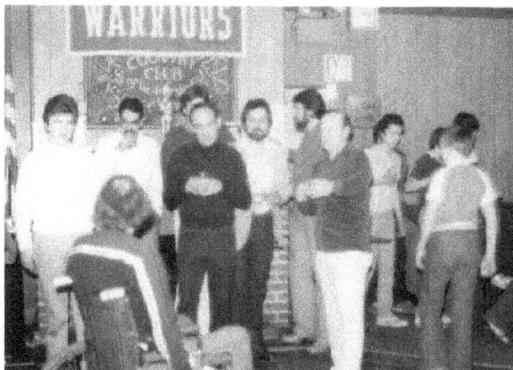

Awards Dinner 1971 – My Father (left center), #1 Fan, receiving an Appreciation Plaque from Jay (right center)

(l to r) Bill Bafundo, Tony Vastola, Jim Oliveto, Jerry Demers, Jim Sherry, Danny Miller

1970 Awards Dinner–Bottom row (l to r) Danny Miller, Tony Vastola, Joe Reich, Jerry Demers, Doug Williams, Jim Oliveto. Back row-George Nardone, Jack Cawley, John Macchiaroli, Kevin McInerney (hidden), Tom McGurl, Bill Bafundo, Jim Sherry,

Joe Reich (center) - 1974 Awards Dinner

1971 Warrior Tackle Team

Joe Regina – Stuyvesant High School, Bronx, NY, 1970

Jackie Cawley - 1969

1969 Warrior Tackle Team

1971

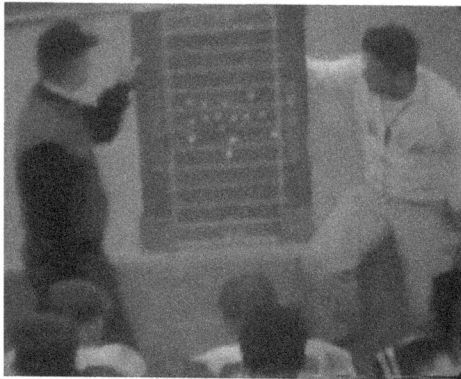
Jay and Tony Vastola – Skull Session

Writers Privilege - Yours truly kicking

Jack Cawley handing off to Frank Botti

1971 Pre-game pep talk. Tonly Vastola (center, red jacket)

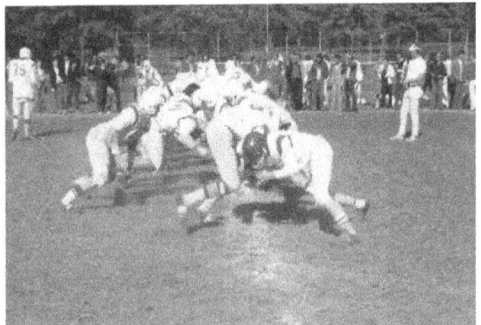
1971 Scrimage at Rice Stadium

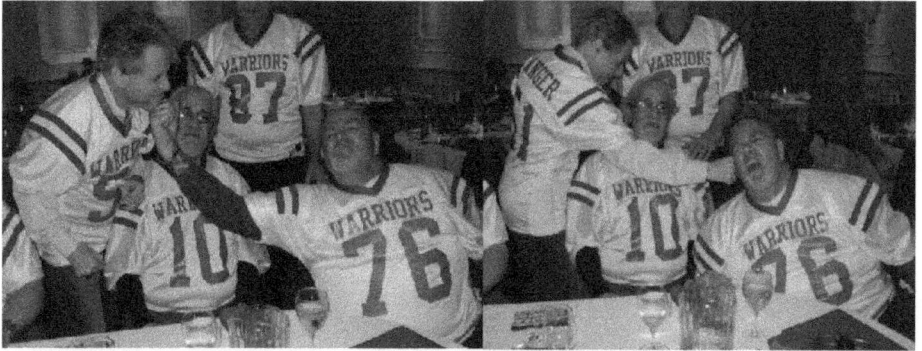

Artie Langer gets rocked by John Macchiaroli, Jeff Ortiz   Sandbox Rematch - Arthur Counters with a Right

Tommy McGurl, Joe Regina (#71), Jimmy Quick, Jackie Cawley, Bob Nieder

John Macchiaroli, Tommy Mastriani, Myself, Jack Cawley, Jeff Ortiz Frank Demers, Jay, Ted McGarrigle, Joe Regina, Tony Arroyo, Tom Piccininni, Vic Anderson

Jim Quick, Jack Cawley. Bob Nieder, Joe Regina Tom McGurl, Jay, Vic Anderson, (bottom row) Tom Mastriani, Tony Arroyo, Jeff Ortiz, John Macchiaroli, Tom Piccininni

1985 Our Lady of Assumption (back row, second from right – Joe Regina, far right – Vic Anderson

1985 - Jay with Assemblyman John Dearie

Coaching Staff - 1987

273

(l to r) Dennis Kandell, Jerry & Joe DeSimone

Javelins – Warrior Football League

Jay & Ricky Demers – Warrior Team

Councilman Cjonja & Joe DeSimone Present Plaque Honoring Jeff Ortiz – Scavello's February 21, 2019

Karen, Jay & Gerri – Ski Weekend – circa 1986

Geri Demers – Ski Weekend – circa 2005

Warrior Cheerleaders - Jennifer Volpe & Kerry Demers (Ages 6 & 8) –1986

Warrior Cheerleaders Competition, New Jersey - 2004

Warrior Cheerleaders Competition, N.J. – First Place - 2004

Bottom Row – Kim Demers, Michelle Howard, Kristi Mincieli, Daniella Mazzella, Jennifer Volpe. Middle Row – Joanne Hubener, Anne Marie Thompsen. Top – Kim Vincent (Eddie Esposito's stepdaughter)

Tori, Gianna & Samantha Volpe - 2006

Rickey, Jerry, Karen & Kerry Demers – Scavello's on the Island, Bronx, N.Y.   Jerry's 80th Birthday - 2018

80th Birthday – Scavello's On the Island   Jay with the "Shot Heard 'Round the World"

Scavello's

Jerry & Geri – Westchester Manor April 21, 2012

Danny Miller & Jerry

Jerry & Joe Regina

Jerry & Geri's Grandchildren – (l to r) Fallon, Callie, Justice, Jade & Amber

Jerry Honored by Bronx County for Service to the Community and its Youth – September 2018

Proclamation presented to Jerry by Senator Jeff Klein (l) & Councilman Mark Gjonaj (r) 2/22/18-Scavello's

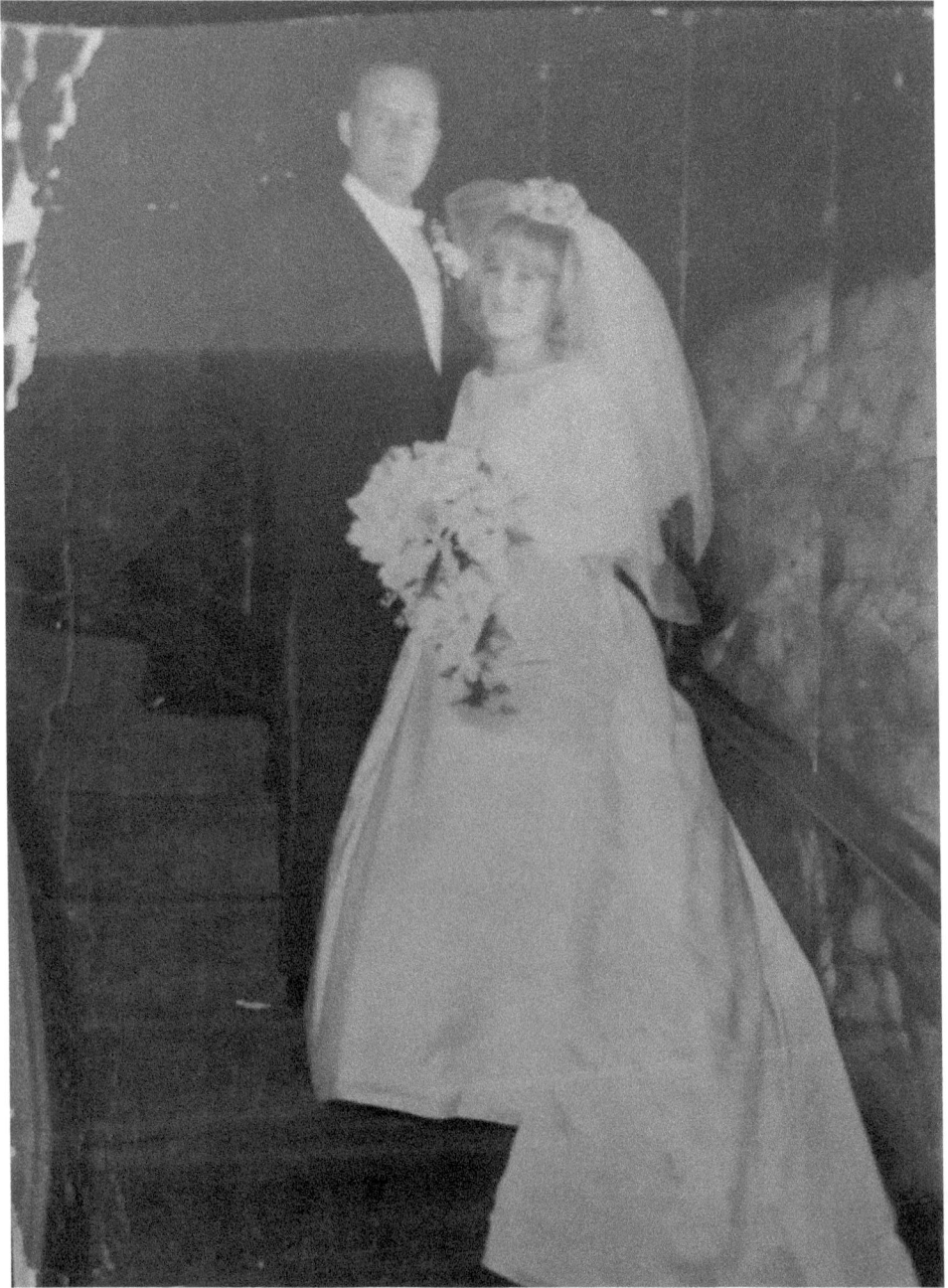

Mr. & Mrs. Demers – January 22, 1966

www.ingramcontent.com/pod-product-compliance
Lightning Source LLC
Chambersburg PA
CBHW030003290326

41934CB00005B/210